The Year 2000 Computer Crisis Legal Guide

Alan M. Gahtan

CARSWELL
Thomson Professional Publishing

The publisher is not engaged in rendering legal, accounting or other professional advice. If legal advice or other expert assistance is required, the services of a competent professional should be sought. The analysis contained herein represents the opinions of the author and should in no way be construed as being official or unofficial policy of any governmental body.

The paper used in this publication meets the minimum requirements of American National Standard for Information Sciences — Permanence of Paper for Printed Library Materials, ANSI Z39.48-1984.

Canadian Cataloguing in Publication Data

Gahtan, Alan M.
 The year 2000 computer crisis legal guide

Includes index.
ISBN 0-459-26011-1

1. Year 2000 date conversion (Computer systems) — Canada.
2. Year 2000 date conversion (Computer systems). 3. Computers — Law and legislation — Canada. 4. Computers — Law and legislation. I. Title.

KE452.C6G33 1998   343.7109'99   C98-931127-9
KF390.5.C6G37 1998

CARSWELL
Thomson Professional Publishing

One Corporate Plaza, 2075 Kennedy Road, Scarborough, Ontario M1T 3V4
Customer Service:
Toronto 1-416-609-3800
Elsewhere in Canada/U.S. 1-800-387-5164
Fax 1-416-298-5094

Dedication

To Suzanne, Jessica, Joshua, Brendan,
and my parents Joseph and Suzette.

Preface

As the year 2000 approaches, many companies are scrambling to minimize their exposure to the Year 2000 problem. While the Year 2000 problem requires a technical response, it also has many management and legal implications. As is becoming evident, the Year 2000 problem has significant implications for all types of entities and virtually any commercial transaction. Many companies have therefore been turning to their legal advisors for assistance.

A significant number of publications have been written to help address the many technical and managerial issues. However, useful information on the relevant legal issues has been lacking. This publication seeks to address this need by highlighting some of the important legal issues related to the Year 2000 computer problem. As such, it should be of interest to business professionals, as to well as their legal advisors.

Now for this disclaimer. This publication should not be viewed as a substitute for legal advice. A business that requires legal advice should retain a professional who has examined the current state of the applicable law and has acquired an understanding of its particular circumstances. Certain examples and references are provided for illustrative purposes and may not constitute a complete statement of the law. The state of the law with respect to Year 2000 issues is changing rapidly. Furthermore, some of the information contained in this publication may only be applicable in certain jurisdictions.

Alan Gahtan
lawyer@gahtan.com

Acknowledgements

I am indebted to a number of individuals who helped make this publication possible. These include Simone Gerrow and Rosa Primiani who performed much of the typing and revisions, Timothy O. Buckley, Michael P. Fitzgibbon, Lisa D.K. Johnson, Donald L. MacDonald, Kevin McGivney, Paul A. D. Mingay, Maria Luisa Osuna, Gordon A. Park, Victoria Prince and John J. Tobin of Borden & Elliot, Lorna Borenstein (Hewlett Packard), Dougal Clark (Bank of Montreal), G. C. Fowler (KPMG), Barbara Hendrickson (Ontario Securities Commission), John LaCalamita (SHL Systemhouse Limited), and other individuals that have chosen to remain anonymous for reviewing drafts of various chapters of the manuscript and providing helpful suggestions. I am particularly grateful to J. Fraser Mann of Borden & Elliot for contributing to the development of some of the sample language and reviewing a draft of the manuscript. I would also like to thank David Bienstock of Carswell and Catherine Campbell (formerly with Carswell) for giving me the opportunity to write this book.

Table of Contents

1

Introduction to the Year 2000 Problem

1.1 ONE PROBLEM OR MANY?

The Year 2000 problem, also known as the Millennium Bug or the Y2K problem, refers to an inability of some systems to operate correctly with dates that reference the year 2000 or after. The Year 2000 problem is not a single problem but actually consists of a number of related problems.[1]

(a) The Two-Digit Year Problem

The most prevalent problem is due to the use of two digits rather than four to represent the year in dates, found in many older computer systems and software programs. The century component of the year is implied rather than being explicitly stored. The assumption works well until a date in the twenty-first century is introduced, causing programs to lose the ability to distinguish between twentieth and twenty-first century dates.

This particular Year 2000 problem had its origin over 30 years ago when memory for computer systems was expensive and programmers came up with ways to save space.[2] The use of two-digit fields to store the year portion

---

1 See Capers Jones, "Dangerous Dates for Software Applications" (March 24, 1998) at <http://www.year2000.com/archive/NFdangers.html>.

2 In 1963, one megabyte of mainframe storage cost $175 per month to lease. By 1972, the price was down to $36 per megabyte per month and by 1983, the price was under $22 per year. By 1996, the cost of memory had dropped by a factor of 10,000 as compared to the cost in 1963. It has been estimated that only 1% more disk storage would have been required to store all four digits of the year. Even if it had been economically justifiable to use two digits to store the year portion of date fields in 1963, by the 1970s the economic costs likely began to outweigh the economic benefits. See Deborah Pitts, "Year 2000

of dates not only resulted in cost savings in respect of memory (especially in databases containing multiple records), but also resulted in efficiencies in system performance, data entry, and display of date information. Early developers probably assumed the systems they were implementing would be replaced long before the century portion of the year fields would become an issue.

These memory-saving techniques were useful when memory was expensive and precious. However, they became a defective standard that everyone kept following both out of habit and to assure that newer software programs would interface with older programs that utilized two digits to represent the year. Therefore, even recently developed systems may be at risk of a Year 2000 problem. Systems with this problem cannot correctly process date information that refers to the year 2000 or after. A date in the year 2000 may be interpreted by such systems as occurring in the year 1900.

(b) Use of Dates as Indicators

A second related problem is the use of certain date fields in database records as indicators rather than to store real date information. The presence of special date values may trigger a pre-programmed action having no relation to dates. Such systems may use the digits "99" in the date field to represent something other than a date in 1999. September 9, 1999 (9/9/99) and December 31, 1999 are common examples. For instance, a dummy date may be inserted into one of the date fields of a payroll record to indicate that the payment was in respect of a bonus rather than regular wages. A dummy date may also be used to indicate an end-of-file marker.

Also, some software programs utilize dummy dates to indicate that the applicable date has not been specified or is not known.[3] For instance, "00" or "00/00/00" may have been used to indicate that the date has not yet been entered and "99," "1/1/99" or some other special date may have been used

---

liability and insurance: is your insurer on the hook?" Year 2000 Computer Crises: The Litigation Summit (November 6-7, 1997) Fulcrum Information Services Inc., San Francisco, California, at 4.

3 The British Standards Institute has issued "A Definition of Year 2000 Conformity Requirements" (the "BSI Definition"), which provides a definition of the expression and the requirements that must be satisfied in equipment and products that use dates and times [Document: DISC PD2000-1. See <http://www.2k-times.com/y2k-p110.htm>]. Note 2.5 to Rule 2 provides *No equipment or product shall use particular date values for special meanings; e.g. "99"* to signify "no end value" or "end of file" or "00" to mean "not applicable" or "beginning of file."

to indicate that no date was applicable or that the date was not known. As systems process information using these dates, they may produce erratic results or stop functioning.[4] A system with this problem may exhibit a problem well before the year 2000.[5]

Dummy dates may also be used as indicators by archival systems. For instance, some archival systems use a dummy date of 9/9/99 to indicate that the file or record should not be deleted by the archiving processes. However, when the year 2000 arrives, the "never destroy" indicator date will be less than the system date, and could result in the deletion of the very records and files that were intended to be permanently retained.

(c) Recognition of the Year 2000 as a Leap Year

Most people are familiar with the basic rule for leap years: if the year can be divided by four then it is a leap year and will contain a 29th day in February. However, there are also two additional rules that take precedence. Century years, although divisible by four, are generally not leap years. Therefore, the year 1900 was not a leap year. However, the final rule is that if a century year can be divided by 400, it is a leap year. According to these rules, the year 2000 is a leap year.

The year 1900 was not a leap year and many programmers, familiar with rules 1 and 2 but not 3, assumed that the year 2000 would not be a leap year either. Systems that do not recognize the Year 2000 as a leap year will not recognize the additional day and calculations involving dates may be incorrect. In addition, systems that need to track the day of the week, such as environmental control systems and security systems, will lose track of the correct day.

(d) Equipment with Embedded Logic

Electricity could be interrupted, telephone networks might collapse and airline flights could be grounded if scheduling programs for pilots and support crews go on the fritz. Social assistance cheques may be delayed—if the mail is moving at all—and automatic teller machines could grind to a halt. Elevators,

---

4 Canadian Institute of Chartered Accountants, *Risk Alert* (January 1998) at 1.
5 If an organization has a year end that is to occur during 1998 then it will need to ensure that its systems are not susceptible to year "99" errors as such systems will start to reference the year "99" as of the 1998 fiscal year.

thinking they have not been inspected since 1900, may descend to the ground floor and shut down.[6]

While not a separate Year 2000 problem, another complication is that Year 2000 problems are not expected to be restricted to what are typically regarded as computing devices but may affect all types of appliances and equipment having computerized components (embedded logic) that are dependent on dates.[7] Systems that may be affected include elevators, HVAC systems, manufacturing systems, financial systems, security systems, PBX phone systems, automobiles, air traffic control systems, diagnostic equipment, and biomedical equipment and devices. Date errors that will arise due to the Year 2000 problem may cause such systems that are not compliant to produce incorrect results, delete data or shut down.[8]

The Nuclear Regulatory Commission, while noting that there are no computerized systems involved in operating nuclear reactors, has sent an "advisory" to utilities warning that the Year 2000 problem is likely to affect plant security, radiation detection and personnel identification.[9]

(e) Interdependencies

While also not a separate problem, another complicating issue is that Year 2000 problems may affect computer systems that are themselves compliant due to electronic linkages between systems. A system designed to operate correctly after the year 2000 may still acquire incorrect data from other systems. A Year 2000 problem can affect products acquired from suppliers and subsequently sold to customers or integrated into products sold to customers. Properly protecting an organization against the Year 2000 problem therefore involves more than simply ensuring that its own systems are compliant.

---

6 John Schofield, "Millennium Mayhem" *Maclean's* (October 27, 1997) at 38.

7 The Year 2000 problem can affect any product, even "low tech" products, that depend on date or time-based calculations for proper operation. Any product containing clocks, clocking algorithms or applications that rely on mathematical calculations based on dates may be affected.

8 The BSI Definition states: *Problems can arise from some means of representing dates in computer equipment and products and from date-logic embedded in purchased goods and services, as the year 2000 approaches and during and after that year. As a result, equipment or products, including embedded control logic, may fail completely, malfunction or cause data to be corrupted. To avoid such problems, organizations must check, and modify if necessary, internally produced equipment and products and similarly check externally supplied equipment and products with their suppliers.*

9 *USA Today* (Wednesday, December 17, 1997) at A2.

An organization, even one that has addressed the above issues, may also be affected due to a dependence on a supplier of a non-computer product or service if such supplier itself experiences a Year 2000 problem. For instance, financial institutions may be very reliant on armoured car services to transport cash between branches. Airlines are vulnerable to disruptions affecting catering and fuel suppliers. Automobile manufacturers typically utilize just-in-time inventory systems and are reliant upon thousands of suppliers, any of whom can create a problem in the production chain.

Regulators have become concerned both with compliance of a company's internal systems, as well as that of its suppliers. For instance, the Federal Financial Institutions Examination Council ("FFIEC") in the United States has stated that "reporting [to the institution's board] must include information on the institution's internal Year 2000 corrective efforts and the ability of the institution's major vendors to provide Year 2000 ready products and services."[10]

1.2 OTHER DATE-RELATED PROBLEMS

Date-related problems are not a hypothetical or a recent phenomena. The Brussels Stock Market had to close, at a cost that exceeded $1 million in commissions, when its computers were confused by an additional leap year day on February 29, 1996. Additional leap year related problems have included a factory in New Zealand that lost about $1 million and difficulty encountered by Arizona's lottery in paying out winnings.[11]

A leap year problem in February 1996 also lead to production problems on January 1, 1997 for a small United States manufacturer. Before the situation could be remedied, liquids hardened in pipelines and resulted in losses amounting to $1 million. A similar leap year problem caused $1 million of damage to an aluminum refinery in Tasmania.[12]

Year 2000 related problems were first encountered in 1970 with systems that had to track 30-year fixed rate mortgages in the United States[13] At least

---

10 See Federal Financial Institutions Examination Council, "Safety and Soundness Guidelines Concerning the Year 2000 Business Risk" (December 17, 1997) at <http://www.ffiec.gov/federal.htm>.

11 See testimony of Comptroller of the Currency, Eugene A. Ludwig, chair of the Federal Financial Institutions Examination Council ("FFIEC") to the House Banking Committee (US) on November 4, 1997.

12 "Industry wakes up to Year 2000 menace" *Fortune* (April 27, 1998) at 163.

13 Most Canadian mortgages are written to a maximum term of five years and therefore the

one Canadian bank, Bank of Montreal, experienced problems in 1975 when projections for 25-year mortgages were miscalculated, forcing limited repair work.[14] Alamo Rent-A-Car experienced a Year 2000 problem back in 1981 when it first encountered British drivers' licences (which are good for 20 years) and found that their system could not handle the date.[15]

Japan also had to deal with date-related conversion issues in 1989 following the death of the Emperor, which required a conversion by the Japanese government and business of date fields to reflect the end of the 64-year "Showa" period and the start of the "Heisei" period.

Another date-related problem expected to occur as we approach the Year 2000 concerns the Global Positioning System ("GPS"), which is used for numerous commercial purposes as well as military purposes. GPS consists of 24 satellites that orbit the earth and send out signals that give their position and the exact date and time. A GPS receiver processes the signals from three or four satellites, and by comparing the exact times at which each signal was received, can determine its location. However, some GPS receivers contain an embedded date problem. The GPS system utilizes a binary field, called a week number, which represents the number of weeks that have passed from a reference date (January 6, 1980). This number will roll over to zero on August 22, 1999. Some manufacturers of GPS receivers did not account for this roll-over and this may lead some non-compliant GPS receivers to fail or malfunction unless upgraded.

Other date-related problems can also be expected to occur after the year 2000. UNIX systems store the date and time as the number of seconds that have elapsed since January 1, 1970. This number is stored as a 32-bit integer that will roll-over to zero on January 19, 2038. Virtually all versions of the C and C++ programming languages will be affected. Due to the high number of embedded programs written in C and C++, this problem may be more serious than the Year 2000 problem. Finally, one of the more common techniques being used to address the Year 2000 problem is merely postponing the problem until some time in the next century. According to Peter de

---

problem did not manifest itself as early in Canada.

14 According to Peter Leblanc, Bank of Montreal's Senior Vice-President of community banking solutions, and Tom Poupore, manager of the bank's Year 2000 project, efforts to fix Year 2000 problems in the 1970s would have displaced a lot of other technology investment that was needed to develop products such as debit cards and on-line banking. See Patrick Brethour, "Getting Bitten by 2000 Bug" *Globe and Mail* (January 7, 1998) at B25.

15 W. Michael Fletcher, *Computer Crisis 2000* (North Vancouver, B.C.: Self-Counsel Press Ltd., 1998) at 81.

Jager, a well-known Year 2000 consultant, many companies are sticking with two-digit year codes and making minor adjustments that will allow their systems to operate for another 20, 30 or 50 years.[16] Even if current systems are replaced by then, replacements may inherit the problem if they are designed to be compatible with existing systems.

1.3 WHEN WILL THE YEAR 2000 PROBLEM OCCUR?

It is not necessary to wait until the year 2000 before systems begin to exhibit problems. A number of Year 2000-related problems have already appeared. While the internal authorization systems used by Visa and MasterCard have been Year 2000 compliant for some time, some credit card authorization terminals utilized by retailers were found to have problems processing credit cards with expiration dates of 2000 or later. This led both credit card issuers to place a freeze (which ran between October 1996 and September 1997) on the issuance of credit cards with expiration dates beyond 1999.

A number of programs with "event horizons" that look into the future or track future dates may have already experienced Year 2000-related problems. Others may experience problems in 1998 or 1999. If a program's event horizon extends into the year 2000, then the program may encounter Year 2000-related problems even prior to the change in the millennium. Examples include:

◆ 30-year mortgages in the United States (1970)
◆ 25-year mortgages in Canada (1975)
◆ 20-year term life insurance (1980)
◆ 5-year mortgages (1995)
◆ 4-year car loans (1996)
◆ 3-year driver licences (1997)
◆ 2-year car registration renewals (1998)[17]
◆ credit cards (depends on expiration date)

---

16 *Maclean's* (October 27, 1997).
17 In Ontario, the Ministry of Transportation had to temporarily discontinue offering a two-year renewal option on vehicle registrations as of January 1998 because its system was not Year 2000 compliant. The problem was quickly resolved and two-year renewals were once again being offered as of early February.

1.4 HOW MUCH WILL IT COST?

A "silver bullet" fix to the Year 2000 problem is not likely to be developed due to the sheer volume, complexity and diversity of the systems at use in typical organizations. The costs of addressing the Year 2000 problem can be significant. Gartner Group, a Connecticut-based computer consulting firm, has projected the costs of addressing the problem at up to US $600 billion (not including litigation that is expected to result). With respect to Canada, the Information Technology Association of Canada has estimated that the costs can run as high as $30-50 billion. Many large corporations are each expecting to spend tens or even hundreds of millions of dollars to analyze their systems and make any required changes.

Some estimates as of late 1997 were:

♦ United States federal government—estimates have ranged between US $2.3 billion and US $30 billion
♦ Canadian federal government $1 billion (May 1997)
♦ CIBC $150-200 million[18]
♦ Bank of Montreal $125 million[19]
♦ Royal Bank $100 million[20]
♦ Canada Post $70 million[21]
♦ London Life $53 million[22]
♦ Manufacturers Life $45 million[23]

A survey, conducted in the fall for the Task Force Year 2000,[24] and released on December 8, 1997, estimated that the Year 2000 problem could cost the Canadian economy a minimum of $12 billion in direct costs to fix the problem. However, this very rough total did not include the unidentified costs of the many businesses that have not begun to address the problem. The survey also acknowledged that costs may also be higher if employees

---

18 CIBC has estimated (Fall 1997) its costs of fixing its Year 2000 problems at $150 to $200 million. Most of this amount would be spent on internal resources. Managers who wish to use outside vendors must give up one position for each $60,000 spent externally. Due to the short period remaining, CIBC, like many organizations, decided to implement a "windowing" solution rather than one involving "screen expansion."

19 The Bank of Montreal's initial cost estimate from early 1994 was $4 million to $5 million. Patrick Brethour, "Getting Bitten by 2000 Bug" *Globe and Mail* (January 7, 1998) at B25.

20 *Maclean's* (October 27, 1997).

21 *Maclean's* (October 27, 1997).

22 Greg Enright, "Are Insurers in Hot Water" *Computing Canada* (November 24, 1997).

23 Greg Enright, "Are Insurers in Hot Water" *Computing Canada* (November 24, 1997).

24 A Year 2000 task force appointed by the Canadian government. See Chapter 3.

with system-oriented skills must be shifted from their regular duties to help fix the problem. Whatever the total bill, the financial impact of the Year 2000 problem is clearly too large to ignore. However, despite the hard work being undertaken and the significant costs expended, there is no guarantee every problem will be caught.

1.5 THE NEED TO TAKE ACTION

> Failure to act may result in business interruption, financial loss, litigation and possibly business failure.[25]

Companies are being placed under increased scrutiny in respect of their Year 2000 compliance efforts by a number of stakeholders, including:

◆ suppliers
◆ customers
◆ lenders and investors
◆ industry analysts
◆ business partners
◆ insurers
◆ bond rating services[26]
◆ regulators

As the year 2000 approaches, many of these stakeholders are likely to become increasingly anxious about the Year 2000 problem and may require the companies to demonstrate that they have implemented a comprehensive program to address the Year 2000 problem.

A company's directors, officers and senior management need to be prepared to respond to inquiries regarding the company's Year 2000 compliance efforts in order to avoid negative consequences. A company that is not taking adequate steps to address the Year 2000 problem, or one whose representatives are unable to demonstrate to stakeholders, especially from the financial press or industry analysts, that it is taking adequate steps may find itself subject to negative consequences in respect to the value of its publicly traded stock. Investors try to anticipate future trends to guide their

---

25 Information Technology Association of Canada, "Challenge 2000: Executive Guide to Year 2000 Computing Solutions" at <http://www.itac.ca/policy/survival.htm>.

26 To the extent that a company is at a high risk of failing in its Year 2000 efforts, debt rating agencies such as Moody's and Standard & Poor's may take the Year 2000 problem into account in rating a company's debt. Downgrading of a company's rating would result in such companies having to offer higher interest rates for new bonds they may wish to issue.

decisions and Year 2000 compliance is becoming an issue. Already, some mutual funds are asking publicly traded companies about what actions they are taking to deal with the Year 2000 problem. Auditors are also paying increasing attention to Year 2000 issues.

(a) Deadlines for Compliance

The deadline for correcting the Year 2000 problem is not the end of 1999 as many believe. Correction to certain types of systems must be completed by the end of 1998 or errors may result.[27] Some regulators are also advising that they expect conversions to be completed by the end of 1998 in order to allow adequate time for testing.[28] For instance:

♦ The Office of the Superintendent of Financial Institutions has stated that it expects most federally regulated financial institutions in Canada to be fully Year 2000 compliant prior to the end of 1998. At a minimum, it expects all institutions should be at the acceptance testing phase.

♦ The United States Office of the Controller of the Currency issued a statement to financial institutions that set December 31, 1998 as a deadline to complete conversion in order to allow a full year for implementation, testing, and any necessary additional corrective action.

♦ The New York Stock Exchange and the National Association of Securities Dealers have "highly recommended" that each member firm accomplish all code changes by the end of 1998, so that 1999 can be used for monitoring the operations of all converted systems and performing quality assurance and interface tests with other organizations.

1.6 TAKING ACTION

The longer a company waits to fix its Year 2000 problem, the less resources will be available to help and the higher the risk of failure. The failure to take appropriate steps as early as possible can also result in a loss of rights, risk of liability, and potentially higher costs down the road. For instance, a basic principle under both negligence and contract law is that a party that suffers damages must act to mitigate its damages. Such a party must take steps to reduce the likelihood of damages occurring, as well as attempt to

---

27 A non-compliant financial system that is used to process information in respect of a fiscal year that begins on February 1, 1999 may experience a problem as the last month of that fiscal year will extend into the year 2000.

28 See Chapter 4.

keep damages to a minimum once they occur. In the event of legal action, a company that did not implement a proper and/or timely compliance program may have a harder time substantiating that it took reasonable steps to mitigate its damages.

Depending on the nature of the failure, a business may be able to revert to manual systems and mitigate some of its losses. However, the failure of a critical system, or the failure of a major supplier or its systems, may have severe consequences on a company's ability to conduct its business. This could lead to loss of business and loss of customers who may quickly switch to Year 2000 compliant competitors. Failure to meet contractual commitments to customers or business partners may also subject the company to liability and associated litigation.

Many companies are implementing projects to address their exposure to Year 2000 problems. These should include comprehensive legal audits to assess their vulnerability to liability claims and an assessment of possible recourse against suppliers of non-compliant products. Another recommended component is to write suppliers in order to ascertain the steps they are taking to ensure that their products and services are or will be Year 2000 compliant. Some customers have indicated that they plan to reduce their dependencies on suppliers that are not able to provide sufficient assurances or proof that they are adequately addressing their risk to the Year 2000 problem.

A customer with a system that is not Year 2000 compliant, who cannot obtain adequate assurances or cooperation from a supplier to address such non-compliance, should take its own steps to attempt to correct the problems, if possible, or if necessary, to replace the non-compliant system. In such event, the customer should provide the supplier with notice of its intention to proceed in order to enhance its ability to later claim for recovery of the costs it incurs.

Some companies have not moved aggressively to deal with the Year 2000 problem. They have assumed that they have only a small number of systems that may experience problems, and that they will replace such systems before the year 2000. Some of these companies may find that such replacements may take longer than anticipated due to interdependencies between systems, and the time required to perform the conversion and implementation activities. In addition, vendors of compliant systems are likely to get busier as less time remains and may suffer personnel shortages.

Implementation of replacement systems may be complicated or delayed by the need to have a more current version of an operating system than that which may be in use at a particular company. Upgrading an operating system may require the installation of upgrades or patches to other programs operated on the same computer, which may result in additional delays. Companies that wait too long before initiating projects to replace non-compliant systems may be found to have failed to exercise proper due diligence.

Companies with a high dependancy on customers and suppliers located outside North America may be at a greater risk. North American companies are generally further ahead in dealing with the Year 2000 problem,[29] while European and Asian/Pacific companies have in general been slower to address Year 2000 issues.[30] European companies are burdened by modifications required to implement dual currency support in anticipation of the European Monetary Union, a task that is expected to be more expensive than Year 2000 conversions. In the case of companies in Asian/Pacific countries, most utilize systems that support double-byte characters required to display local languages. Such systems cannot easily utilize many of the automated conversion tools that have been developed for the North American market.

It should be noted that certain industries, even within North America, may have more difficulty identifying and correcting Year 2000 problems. For instance, many manufacturing and process control systems contain embedded logic, some of which contain software written as long ago as 1975. Industries where participants are highly reliant on a large number of external suppliers or that are highly dependent on electronic links with each other and/or other parties may also have a higher exposure to Year 2000 problems.

The health care sector may also be at high risk. According to a report by the Gartner Group presented at the 1998 Annual Healthcare Information and Management Systems Society conference and exhibition in February 1998, seven out of eight health care organizations risk Year 2000-related systems failures largely because of their lack of responsiveness. Health industry executives at the conference indicated that, far more critical than potential failures in information systems that track everything from patient

---

29 Companies in the United Kingdom and Australia have also shown leadership in addressing the Year 2000 problem.
30 The United States Federal Reserve Bank announced plans to coordinate upgrades of systems in use by foreign banks doing business with the United States. It is concerned that bad data from a computer that has not been fixed (particularly from Asian banks, which are making little progress in addressing Year 2000 issues) can contaminate a system that has been fixed.

records to accounting information, was the lack of effort being made to diagnose the impact of the Year 2000 problem on biomedical equipment such as ventilators and other life-support systems with embedded hardware and software.[31]

Most types of medical equipment are unlikely to be adversely affected by the Year 2000 problem. Some devices such as electrocardiograph recorders, patient monitors, and ultrasound scanners may display date information that is incorrect but such problems are unlikely to affect patient care. However, a subset of devices may actually fail or operate incorrectly. Given the limited time remaining, it will not be possible to test every device and system, and some devices may simply not be possible to test. It will therefore be important for hospitals to work with their suppliers and to prioritize their testing resources.[32]

The Food and Drug Administration ("FDA") in the United States has set up an on-line database with information regarding the Year 2000 compliance of various medical devices. It can be accessed at <http:/208.192.104.178/Y2K/Y2Ksearch.cfm>. Canadian federal regulators are reportedly developing a similar facility.

1.7 CHALLENGES

> While anything is possible, experts seem to agree that a simple or all encompassing solution to the conversion problem is very unlikely. Rather, just the opposite circumstances appear to be true: that a Year 2000 conversion requires extensive planning, organization, commitment and follow through; that consulting expertise in this area is limited; and that competition for these resources will accelerate rapidly as the Year 2000 approaches.[33]

Many companies are finding the scope of their Year 2000 compliance project to be daunting. In many cases, companies are finding themselves behind schedule, especially in areas outside the Information Technology ("IT") department. Many have underestimated the efforts, costs, and time required to ensure that non-IT products and services used or acquired by the organization are compliant.

---

31 The Year 2000 team at the Hospital of St. Raphael, an acute care facility in New Haven, Connecticut, is reported to have uncovered 18 ventilators that were noncompliant.

32 Anthony J. Montagnolo, "Guess What? Medical Devices Hold Year 2000 Surprises, Too!" *Health Measures* at <http://www.healthmeasures.com/>.

33 The Information Technology Association of America, "Start Preparing for Your Year 2000 Software Conversion Today" at <http://www.itaa.org/yr2000bg.htm>.

The most prevalent reason many companies are citing for initially under-estimating the scope of the problem is that it was thought to be an IT problem. However, these companies soon realized that the solution involves much more than simply correcting their internal software. Properly addressing the problem involves almost every aspect of the business. All types of equipment containing embedded logic must be included in the review, as well as an investigation, and in some cases verification of the Year 2000 compliance of suppliers and other parties.

The Year 2000 problem is compounded by the time required to analyze the problem and carry out the necessary conversion and testing, especially for large or complex computer systems. Government agencies and companies with a long acquisition cycle may be at a further disadvantage.[34] Some agencies and companies are acknowledging that insufficient time remains to correct all systems in time and are instead focusing their efforts on the correction of only their critical systems.

In these cases, the importance of each system to the business must be assessed. This involves evaluating how critical a system is to the uninter-rupted operation of the company and a consideration of legal compliance requirements. If a company has a documented disaster recovery plan, reference to such a plan may help prioritize work for Year 2000 compliance purposes.

Even a Year 2000 compliant version of a program may allow a user-written application, such as a macro or a script, to request a two-digit year. This is an additional problem that must be addressed. For instance, Microsoft reports that while all of its operating systems, including MS-DOS, were designed with the ability to handle four-digit dates well into the next century, users can enter two-digit shortcuts that are then stored as four-digit dates by Microsoft products based on documented assumptions. However, since there is no industry-wide standard on how to interpret two-digit shortcuts, the various PC applications in use today may interpret a two-digit year differently. As a result, errors can occur when such dates are entered,

---

34 In a letter sent to Deputy Ministers of the Canadian government by the Information Technology Association of Canada ("ITAC") and the Canadian Information Processing Society, ITAC President Gaylen Duncan stated: "Existing procurement practices are hindering the acquisition of needed products and services. An RFP released in full compliance with NAFTA requirements takes 6-9 months to complete, excluding Treasury Board reviews and budgetary meetings. At the present time, however, only a trickle of RFPs has been forthcoming. Without a faster budgeting and procurement cycle, federal departments may not have enough time to complete the work required."

displayed or exchanged, whether between different applications within the same company or between different business entities.

As an example, Microsoft Excel versions 4, 5 and 7 interpret two-digit years of "00" to "19" as shortcuts for "2000" to "2019." However, Excel 97 (and Access 97) interpret two-digit years from "00" to "29" as shortcuts for "2000" to "2029." Consequently, "21" will be interpreted as "2021" by Excel 97 and Access 97, but as "1921" by Excel versions 4, 5 and 7. All versions of both applications will interpret "30" as corresponding to "1930."

Many companies, including the major financial institutions, are addressing the Year 2000 problem using "windowing solutions" rather than the more obvious solution of adding two digits to the date field. In many cases, solutions based on adding two digits have been found to be more time consuming and expensive. However, implementation of a windowing solution requires agreement on common standards, both within the company and between companies that exchange data electronically.

Another challenge posed by the Year 2000 problem concerns testing. Any software that has time limits (*i.e.*, expiration dates) could be disabled due to Year 2000 testing activities. Year 2000 testing may also trigger problems such as causing security certificates to expire or deleting "old" appointments or messages in calendar/e-mail applications.

Another issue arises from the requirement to retain certain data for legal or regulatory purposes. Modifying programs to make them Year 2000 compliant may make archival data inaccessible to the corrected programs. It may therefore be necessary to retain unmodified versions of the corrected programs to provide access to such archived data. An alternative is to convert all archived data so that it is compatible with the modified programs.

Companies with potential Year 2000 problems are becoming increasingly reluctant to discuss the magnitude of their Year 2000 corrective work. They may fear that such information may be utilized by future litigants in the event the company's Year 2000 problems are not corrected in time. It is therefore becoming more difficult to share knowledge and ascertain the status of various products and companies.

To further complicate matters, various terms being used by vendors, such as "Year 2000 Ready", and "Year 2000 Compliant" do not have an agreed-upon meaning.

1.8 TURNING PROBLEMS INTO OPPORTUNITIES

The Year 2000 problem is being seized as an opportunity by some companies. Those who are able to complete their conversion and compliance efforts early hope to market this fact to potential customers who may be nervous about continued dealings with their competitors who may be further behind in their efforts. Some companies in this category are even contemplating marketing their expertise to others. IT managers have also recognized that a Year 2000 project can serve as a catalyst for implementation of an asset management system and a justification for rationalizing the number of applications and systems that have proliferated in recent years. Ancillary benefits of a Year 2000 project can be a more stable and efficient infrastructure, as well as the standardization on a common architecture.

IT service providers are profiting from the Year 2000 problem through fees earned providing consulting and conversion services. However, the opportunity to work closely with customers on Year 2000 projects, and intimate knowledge gained about customer systems, will also provide them with a better ability to market outsourcing options to such customers down the road.

2

Liability Issues

2.1 Relationships Where Liability May Arise

There are a number of potential sources of liability associated with the Year 2000 problem for a company and its directors and officers. The following are some of the more common types of relationships under which such liability may arise:

◆ supplier to customer
  – supply of software and hardware products
  – maintenance services
  – outsourcing services
  – conversion services
  – consulting and integration services
  – non-computer products and services that are disrupted due to a Year 2000 problem (including government services)
◆ director/officer to company/shareholder
◆ vendor of a business to a purchaser (for breach of warranty or failure to disclose)
◆ investee/debtor to an investor/creditor
◆ manufacturer/distributor to a user of product
◆ insurer to an insured (or an insurance broker to an insured)
◆ landlord to a tenant/visitor
◆ employer to an employee (*i.e.*, obligation to provide a safe work environment)
◆ regulated entity to the government/regulator

Aside from anticipated litigation directly related to the Year 2000 problem, many companies are expecting to deal with their Year 2000 problems by replacing existing non-compliant systems. Due to the short time remaining for implementation, it is likely that at least some of these projects will experience delays or may be implemented without adequate testing. These will also likely generate additional claims for damages. In some of these cases, customers may be at least partially responsible for not leaving sufficient time to allow for proper implementation.

It should be noted that this chapter utilizes the terms customer and supplier, in lieu of buyer and seller as is found in most sale of goods legislation. This is done to remain consistent with the remainder of this publication.

2.2 GROUNDS FOR LIABILITY

There are several legal theories that may support liability for Year 2000-related problems. These include:

- breach of contract
  - explicit Year 2000 warranty
  - failure to conform to specifications (functional, technical or performance) at delivery or as part of ongoing maintenance obligations
- negligence
  - negligent design
  - negligent advice
  - failure to disclose/duty to warn
- misrepresentations
  - fraudulent misrepresentations
  - negligent misrepresentations
  - statutory liability for misrepresentations
- breach of fiduciary duty
- product liability
- breach of implied warranties
- breach of statutory obligations or requirements
- intellectual property infringement[1]

This chapter does not seek to address all issues relating to the allocation of liability or all theories of liability in respect of the Year 2000 problem. Potential defences and the measure of damages are also not considered in detail. The objective is to highlight some of the more obvious grounds of potential liability.

A better understanding of rights and obligations can allow customers and suppliers to take steps to preserve rights and mitigate liability. In some cases, a failure of a customer to take timely action to address the Year 2000

---

1 This issue is discussed in greater detail in Chapter 10.

problem may result in a loss of rights. For instance, a customer may be found to have been contributorily negligent, to have failed to act reasonably to mitigate its damages, or to have lost a right to reject previously accepted goods or to revoke a contract. Similarly, the failure of a supplier to notify a customer of a known defect may result in liability. While timely action should be taken to address these issues, the attention of affected parties should not be deflected onto lawsuits rather then being focused on addressing Year 2000 problems as soon as possible.

(a) Breach of Contract

A common claim may be that the supply of a product that was not Year 2000 compliant constituted a breach of a term of the contract, including possibly an express warranty.[2] For instance, a customer may claim that date-related errors constitute a failure of the product to conform to its specifications (if these are spelled out in detail), including those dealing with dates and date calculations, as required under a licence agreement or other contract relating to the sale of the product.[3]

Similar arguments might be made in respect of an obligation to correct a Year 2000 problem pursuant to a maintenance agreement. Many such agreements contain an obligation to fix bugs or deficiencies. Depending on the language utilized in such agreements, a Year 2000 problem may constitute the type of problem that must be corrected at no charge to the customer if the supplier is providing maintenance services.[4]

Certain contractual terms, such as the requirement for software (or other product) to be reasonably capable of achieving its intended purpose or to be capable of continued operation for a certain minimum expected life, may be implied. If both parties contemplated that the software should be capable of operating properly beyond 1999, then its failure to do so may constitute a breach of the contract. On the other hand, it is possible that at the time the software was acquired, both parties anticipated that the customer would replace, or at least upgrade, the software prior to the year 2000. One factor to be considered in assessing the expectation of the parties might be the

---

2 However, it should be noted that many express warranties are limited in duration. Thirty days, ninety days and one-year durations are common. They may also be subject to other exclusions and limitations contained in the contract.

3 A failure to correctly calculate the duration between two dates or to recognize a date after the year 1999 may constitute a failure to correspond to applicable specifications.

4 Retailers and distributors of third-party products who provide their own extended warranties may be particularly at risk.

length of the license (*e.g.* whether it was for a "perpetual licence" or a license for a minimum period that extended beyond the year 1999).

In the case of a "perpetual licence," the perpetual term aspect may be discounted by a court. A term of definite duration that extends beyond the year 1999 may be more relevant. In this respect, a number of licence agreements, particularly agreements drafted in the United States, have terms of 21 or 99 years. These may have been inserted to avoid an interpretation of the transaction as a sale. They may, however, constitute a trap for the supplier with respect to the Year 2000 problem, as they may be a factor used by a customer to argue that the parties intended that the software would continue to be used after the year 1999.

With respect to any implied terms as to the expected life of a product, suppliers will likely argue that they are continually improving their products and that the expectation of both parties was that the licensee would implement new versions of the product (*i.e.*, a planned obsolescence argument). As evidence, they may cite provisions of maintenance agreements that require the customer to implement new updates within a certain period of release or which may release the supplier of maintenance obligations if such updates are not implemented.

Even if the presence of a Year 2000 problem, or the reluctance of a supplier to remedy such a problem, is a clear breach of the agreement, there may be contractual limitations on the supplier's liability.[5] These types of limitations are often upheld by courts. However, in certain circumstances, a court may refuse to enforce such limitations (particularly where the limitations are not clear). Contractual obligations, including associated contractual exclusions and limitations, are discussed in more detail in Chapter 11.

In the case of products that are subject to the *Uniform Commercial Code* (the "UCC") in the United States (discussed later in this chapter), a customer may have a right to revoke the contract within a reasonable time of acquiring knowledge of, or when it should have acquired knowledge of, a material defect.[6] This may have a significant impact on the damages that are recoverable because under the UCC, where effective revocation of acceptance has occurred, consequential damages may be recoverable.

---

5 For instance, the agreement may exclude the liability of the supplier for certain types of losses (*e.g.*, indirect or consequential damages). The agreement may also limit the supplier's total liability to the amount of money received from the customer.

6 See UCC section 2-608. The UCC is a body of legislation that, among other things, governs the sale of goods.

(b) Negligence

Under the law of negligence, a person or company can be found liable for a foreseeable loss or injury resulting from a failure to exercise a reasonable standard of care in respect of a person to whom they owed a duty of care.[7] Generally, a supplier will owe a duty of care to a party, such as a customer, who comes into contact with their product. The duty is not limited to those persons with whom the supplier has entered into a contractual relationship. In cases where a contract exists between the parties, the duty of care arising from the law of negligence can supplement any contractual obligations.

Damages that can result from the supply of non-compliant products or services include: (1) personal injury; (2) property damage; and (3) economic losses. If personal injury results due to a Year 2000 problem, then it is likely that claims in negligence, contract and strict liability (depending on the jurisdiction) can be made. If damages are purely economic in nature or limited to property damage then the right to claim such damages may be limited depending on the jurisdiction. For instance, in some United States jurisdictions, the recovery of purely economic losses may not be applicable to certain types of claims such as negligent misrepresentation or professional negligence. It should be noted that, in recent years, Canadian courts have been leaning towards the granting of relief for purely economic losses in respect of claims of negligence.

Another issue that may arise in respect of a claim for negligence is whether the defendants can assert contributory negligence as a defence. In some cases, potential plaintiffs may have had notice of Year 2000 problems and may have neglected to take timely action to address deficiencies. Such contributory negligence on their part may reduce any damages they may otherwise be entitled to claim. Other tort defenses (causation and foreseeability issues, statutes of limitation, etc.) may also be applicable.

(i) Negligent Design

A duty of care is owed by manufacturers to users of their products not to design or manufacture their product negligently. A supplier may be found liable if it failed to exercise reasonable care in the design of a product. A claim may be made that software or hardware developers were negligent in

---

7 However, not every error or omission that results in a loss or damage will give rise to a claim in negligence. It must be shown that the defendant failed to meet the standard of care that would be exercised by a reasonable person in the position of the defendant.

the design and development of a system because they did not provide support for the change in the millennium.

The work of developers and vendors will be measured against a yardstick defined by the knowledge, skill and expertise of competent and experienced developers and vendors. The standard to which developers and vendors will be held may depend on the general practice in the industry at the time the product was designed. It would be more likely that a developer of a product that was designed in the recent past would be held to have breached such a standard of care than the developer of a product that was designed ten or twenty years ago.

(ii) Negligent Advice

Persons or companies contemplating a significant acquisition or investment frequently seek and rely on the advice of third parties who possess, or are assumed to possess, special knowledge concerning the proposed acquisition.[8] Other professionals, including lawyers, may be used to assist with the negotiation and documentation of the acquisition.

A duty of care to exercise reasonable skill and care in giving advice is owed by professionals and others who hold themselves out as experts in an area.[9] The trend has been to impose this duty of care not only on professionals but also on other parties engaged in business or who have a special relationship with the party to whom the advice is given. A consultant retained by a customer, who holds himself out as possessing special skill and knowledge to give advice relating to the products or services being considered by the customer, may be liable in negligence for advice that falls below the then applicable standard of reasonable skill and care.[10]

Consultants are frequently used to assist in the selection and implementation of computer products. They may provide assistance with preparing a Request for Proposal ("RFP") and in translating the customer's requirements into functional specifications. They may also provide assistance in the review of proposals received from potential suppliers and with any required follow-up inquiries.

---

8 The proposed acquisition may be a computer system.
9 Similar liability is imposed by article 1053 of the Civil Code of the Province of Québec.
10 In the United States, the vast majority of federal and state courts have refused to recognize the tort theory of computer malpractice.

If a court accepts that the applicable standard of care required such a consultant to consider the Year 2000 problem, then a consultant who participated in the acquisition of a computer system (or equipment containing date sensitive logic) in recent years may be found liable to the customer for damages incurred due to the presence of a Year 2000 problem as a result of any failure by the consultant to include a requirement in the specifications that the system be capable of uninterrupted operation past the year 1999.

Lawyers who assist in the negotiation and drafting of contracts relating to the acquisition of products and services, mergers and acquisitions, financings or other commercial transactions may also be liable if they fail to adequately consider the Year 2000 problem and suggest appropriate provisions to protect the interests of their clients. An interesting issue may be the extent to which a lawyer who drafted a contract that failed to properly address Year 2000 issues may subsequently provide advice in respect of such contract and the Year 2000 obligations of the parties without breaching his or her professional responsibility or ethics rules (*i.e.*, because the client may have a claim against the lawyer).

Other professionals may also find themselves subject to a Year 2000-related claim. For example, claims may be made against insurance agents or brokers who may have failed to exercise adequate due diligence in respect of coverage for potential Year 2000 losses when recommending policies.

(iii) Failure to Disclose

The law of negligence also imposes a duty on manufacturers and suppliers to warn users about dangers of a product.[11] The standard of care to be met by manufacturers in ensuring that users are properly warned of dangers in their products may be higher for some types of products, such as medical products, which have a significant capacity to injure. In such cases there may be a heavy onus to provide clear, complete and current information concerning the dangers inherent in the ordinary use of the product. The duty applies not only to dangers known at the time of sale but also applies to dangers discovered after the product is sold and delivered. The duty to warn may also apply to problems in a product that may result in damages to users if not disclosed. Therefore, suppliers who are aware of Year 2000 problems

---

11 The Supreme Court of Canada, in *Hollis v. Dow Corning Corp.* [1995] 4 S.C.R. 634, reiterated the duty of a manufacturer to warn consumers of dangers inherent in the use of its product of which it has knowledge or ought to have knowledge.

with their products may need to inform customers of such problems if it is foreseeable that the product will still be in use by some customers at the time that problems are anticipated to occur. The appropriate steps should be carefully considered in consultation with legal counsel.[12]

The more a user knows about problems and risks inherent in a product they are using, the more inclined a court will be to find him or her contributorily negligent if the continued use of the product results in damages. In this respect, some suppliers are taking steps to reduce their potential liability by sending notices to customers who are known to be using products that are not Year 2000 compliant.

Some suppliers have established Web-accessible databases containing information regarding the Year 2000 readiness of various products, as well as a number of regional Year 2000 support centres to assist customers in ascertaining the Year 2000 status of products they utilize. These initiatives may also include streamlining the processing of inquiry letters.

In some cases, suppliers have also sent notifications to customers of older products with known Year 2000 incompatibilities. A supplier with knowledge of the problem, particularly where it has developed fixes, should advise customers of the potential problem and solutions. Suppliers should discuss this issue with their legal counsel because the legal obligations will depend on the factual circumstances.

Liability for a failure to disclose Year 2000-related problems will arise in circumstances other than those involving technology transactions. For instance, a company may be subject to obligations under securities legislation requiring disclosure of material information. This may require disclosure of a company's exposure to the Year 2000 issue, including anticipated costs to address any problem. The company's directors, as well as other signatories, may also be liable for material misstatements and omissions in securities-related filings. This topic is discussed in more detail in Chapter 5.

---

12 Other types of relationships may also create an obligation on one party to notify another that danger exists, or damage could result, unless certain steps are taken to avoid such danger or damage.

(c) Misrepresentations

(i) Fraudulent Misrepresentations

Customers will need to review what representations were made by suppliers concerning products that are not Year 2000 compliant. Suppliers may be liable for statements concerning Year 2000 compliance made to a customer during negotiations for the acquisition of their product or the ability of their product to continue normal operations after the year 1999. Suppliers may also be liable for any misrepresentation made in respect of services, including Year 2000 consulting or conversion services. This could include, for instance, a representation that they will be able to guarantee the identification and correction of all non-compliant program code being utilized by a customer if this is not the case.

To be actionable, the misrepresentation must have been part of the preliminary bargaining and not incorporated as a term in the contract between the parties—if it is incorporated within the contract then the customer's recourse would be for breach of contract. The misrepresentation must have been made as a statement of fact and not as a mere expression of an opinion. Furthermore, it must have been made to induce the customer to enter into the contract and the contract must in fact have been made.

If the misrepresentation by the supplier was innocent, the customer's only remedy may be rescission. However, this remedy is often impossible or at least impractical for the customer. The availability of more extensive remedies may require the customer to establish fraud or negligence on the part of the supplier. In order for a customer to establish that a false statement was made fraudulently, the customer must show that the statement was made knowingly, without belief in its truth, or recklessly, careless of whether it be true or false.[13]

A customer of computer products may be induced to contract with a supplier as a result of a false representation of fact concerning the products. Where a statement is made by or on behalf of the supplier with knowledge of its falsehood, or is made recklessly, without belief in its truth, with the intention that it be acted upon by the customer, and the customer is in fact

---

13 *Derry v. Peek* (1889), 14 A.C. 337 (H.L.). Note that the exact formulation of the requirements may vary between jurisdictions.

induced to act upon it, the supplier may be liable to the customer for the damages sustained by the customer as a result of the deceit.[14]

Circumstances that may be held to constitute fraud include situations where a supplier:

♦ knows that the product will malfunction on or after the year 2000 and continues to sell such products and to represent that the product is Year 2000 compliant;
♦ represents that it can correct Year 2000 problems in its products or services [by a certain date] when the supplier knows at the time of making the promise that this would be impossible to achieve;
♦ represents that it will provide a Year 2000 upgrade for a product when the supplier knows that it will actually discontinue the product; or
♦ sells a product or licenses software in the late 1990s, knowing that an upgrade will be required and that it will charge a cost for that upgrade (or will only provide the upgrade to customers who subscribe to ongoing maintenance).

In some cases, statements made to a customer during negotiations for the acquisition of a product may lack the necessary intent to support a cause of action for fraud. This may be the case where the supplier did not intentionally deceive the customer (*i.e.*, deliberately and knowingly attempt to deceive). In certain cases such statements may be held to constitute an express warranty as to the fitness of the product for the customer's intended purpose (and therefore the proper cause of action that would be brought against the supplier would be for breach of contact). Such statements may also support an action for negligent misrepresentation.[15]

An allegation of fraud should not be made lightly. It is usually difficult to establish all the necessary elements and there can be negative consequences if the fraud claim is unsuccessful.

---

14 *Sookman Computer Law: Acquiring and Protecting Computer Technology*, (Toronto: Carswell, 1992—Release 1) at section 2.18(a), citing *Parna v. G.S. Properties Ltd.*, [1968] 1 O.R. 626 (Ont. H.C.), varied [1969] 2 O.R. 346 (C.A.).
15 See section 2-313 of the UCC, which deals with a breach of express warranties. Any affirmation of fact that becomes part of the bargain may constitute an express warranty. Pursuant to this section, marketing materials, correspondence and statements have all been found to constitute express warranties depending on the circumstances.

(ii) Negligent Misrepresentation by Suppliers

Depending on the circumstances and the nature of the relationship, a supplier may be found liable for the negligent provision of advice relating to its products. This may include a representation that its product will be suitable for the customer's current requirements and for a reasonable future time, where the supplier failed to consider the potential Year 2000 problems in its product.

The elements that would need to be shown in an action for negligent misrepresentation are:[16]

♦ a false statement negligently made (such as that the product can continue to meet the customer's requirements for the next [x] years, which time frame extends past the year 1999);
♦ a special relationship giving rise to a duty of care exists (such a duty can arise when the person making the statements is possessed with special skills and/or knowledge);
♦ a reasonable person would know that the other contracting party (*i.e.*, the customer) is relying and in fact actually does rely, on that skill; and
♦ a loss was suffered as a consequence of that reliance.

An action for negligent misrepresentation, in the majority of United States jurisdictions, requires the plaintiff to prove that:

♦ the defendant made a representation in the course of its business or in a transaction in which it had a pecuniary interest;
♦ the defendant supplied false information;
♦ the defendant did not exercise reasonable care or competence in obtaining or communicating the information; and
♦ the plaintiff suffered pecuniary loss by justifiably relying on the representation.

Some jurisdictions also require that the plaintiff be unaware of the falsity of the representation. A minority of jurisdictions require that the defendant be in the business of "supplying information," and that the information be

---

16 The following is an adaption of the elements for negligent misrepresentation that were set out by the court in *Jonas & Erickson Software v. Fitz-Wright Co.* (1991), 24 A.C.W.S. (3d) 166 (B.C.S.C.).

provided to the plaintiff for their guidance in business relations with third parties.[17]

In many of the above situations, the relationship between the parties may be governed by a contract. However, even in such a case, it may be advantageous to bring a separate action in negligence in order to circumvent exculpatory provisions or limitation period problems.

It should be noted that a number of courts in the United States have refused to permit recovery for negligent advice given by a computer supplier to a customer where the relationship was governed by contract.[18] The results may differ in an appropriate situation where the existence of some special relationships of trust and confidence between the parties can be established.

(iii) Statutory Liability for Misrepresentations

The law affecting misleading representations by suppliers of goods and services is codified in some jurisdictions. For instance, section 52(1) of the *Competition Act* (Canada) provides:[19]

> No person shall, for the purpose of promoting, directly or indirectly, the supply or use of a product or for the purpose of promoting, directly or indirectly, any business interest, by any means whatsoever, (a) make a representation to the public that is false or misleading in a material respect; (b) make a representation to the public in the form of a statement, warranty or guarantee of the performance, efficacy or length of life of a product that is not based on an adequate and proper test thereof, the proof of which lies upon the person making the representation.

This provision appears to be broad enough to cover misleading representations concerning a product's ability to operate normally after the year 2000. It would also appear to cover a warranty or certificate as to the Year 2000 compliance of a product that is given based on a supplier's honest belief but without "adequate and proper" testing having been conducted.[20]

---

17 Stephen L. Hock, "Computer Manufacturer and Vendor Liability" *Year 2000 Computer Crisis: The Litigation Summit* (November 6-7, 1997) Fulcrum Information Services Inc., San Francisco, California.

18 See *Sookman Computer Law: Acquiring and Protecting Computer Technology* (Toronto: Carswell, 1992-Release 1) at section 2.18(b).

19 R.S.C. 1985, c. C-34.

20 The *Competition Act* also prohibits the publication of the results of testing of a product that cannot be corroborated. Suppliers would therefore be well advised to keep careful records of any testing conducted in respect of Year 2000 compliance.

It is possible that this provision, or comparable provisions in other jurisdictions, could be relied on by a purchaser of a product with an advertised operating life that would extend beyond the year 1999 but where such product contains a date problem that precludes normal operation after the year 1999.

Other legislation may also deal with misleading advertising. For instance, Ontario's Business Practices Act[21] declares it to be an "unfair practice" to make "a false, misleading or deceptive consumer representation," which may include a wide variety of representations including performance characteristics that the goods or services do not have. Another example is the *California Consumer Legal Remedies Act,* which imposes liability for certain unfair and deceptive business practices.[22]

Many Year 2000 related lawsuits can be expected to include a claim based on legislation dealing with business practices. For example, in *Atlaz v. Software Business Technologies,*[23] the complaint alleged "fraudulent and unfair business practices" in violation of California law:

> The misrepresentations and non-disclosure by defendants of the material facts concerning the Year 2000 Problem contained in the SBT Pro Series software packages constitute an unfair business act or practice within the meaning of Business and Professions Code Section 17200 because defendants knew or should have been aware at all relevant times that the SBT Pro Series software packages contained such material problems.

Legislation governing unfair business practices and misleading advertising typically gives government agencies the authority to prohibit misleading advertising. However, such legislation may also provide remedies to consumers who were affected by the misleading statements. In some cases, consumers subjected to an unfair practice are given the right to rescind the contract. Where rescission is not possible, the consumer may be entitled to recover the amount by which the amount paid exceeds the fair market value of the goods or services received under the contract or damages, or both. In addition, a court may be expressly authorized to award exemplary or punitive damages against a supplier that engages in an unfair practice.

---

21 R.S.O. 1990, c. B.18.

22 West's Ann. Cal. Civ. Code Title 1.S, *California Code,* section 1750.

23 *Atlaz Int'l Ltd. v. Software Business Tech. Inc.,* No. 172539, filed December 3, 1997 in California's Marin County Superior Court.

(d) Breach of Fiduciary Duty

Liability may be imposed on the basis of a breach of a fiduciary duty. Lawsuits against directors and officers could be triggered by "earning surprises" or drops in share values due to a failure of the company to take appropriate and timely action to deal with the Year 2000 problem. Plaintiffs will attempt to show that the directors and officers failed to exercise due care in assessing and responding to the Year 2000 problem.

Directors and officers can also be liable for actions they take (*i.e.*, selling securities of the corporation) while in possession of material, non-public information regarding the Year 2000 problems faced by the corporation. The obligations and duties of directors and officers is considered in more detail in Chapter 7.

(e) Product Liability

A customer who suffers a loss or injury due to a Year 2000 defect in a product will likely bring an action against the retailer. However, this approach has a number of weaknesses. For example, the retailer may be or become insolvent or otherwise discontinue the business. Another problem is the difficulty of obtaining discovery against the manufacturer who is more likely to have possession of the required documents and knowledge of the pertinent facts.

A manufacturer may be directly liable to an end user of a defective product. Anglo-Canadian courts have primarily relied on theories of collateral contracts. Under these theories a manufacturer may be liable for breach of an express warranty if the warranty is intended to induce the customer to order the manufacturer's product from another person. However, certain requirements may need to be met The warranty must be:

♦ an express representation;
♦ intended to have contractual force;
♦ known by the customer prior to the purchase; and
♦ actually relied on.

Numerous difficulties remain with this approach. They were recognized by the Ontario Law Reform Commission, which proposed a number of recommendations unsuccessfully introduced into law.[24] However, other provinces, including Saskatchewan, New Brunswick and Quebec, have moved to abolish the problem of privity for consumer warranty claims.

The United Kingdom has also enacted reforms under its *Consumer Protection Act 1987*, pursuant to which liability may attach to the following parties:[25]

♦ the producer of the product;
♦ a person who holds him- or herself out as being the producer (*i.e.*, applies his or her label to a product manufactured by someone else);
♦ the person who imported it into the European Union in the course of business;
♦ where the "producer" cannot be identified in a reasonable time, the person who supplied it such as a retailer or wholesaler.

The doctrine of product liability has developed much further in the United States and is grounded in tort law.[26] Manufacturers and other sellers in the supply chain are held liable to a strict liability standard for selling a product in a defective condition that is unreasonably dangerous to the user or consumer. However, a common defence has been "obvious danger." In the past this has been construed to mean a danger relating to a possible physical injury. Suppliers may attempt to extend this to argue that plaintiffs were aware of the risk that a product that utilized dates may encounter a problem in the year 2000.

As noted above, causes of action in negligence may also be applicable.

(f) Implied Warranties

(i) Implied Warranties and Conditions under Sale of Goods Legislation

Aside from express warranties contained in acquisition contracts, certain implied warranties and conditions imposed by law may also be applicable.

---

24 The Commission's recommendations were incorporated into Bill 110, the *Consumer Products Warranties Act*, 1976, which received first reading on June 16, 1976, but did not proceed to become law.

25 *Consumer Protection Act 1987* (U.K.) 1987, c. 43. See Tarlo Lyons, *Legal Liability and the Millennium Date Change Problem*. (U.K. law firm publication)

26 See also UCC Article 2-318.

For the most part, these have been codified in consumer protection and sale of goods legislation (or the *Uniform Commercial Code*, in the United States). The Ontario *Sale of Goods Act*[27] refers to implied *conditions* whereas the *Uniform Commercial Code* refers to *warranties*. Under contract law, a breach of a condition is treated more seriously than a breach of a warranty and provides the non-breaching party with additional remedies.

Although there may be arguments regarding whether a product that is not Year 2000 compliant is or is not of "merchantable quality" or "fit for purpose," the closer to the year 2000 that a product is acquired, the more likely these implied warranties and conditions will be held to include Year 2000 compliance.

Correspondence with Description—If a transaction involves the sale of goods by description, there will be an implied condition that the goods will correspond with the description. This condition may be applicable even where the customer has an opportunity to inspect the goods if the customer relies on the description. This implied condition is not likely to be very useful in respect of Year 2000 issues. It has generally been interpreted by Canadian courts as being directed to the identification of goods and not to their quality.

Fitness for Purpose—The *Sale of Goods Act* in Ontario, and comparable legislation in other provinces, implies a condition that the goods will be reasonably fit for their purpose. Certain Year 2000 problems may result in a court finding that the product was not fit for its purpose. However, certain requirements must be met in order for this to occur:

(1) the goods must be of the type supplied in the course of the supplier's business;[28]
(2) the supplier must have knowledge of the buyer's intended purpose for the goods; and
(3) there must be reliance on the supplier's skill or judgment.

Under the *Uniform Commercial Code* in the United States, there is an implied warranty of fitness for purpose, where:

(1) the supplier, at the time of contracting, has reason to know any particular purpose for which the goods are required; and

---

27 R.S.O. 1980, c. 462.
28 The purpose of this is to exclude private sales.

(2) where the customer is relying on the supplier's skill or judgment to select or supply suitable goods.

The implementation of the UCC in some jurisdictions does not require a direct contractual relationship between the parties in order for any implied warranties to apply. In such situations, manufacturers who sell their products through intermediaries may still be liable to customers for breach of such warranties.

Even in the case where no purpose is expressly stated, it may nonetheless be obvious from the character of the goods. In some cases a requirement that the goods continue to operate after the year 1999 may not be difficult to prove.

Implied Condition of Merchantability—The Ontario *Sale of Goods Act*, as well as comparable legislation in other jurisdictions, contains a condition that goods will be of a "merchantable quality." This condition will be breached if the goods are unfit for any purpose for which they would ordinarily be used. The condition is applicable where goods are bought by description from a supplier who deals with goods of that description (but need not be the manufacturer).

In the United States, a warranty of merchantability, unless properly disclaimed, becomes part of every contract to which the UCC applies in which the seller is a merchant with respect to the goods provided in the contract. Other warranties may be implied based on previous dealings between the parties or industry practice.[29]

If the customer has examined the goods, there is no implied condition in regards to defects that such examination ought to have revealed. Therefore, where a contract requires that a customer perform acceptance testing specifically in respect of date functions or Year 2000 issues, the implied condition of merchantability may be negated.

(ii) Applicability of Sale of Goods Legislation

The implied warranties and conditions arising under sale of goods legislation are applicable to transactions that involve a "sale of goods." They will not be applicable to a contract for work and materials.

---

29 See UCC 2-314(3) and UCC 2-316(3)(c).

Under Ontario's *Sale of Goods Act*, in order for a contract to constitute a contract for the "sale of goods," it must involve the transfer, or agreement to transfer, property in goods by a seller to a buyer for a monetary consideration. The word "goods" is defined to include "all chattels personal, other than things in action and money." With respect to "chattels personal," only "choses in possession" come within the statutory definition of "goods." "Choses or things in possession" includes "all things that are at once tangible, moveable, and visible, and of which possession can be taken."

With respect to information technology products, the sale of hardware clearly fall within the ambit of sale of goods legislation. Courts have also predominantly treated sale transactions involving a combination of hardware and software as a sale of goods. Numerous decisions in the United States have also treated transactions involving the supply of complete systems as "transactions in goods" to which the UCC applied.

The supply of services probably would not be considered a transaction to which sale of goods legislation or the UCC would apply. However, the picture is less clear in respect of transactions involving software only. In the United States, transactions involving pre-packaged software have been held to be transactions in goods to which the UCC applies. In some cases, even custom programming has been found to constitute a "transaction in goods." An important consideration in many cases is whether the service aspect predominates.

In Canada, provincial sale of goods legislation will not likely apply to pre-packaged software (supplied pursuant to licence agreements that expressly provide that no property in the software will be acquired by the licensee) if the software is not supplied as part of a larger transaction to which the sale of goods legislation would otherwise apply.[30] Likewise, a transaction in which only custom programming is provided will likely be characterized as a contract for the supply of services, not subject to provincial sale of goods legislation.

The result is similar under the United Kingdom's *Sale of Goods Act* (1979).[31] That statute implies terms of merchantable quality and fitness for purpose into agreements for packaged software provided on disk where ownership of the disk is transferred to the customer. Where software is

---

30 The supply of pre-packaged software would, however, fall within the ambit of sale of goods legislation if the software is "sold."

31 *Sale of Goods Act 1979* (U.K.), 1979, c. 54.

installed by the supplier and no media is provided then these terms may not apply.

The initial version of a software program may have been acquired as part of a transaction to which the sale of goods legislation would apply (*i.e.*, as part of a system). However, the more recent version of the software actually in use by a customer may have been acquired through a transaction that does not fall within the scope of such legislation.[32]

With respect to transactions not subject to sale of goods legislation, such as the provision of "services," the common law, or other legislation may require the supplier to exercise reasonable skill and care, and to perform the work in a good and professional manner (but would not necessarily require that a particular result be achieved). For example, such standards may be applicable to services performed by a consultant or system integrator in recommending a system to be acquired by a customer from another party. The implied warranties of merchantability and fitness for purpose may also be applicable to goods supplied as an incidental under a contract that is primarily for services.

(iii) Disclaimer of Implied Warranties and Conditions

The legislation under which the implied warranties and conditions arise will generally permit them to be negated or varied by the express agreement of the parties. It is common for suppliers to disclaim all implied warranties and conditions in any written agreements that are entered into with customers. In most jurisdictions, such disclaimers, if drafted properly, will be enforceable.

In some cases, courts will try to protect rights provided under legislation and will restrict the circumstances in which a supplier may absolve itself of liability under implied warranties. One technique is to examine the exact words that are used in the disclaimer. If they do not precisely describe the type of liability disclaimed, then courts may find that the implied liability is still applicable. For instance, if a supplier includes a disclaimer of "all warranties implied by statute," a court may still hold such a supplier liable under implied "conditions."

Courts may also refuse to give effect to an exemption clause where:

---

32 Consider an update downloaded from a supplier's web site.

- the seller attempts to completely exempt itself from liability such that it may default on its bargain with impunity;
- the disclaimer is not sufficiently prominent so as to provide reasonable notice; or
- the exclusion is not reasonable.[33]

Finally, where the transaction involves a consumer, many jurisdictions do not permit the disclaimer of the implied warranties and conditions provided under sale of goods legislation.

2.3 BREACH OF STATUTORY DUTIES

Liability under various regulatory requirements may arise due to Year 2000 problems. A failure to utilize a compliant system that results in incorrect results, or interferes with a company's ability to process data, can result in a breach of regulatory or statutory obligations to which the company may be subject, including those relating to or imposed by:

- securities commissions
- government regulators
- tax authorities
- customs
- agricultural boards
- employee records
- pension calculations[34]
- privacy
- credit reporting

As regulators become more aware of Year 2000 problems, new requirements designed to directly address Year 2000 issues may be imposed.

---

33 The United Kingdom's *Unfair Contract Terms Act* (U.K.) 1977, c. 50, will void any unreasonable exclusions of implied terms in a contract. See also *St. Albans City and District Council v. International Computers Ltd.* [1996] 4 All E.R. 481 (C.A.), a UK decision of the Court of Appeals that held that in the case of packaged software delivered on disk where the customer obtains ownership of the disks, warranties implied by sale of goods legislation may only be excluded if it is reasonable to do so.

34 An error in the calculation of retirement benefits may result in liability. In the United States, see the *Employee Retirement Income Security Act of 1974*, 29 U.S.C. Sec 1001 ("ERISA").

2.4 DUTY TO MITIGATE

A basic principle under both negligence and contract law is that a party that suffers damages must act to mitigate its damages. If a customer cannot convince a supplier to make a system Year 2000 compliant then the customer should take reasonable steps to correct the problem on its own or to replace the system.

2.5 LIMITATION PERIODS

A party's ability to bring a claim may be limited by limitation periods. If a lawsuit is not initiated within the applicable period of time, the claim becomes "statute barred." There are a variety of reasons that have been advanced to explain the use of limitation periods.[35] They do exist and must be considered.

Each jurisdiction usually has general statutes of limitation.[36] There may also be other (and in most cases, shorter) limitation periods that are scattered in many other statutes that are applicable to a wide variety of causes of action. In some cases, notice provisions may also be applicable.

The statutory limitation periods applicable to breach of contract or to negligence, two of the more common causes of action likely to be considered in respect to Year 2000 problems, will depend on the particular jurisdiction. The period is as long as six years in some jurisdictions but may be *much shorter* elsewhere.[37] While the applicable limitation period may be similar for both causes of action, the start of the period will typically differ. This is because the limitation period starts to run when the "cause of action has accrued." However, when a cause of action accrues may differ for a breach of contract as compared to a negligent act.

---

35 Graeme Mew, *The Law of Limitations* (Markham: Butterworths, 1991). Chapter 1, section 3 lists four broad categories: (1) the defendant is entitled to peace of mind some point in time after the occurrence of conduct that might be actionable; (2) evidentiary concerns; (3) economic concerns; and (4) judgmental reasons.

36 In Ontario the applicable statute is the *Limitations Act*, R.S.O. 1980, c. 240.

37 The general limitation period in some provinces is as short as two years. In the United States, in a transaction governed by the UCC, an action must generally be commenced no later than four years after the action accrues. See UCC 2-725(1) [1996]. Generally, an action accrues when delivery is made, even if the buyer is unaware that the product or goods are defective. In an action for negligence, the action may not accrue until the initial failure of the product or goods.

An action for breach of contract arises at the time a breach occurs. It is not necessary for the plaintiff to have suffered damages. A breach of contract may occur at the time the defective product is delivered to the plaintiff. In contrast, damage may be necessary before a cause of action can lie in negligence. Causes of action in negligence, and possibly in contract, may not arise, and the associated limitation period may not commence, until a plaintiff discovers or ought to have discovered the material facts on which the claim is based.

In some cases, the same conduct may provide the basis for actions for breach of contract and negligence. In situations where the action for breach of contract may be barred by a limitation statute, a plaintiff may be able to proceed with an action for negligence.

It should be noted that limitation periods may not be enforceable in all circumstances. For instance, a court may find the following to be exceptions:

- ◆ **Agreement.** In some jurisdictions, the parties can contractually agree not to enforce a limitation period by fulfilling the requirements of an enforceable contract (including consideration).
- ◆ **Waiver.** A person can knowingly waive the benefit of a limitation period. A waiver can be express or implied. Generally, settlement discussions between the parties should not lead to an inference that a defendant has waived limitation period defences that it would otherwise be able to raise. However, in some jurisdictions, settlement discussions after expiry of a limitation period may constitute confirmation by a defendant of a plaintiff's claim.[38]
- ◆ **Estoppel.** The doctrine of estoppel prevents a person who makes a representation, that is detrimentally relied upon by another party, from then following a course of action that is contrary to the original representation. In some circumstances, a supplier who tells a customer to hold off a lawsuit because a Year 2000 version of the product is imminent may have a difficult time later trying to claim that the customer's lawsuit is barred by a limitation period. It is recommended that a customer not take any chances and file a statement of claim to protect its rights.
- ◆ **Acknowledgement.** Acknowledgement of a simple contract or a confirmation of a cause of action may have an effect on the expiry of time. A licensor, that may be under an obligation pursuant to an agreement

---

38 Graeme Mew, *The Law of Limitations* (Markham: Butterworths, 1991), in Chapter 6.3, (Settlement Negotiations).

that might otherwise become unenforceable due to an expiry of a limitation period, could potentially acknowledge its liability in a response to a customer inquiry letter concerning Year 2000 compliance of its product and thereby extend the applicable period.

♦ **Fraud.** Common law principles as well as the provisions of some statutes of limitations may exclude the application of a limitation period where fraud or deceit is involved. It is therefore possible that a party that acts fraudulently or deceitfully in respect of its dealings with others on a Year 2000 problem may be precluded from relying on any applicable limitation periods.

There are many variations and exceptions to limitation periods and the foregoing discussion should be viewed as general principles rather than as a complete guide in respect of a particular legal situation. For instance, the laws governing many professionals may contain provisions that may provide for a much shorter limitation period or may effect when a limitation period starts running. For instance, limitation periods contained in legislation governing hospitals or medical practitioners typically provide for a limitation period that may be as short as one or two years.

In some cases it may be too late to wait until the year 2000 to initiate a claim. It may be critical to issue a claim as soon as possible in order to prevent the claim from becoming barred by a limitation period. A party with a potential claim should consult its legal advisor as soon as possible so that appropriate action can be taken immediately if necessary to preserve that party's rights.

3

Government Response/Initiatives

3.1 CANADIAN GOVERNMENT RESPONSE

(a) Introduction

> The Government of Canada's priority with regard to the Year 2000 challenge is to ensure the safety, security and economic well-being of all Canadians by providing uninterrupted government service in key areas.[1]

In Canada, the Treasury Board Secretariat has assumed the role of coordinating and monitoring the Canadian government's internal efforts to address the Year 2000 problem. The Treasury Board has indicated that it will exercise every possible effect to accomplish the Year 2000 priorities and ensure appropriate actions are taken. This follows the establishment by the Treasury Board in the Spring of 1996 of the Chief Information Officer (CIO) Year 2000 Project Office to work with departments and agencies to identify and find solutions to common problems.

Other government departments have also assumed various functions to support the federal government's compliance efforts. Public Works and Government Services Canada ("PWGSC") has set up a permanent Year 2000 procurement office to facilitate the procurement process and assist departments with procurement issues. Government Telecommunications and Informatics Services ("GTIS") of PWGSC has been working on the

---

1 Treasury Board of Canada Secretariat, "The Chief Information Officer Year 2000 Project Office" at <http://www.info2000.gc.ca/general/office.asp>. See also <http://www.info 2000.gc.ca>.

vendor compliance issue and has set up a repository of the compliance status of thousands of software packages.[2]

(b) 1997 Report of the Auditor General/Effect on Government

The Year 2000 computer problem can have a significant adverse effect on government programs and operations. In particular, systems that are most critical in supporting major programs may fail and could affect public health and safety and other essential services to the public. Aside from the direct fallout of systems errors or failures, Canadians' confidence in the public service may also be at stake.

This warning is contained in the *1997 Report of the Auditor General* (the "Auditor's Report"), released by the Office of the Auditor General of Canada.[3] In response, the federal government indicated that it has accorded the Year 2000 computer problem its highest level of priority.

The Auditor's Report examined the risks and exposures as of April 30, 1997 that government programs and operations face as a result of the Year 2000 threat. It expressed concern that if progress were to continue at the rate observed, it would likely be too slow to overcome the Year 2000 problem. Systems that support major programs and essential services may fail, and continuous delivery of these programs and services could be at risk. The potential consequences for the government could manifest themselves as health and safety concerns, financial implications, disruption to essential services for the public, or legal ramifications.

The costs for fixing the Year 2000 are expected to be significant. As of early May 1997, the Treasury Board Secretariat estimated $1 billion as the overall cost of making government systems compliant for the year 2000. It was anticipated that some departments may request significant incremental funding, potentially totalling hundreds of millions of dollars.

The Auditor's Report recommended that departments and agencies target implementation for April 1, 1998 in order to allow one full business cycle for testing. This follows the general practice being advanced by the information technology industry that organizations have all compliant systems implemented by the start of one full business cycle in advance of 2000.

---

2 See <http://vend2000.gc.ca>.

3 The Auditor's Report is available at <http://www.oag-bvg.gc.ca/>.

At the conclusion of the inventory, assessment, and planning phase, many government departments may realize that there is insufficient time to convert all systems. Some departments will therefore need to consider the use of systems triage in order to deal with their Year 2000 problems. This means that where it has been determined that not all systems can be salvaged in time, priority ought to be given to those that would benefit most from the remaining time and resources. In the Year 2000 context, top priority needs to be assigned to systems that are critical to an organization's business lines or program mandate.

According to the Auditor's Report another crucial area that needs to be addressed is the development of contingency plans. Government agencies, like their private sector counterparts, must plan for the possibility that some systems, upon reaching 2000, may not continue to function as designed. Many organizations have various forms of disaster recovery plans and backup systems in place. However, it is unlikely that these measures alone will be sufficient in the event that systems fail as a result of Year 2000.

An examination of legal issues related to Year 2000 compliance was also identified as an area justifying further study. According to the Auditor's Report, analysis of the legal implications of Year 2000 had been primarily in the area of contracting and contract administration. Limited work had been done to examine and analyze other possible legal implications for the government that may result from Year 2000.

The Auditor's Report stated that there would be merit in conducting legal analyses so that departments and agencies can receive guidance and advice on precautionary measures to take as appropriate. This advice mirrors the practice in the private sector where many organizations are conducting legal audits to identify appropriate actions that need to be taken to reduce their potential liability for Year 2000 computer problems.

(c) Task Force Year 2000

On September 2, 1997, Canadian Industry Minister John Manley announced the creation of a federal "Task Force Year 2000," chaired by BCE Inc. President and Chief Operating Officer Jean Monty and including 13 other chief executives of Canadian companies[4] to look at the Year 2000 problem.

---

4 The representatives were selected from a number of key economic sectors (banking, insurance, transportation, manufacturing, telecommunications, information technology, resource-based, retail, and service) and from small and medium-sized businesses.

The mandate of the Task Force was to assess the nature and scope of the electronic challenge in Canada, the state of industry preparedness to deal with issues related to Year 2000 computer risk, and to provide leadership and advice on how these risks could be reduced.

Even though the Canadian government stated that it considers the Year 2000 problem as an issue for businesses to solve, it was recognized that the government would nevertheless be held accountable by the public and that the Year 2000 problem is a national competitive issue. There is also a desire to improve communications regarding this problem so that different companies do not need to each reinvent the wheel. One of the purposes of the Task Force was therefore to help share best practices between organizations.

Statistics Canada was asked to survey small and medium-sized businesses on their concerns and preparations for meeting the Year 2000 problem. The results of a survey, conducted in the fall of 1997 (and released on December 8, 1997), provided some insight on the Year 2000 preparedness of Canadian business. Initial findings indicated that less than half of Canadian companies had taken action to address the Year 2000 problem. Nine percent of companies were not even aware that there was a Year 2000 problem. The survey results also confirmed that companies in some sectors, for instance finance and insurance, had been more diligent in addressing the problem.

The survey results indicated that 46% of all companies said they were aware of the issue but had not done anything about it. Of those in that category, 27% said they were not worried about the problem yet because there would be sufficient time to fix it later. About a quarter said it was not an important issue for their company because they used computer systems only minimally.[5]

In addition, while a company's use of computer systems may be minimal, it may nevertheless be vulnerable to Year 2000-related failures of embedded systems that are utilized in the business. Those same companies likely do not employ computer professionals who could warn them of potential problems in such embedded systems.

---

5 It is submitted that some firms in the former group may be underestimating the time required to convert an existing system, particularly as resources become more scarce. Those in the latter group need to consider the effect on their business if a Year 2000 problem is experienced by a key supplier.

Task Force Year 2000 released its report, *A Call for Action* in February, 1998. The Task Force was originally planning to make its report public in May, but moved up the deadline because of the urgent need to take action. The report reviewed the various actions that have been taken by securities regulators, the Canadian Institute of Chartered Accountants, and others, and made key recommendations to give impetus to the actions that must be taken in order to prepare Canadian business and industry for the year 2000.

In furtherance of its objective to communicate the importance of the Year 2000 problem, and encourage the private sector to transform awareness into formal action, the Task Force implemented a $4 million communications campaign. It called on the media to continue to report on the efforts of all parties in meeting the Year 2000 challenge, monitor the effective implementation of Task Force recommendations and, in the case of electronic and print media, to develop and distribute regular messages of public interest to increase awareness and encourage action. The Task Force is also seeking assistance from national, provincial and regional associations. They have been asked to immediately take a more proactive awareness and support role on Year 2000 preparedness and publicly report on initiatives taken if they have not yet done so.

3.2 UNITED STATES GOVERNMENT RESPONSES

There have been initiatives for the establishment of a national commission in the United States. Bill S.22 sought to establish a commission, to be known as the "National Commission to Address the Year 2000 Computer Problem," which would have compiled a report for Congress and the President.[6] If it had been enacted, the Bill would have required the Commission to conduct an analysis of the history and background concerning the reasons for the occurrence of the Year 2000 computer problem, as well as a legal analysis of responsibilities for costs.[7] More recently, in December 1997, the President of the Information Technology Association of America ("ITAA") called on President Clinton to create a "National Year 2000 Task Force."

On February 4, 1998, President Clinton issued an Executive Order to establish the President's Council on Year 2000 Conversion. The Executive Order also states that it shall be the policy of the executive branch that agencies shall (i) assure that no critical Federal program experiences

---

6 Senate Bill S.22, January 21, 1997 (105th Congress 1st Session).
7 Section 7.

disruption because of the Year 2000 problem; (ii) assist and cooperate with State, local and tribal governments to address the Year 2000 problem where those governments depend on Federal information or information technology or the Federal Government is dependent on those governments to perform critical missions; (iii) cooperate with the private sector operators of critical national and local systems, including the banking and financial system, the telecommunication system, the public health system, the transportation system, and the electric power generation system, in addressing the Year 2000 problem; and (iv) communicate with the foreign counterparts to raise awareness of and generate cooperative international arrangements to address the Year 2000 problem.

The Office of Management and Budget ("OMB") has assumed part of the responsibility for making sure other federal agencies take appropriate action to address the Year 2000 problem. The OMB sent a report to Congress (December 16, 1997) describing how federal agencies are handling the Year 2000 problem. Each agency was graded on its progress with the Department of Transportation identified as an area of serious concern. The report stated that vital national computer operations responsible for the air traffic control system are "at high risk of system failure" at the turn of the century.[8]

Governments are suppliers of a number of vital goods and services. Many are finding that their operations are susceptible or potentially susceptible to Year 2000 problems and have begun exploring ways of potentially protecting themselves in the event they experience a disruption in their ability to deliver.

Some United States state governments, including Georgia, Oregon, Indiana, Utah, California and Virginia,[9] are considering legislation to provide immunity for the state government from class action lawsuits brought in respect of the Year 2000 problem. At least one state, Nevada, has passed legislation to protect itself from potential liability arising from Year 2000 failures of its systems.[10] Nevada's legislation, which covers Year 2000

---

8 M.J. Zuckerman and Anthony DeBarros, "Avoiding Digital Disaster" *U.S.A. Today* (December 17, 1997) (cover page). Within less than one month, IBM indicated that certain computers in use for air traffic control are not Year 2000 compliant and can be expected to fail if not replaced.

9 For instance, see the Virginia *Tort Claims Act*, HB 277. The bill would change the state's limited waiver of immunity under its *Tort Claims Act* to retain Sovereign immunity from Year 2000 suits filed in state courts.

10 SB-180.

actions arising from torts, contractual disputes and civil rights claims, extends the immunity until the end of the year 2005.

States enjoy sovereign immunity, but for political reasons, waive that immunity. Nevada's legislation reinstates that immunity for the purposes of Year 2000 damages. However, Nevada was fortunate in that its waiver of immunity was a matter of statutory law and not written into the state's constitution. It was therefore possible to pass the Year 2000 immunity legislation as an amendment to an existing statute rather than requiring an amendment to the state's constitution—a more costly and time-consuming task. Other states may not be as fortunate.

The United States federal government has also considered adopting legislation requiring that systems supplied to the government be Year 2000 compliant. One legislative proposal would require all new computer hardware and software purchased by the government be able to process dates properly in the year 2000.[11]

3.3 RESPONSES FROM OTHER GOVERNMENTS

The United Kingdom's Government established a "Taskforce 2000"[12] in order to raise public awareness of the Year 2000 problem. The United Kingdom also observed the world's first Year 2000 awareness week in December 1997, which included numerous conferences and debates. The National Health Service in the United Kingdom has been attempting to raise awareness and has undertaken a program to inform hospital and health-service managers of their exposure to Year 2000 risks and to provide them with a variety of guides and other resources to assist them in developing and implementing their Year 2000 programs. The United Kingdom's House of Commons Select Committee on Science and Technology issued a sweeping report on April 1, 1998 in respect of the Year 2000 problem.[13] Most of the conclusions and recommendations focused on efforts required to address Year 2000 issues in respect of government operations. Other conclusions and recommendations included the following:

---

11 Reported by Reuters on July 11, 1997.
12 <http://www.taskforce2000.co.uk/>
13 UK House of Commons, Science and Technology Committee, "Science and Technology—Second Report" (April 1, 1998). Available at <http://www.parliament.the-stationery-office.co.uk/pa/cm199798/cmselect/cmsctech/342ii/st0202.htm>.

♦ Organizations should not consider legal action as a primary remedy to Year 2000 problems but as a last resort and should not plan to enter litigation in preference to taking preventative action now;

♦ The risk of legal action on the part of those affected by century date-related failures reinforces the need for all organizations to undertake thorough Year 2000 preparations to ensure that their systems, products and services are millennium ready. It should also be seen as a reason to keep thorough and accurate records of all remedial measures in case called upon by the courts to demonstrate that all reasonable steps to avoid system failures were taken;

♦ Development of a standard checklist to enable businesses to report progress in a common form;

♦ Rejection of the right to charge for upgrades necessitated by non-compliance of existing equipment. Depending on the age of the current system and the terms under which it was supplied, companies have an obligation to provide suitable upgrades or replacements free of charge;

♦ Wide dissemination, in clear and non-technical terms, of the information needed to test domestic equipment for millennium compliance;

♦ The need for prioritization should be stressed (*i.e.*, time may not remain to address all systems and there is a need to prioritize the remaining time in order to ensure that problems in critical systems are addressed); and

♦ Commissioning of a quarterly survey on progress in the business sector, broken down into categories including core services such as transport, telecommunications and other critical public services (and that the results of the survey are made publicly available).

3.4 LEGISLATIVE RESPONSES

A number of countries are considering a legislative approach to the Year 2000 problem. The United States has seen some initiatives for legislation arising from Silicon Valley (California Assembly Bill 1710) to provide a safe harbour for the computer industry, which many in the United States consider to be a strategic industry.[14] Congress has passed legislation giving more power to federal regulators of financial institutions to deal with the Year 2000 problem and is considering safe harbours for regulated industries such as banking and securities. However, in Canada, the Minister of

---

14 California Assembly bill AB-1710 would limit the financial liability for Year 2000 damages to bodily injury and reasonable costs, excluding emotional and punitive damages.

Industry has stated that legislation in Canada would take too long and would never happen.

The Information Technology Association of America ("ITAA") maintains a list of the various legislative initiatives in the United States relating to the Year 2000 problem.

3.5 YEAR 2000 WARRANTIES

The Canadian federal government has developed some Year 2000 warranty provisions to be included in agreements made by suppliers with the Canadian government. The text of these warranties is accessible from the Industry Canada Web site.[15] Various United States federal agencies and a number of state governments have also adopted Year 2000 warranty language that must be incorporated into agreements made by suppliers with such states.

---

15 <http://strategis.ic.gc.ca/year2000>

4

Regulators and the Year 2000 Problem

Canada's Task Force Year 2000 recognized the important role government can play in encouraging the private sector to take appropriate action to address the Year 2000 problem. It recommended that by April 1, 1998 regulators at all levels of government complete an assessment of the impacts that Year 2000 computer failures in their regulated industries would have on their regulatory objectives; revise, where appropriate, their compliance assessment procedures; and exert, where possible, moral suasion on their regulated industries regarding the importance of Year 2000 preparedness.[1]

The discussion that follows in this chapter focuses on financial institutions and participants in the securities industry. However, it illustrates the concerns, and possibly the approaches, of regulators responsible for overseeing other sectors.

4.1 OVERVIEW

In Canada, the Office of the Superintendent of Financial Institutions ("OSFI") is the federal regulator responsible for overseeing all federally regulated financial institutions including banks, certain trust companies, insurance companies, and credit associations. OSFI wrote to those institutions regarding the Year 2000 problem[2] stating:

---

1 Task Force Year 2000 Recommendation 13.
2 Letter dated September 25, 1997 regarding "Year 2000 Project." The letter also included a "Best Practices" paper. See <http://www.osfi-bsif.gc.ca/Publications/yr2000.htm>. With respect to securities dealers, while these entities are regulated provincially, a number of such dealers are subsidiaries of federally regulated banks. As a result, any

> As January 1, 2000 approaches, there is growing concern about institutions' and corporate entities' preparedness to deal with year 2000 technology issues. Experts believe that even the largest and best-prepared organizations may encounter problems with the year 2000 date change because of its broad impact on computer systems. Technological advancements, globalization and competition for resources make processes to assess and implement year 2000 preparedness both complex and costly. Some financial institutions have developed comprehensive, broad-based plans while others have focussed their efforts on internal computer applications.

OSFI went on to state that its staff would continue to assess individual institution's Year 2000 preparedness, including a review of:

♦ whether and how the institution has assessed and developed a strategy;
♦ the accountability framework, including involvement of internal audit, compliance and legal departments;
♦ key deliverables for internal operating systems as well as for application systems provided by third parties;
♦ progress against project development milestones and the implementation schedule;
♦ the assessment made by the institution of the Year 2000 preparedness of its major clients; and
♦ presentations to the board of directors to confirm that they have been briefed.

In the United States, the staff of the Securities and Exchange Commission ("SEC") undertook an examination of the state of its internal preparedness as well as that of the American securities industry and public companies to properly handle the information processing challenges associated with the millennium change. Their effort culminated in a *Report to the Congress on the Readiness of the United States Securities Industry and Public Companies To Meet the Information Processing Challenges of the Year 2000*, United States Securities and Exchange Commission (June 1997) (the "SEC Report").[3]

The difficulty of addressing the Year 2000 problem was recognized in the SEC Report. The SEC staff stated:

> It is not, and will not, be possible for any single entity or collective enterprise to represent that it has achieved complete Year 2000 compliance and thus to guarantee its remediation efforts. The problem is simply too complex for such

---

recommendations made by OSFI are also likely to influence the actions taken by such dealers to deal with Year 2000 issues.

3 A copy of the report is available at <http://www.sec.gov/news/studies/yr2000.htm>.

a claim to have legitimacy. Efforts to solve Year 2000 problems are best described as "risk mitigation." Success in the effort will have been achieved if the number and seriousness of any technical failures is minimized, and they are quickly identified and repaired if they do occur.[4]

4.2 ACTIONS BY REGULATORS

The SEC's Division of Market Regulation has performed a review of United States stock exchanges, NASDAQ, and clearing organizations (self-regulating organizations or "SROs") within its jurisdiction. It has incorporated Year 2000 issues into its routine reviews of SRO automated systems, and monitors SRO progress towards correcting Year 2000 problems. With respect to its regulated entities, the SEC indicated that it will continue its examinations and inspections programs to ensure that securities markets participants continue to vigorously address the Year 2000 problem. The staff will work closely with the SROs and will follow the progress and findings of their membership inspection programs as well.[5]

In March 1998, the SEC announced a plan to require most broker dealers and non-bank transfer agents to make special progress reports to the Commission during 1998 and 1999. The new reports would require firms to disclose information on the plans they have underway and the costs involved in their Year 2000 efforts. The SEC is also considering requiring such firms to hire independent public accountants to give an opinion on whether there is a reasonable basis for the statements regarding Year 2000 preparations.

Other regulators have also taken an interest in encouraging compliance or at least determining the scope of the potential problem. For instance, the New Jersey Department of Banking and Insurance requires regulated banks and insurance companies to complete a Year 2000 questionnaire.[6] Other government regulators and agencies may consider mandating compliance for regulated industries where a Year 2000-related failure may have a serious negative impact on the public or where the failure of one entity may place other entities at risk.

---

4 SEC Report, Executive Summary.
5 SEC Report, Executive Summary.
6 Order no. A97-129, "In the Matter of the Effect of the Year 2000 on Computer Systems for Entities Subject to Periodic Examination by the Department of Banking and Insurance" (May 21, 1997).

In some industries, regulators have already begun to take action against entities perceived to be moving too slowly to resolve their Year 2000 issues. For instance, in the financial services sector, federal and state banking regulators have taken action against three Georgia banks that had not made adequate preparations to deal with the Year 2000 problem. The Federal Deposit Insurance Corporation ("FDIC") and the Georgia Department of Banking and Finance issued a joint order against the Farmers and Merchants Bank of Eatonton, the Farmers Bank of Union Point, and the First Bank of Coastal Georgia in Pembrooke.[7] The order requires the banks to implement a compliance and monitoring program, and requires the submission of written compliance reports to the FDIC on a quarterly basis.

A similar order was issued by the Federal Reserve Board against Putnam-Greene Financial Corp., the parent company of the three banks. These orders represent the first enforcement actions against American financial institutions for failing to adequately address the Year 2000 problem.

The United States Treasury Department is pressuring other banks to upgrade their systems no later than December 1998 or risk losing their insurance protection.[8] Similar action by other regulators can be expected, particularly in industries with significant linkages between the regulated entities such that a failure of one entity can trigger a cascade effect.

Securities regulators in Canada are also concerned about the Year 2000 problem. In November 1997, the Chair of the Ontario Securities Commission ("OSC") sent letters to SROs (such as the Investment Dealer Association and the Toronto Stock Exchange), and registrants (such as securities dealers and other persons required to be registered under the *Securities Act*), asking them to advise the Commission on the steps they are taking to address the Year 2000 problem, and suggesting that they form industry-wide committees to coordinate their efforts in addressing Year 2000 compliance issues.

The OSC also participated in the notice sent by the Canadian Securities Administrators ("CSA").[9] CSA Notice 31-301, issued on November 21, 1997, advises that:[10]

> [t]he members of the CSA are concerned that many securities market participants may not be adequately addressing the risks associated with the Year

---

7 *In the Matter of Farmers and Merchants Bank Eatonton, Georgia*, FDIC-97-084b.

8 *USA Today* (December 17, 1997) at A2.

9 The CSA is a group of Canadian securities regulators from each of the provinces.

10 (1997) 20 OSCB 6058.

2000. It is essential because of the inter-connection of the securities markets that all market participants be Year 2000 compliant. The failure of any individual market participants to deal with this issue could very well impact on other market participants.

The CSA Notice goes on to advise that the risks the Year 2000 problem poses must therefore be carefully identified and addressed. In order to assist all parties in understanding and identifying the risks, the CSA attached a statement of the Technical Committee of the International Organization of Securities Commissions[11] regarding Year 2000 computer problems. The OSC is also working with the International Organization of Securities Commissions, which has a working group that is addressing Year 2000 issues.

Greater involvement by regulators from other sectors is also expected. For instance, the Health Canada[12] and the Food and Drug Administration ("FDA") are expected to assume greater involvement in addressing potential Year 2000 problems in medical devices. Each has sent letters to manufacturers of medical devices asking for information regarding Year 2000 compliance and has disclosed plans to post the responses on Web sites.

4.3 ACTIONS BY SELF-REGULATORY ORGANIZATIONS

Self-Regulatory Organizations have also been assuming an important role in addressing the Year 2000 problem. According to the SEC Report, the New York Stock Exchange ("NYSE") has used its examination program to educate its members about the problem. During examinations, NYSE examiners have notified members of the problem and informally inquired as to the members' remedial actions.

In Information Memorandum Number 97-30, (May 22, 1997), the NYSE informed its members that it expects each to have a designated senior official with responsibility to oversee a Year 2000 project. The NYSE expects its members to identify the magnitude of the problem within their

---

11 <http://www.iosco.org/>. See also the Press Communiqué concerning a Round Table on Year 2000 that was hosted by the Bank for International Settlements and jointly sponsored by the Basle Committee on Banking Supervision ("Basle Committee"), the Committee on Payment and Settlement Systems ("CPSS"), the International Association of Insurance Advisors ("IAIS"), and the International Organization of Securities Commissions ("IOSCO"). <http://www.bis.org/press/p980409.htm>.

12 For Health Canada, see <http://www.hc-sc.gc.ca/>. For information concerning the Year 2000 problem in respect of medical equipment, see also <http://www.y2k.gov.au/biomed/>.

organizations, establish realistic and aggressive time frames for completing necessary program revisions, and have a target completion date of December 1998, with the balance of 1999 available for system testing and adjustments. As part of its Information Memorandum, the NYSE also requested its members to complete a questionnaire describing each firm's Year 2000 compliance project. The NYSE indicated that it would use the information to assess the impact of the problem on its member organizations, and also to provide a basis for its surveillance staff to monitor each organization's progress to a timely completion.

The National Association of Securities Dealers, Inc. ("NASD") has indicated its commitment to the coordination of the efforts within the United States securities industry to meet the Year 2000 challenge. The NASD informed the SEC that it has also used its examination program to educate members about the Year 2000 problem. In June 1996, Educational Circular Number 96-16 was issued to District Directors, informing them of the problem, and instructing them to have examiners ask members what steps they were taking to prepare for the Year 2000. The purpose of this inquiry was to "raise members' awareness about this problem."[13]

NASD has recognized that its members should have received sufficient notice of the Year 2000 problem through news and magazine articles, web pages and special hearings in Congress. In Notice to Members Number 97-16 (March 1997), the NASD informed its members that if they have not already done so, all members are urged to initiate their Year 2000 project. It indicated that every "member has a responsibility to analyze the readiness of their internal computer systems for the [Year 2000] challenge. In particular, members who use automated programs to satisfy their regulatory and compliance responsibilities must ensure that those systems are able to function on and after January 1, 2000. Computer failures related to [Year 2000] problems generally will be considered neither a defence to violations of a firm's regulatory or compliance responsibilities nor a mitigation of sanctions for such violations." NASD also urged its members to contact vendors of software and hardware products they use to ensure they are addressing the Year 2000 problem.

Self-Regulatory Organizations in Canada have also taken coordinated action to address the Year 2000 problem. A task force was convened in 1997 to study the issue and assist the G-30 committee in understanding the

---

13 SEC Report, Section 6(2)(2).

potential impact of the millennium change and the means of preparing for it in advance.[14]

The Investment Dealers Association of Canada ("IDA") has established a Year 2000 Committee that consists of representatives of IDA members and invited representatives of some vendors to the securities industry. As well, the Canadian Depository for Securities Limited ("CDS") has established a Year 2000 Committee made up of representatives from the IDA, banks, trust companies, the Montreal, Toronto, Alberta and Vancouver Stock Exchanges, as well as the major service bureaus.[15] CDS' Year 2000 Committee is responsible for reviewing CDS' progress on Year 2000 remediation efforts and coordinating Year 2000 testing activities in the securities industry. A major concern being addressed by CDS is the risk of contamination that may arise if incorrect data is transferred undetected from a non-compliant participant to counterparties and other participants. Another risk is that a major participant that experiences a problem may need to pull out of the system, potentially interfering with the efficient operation of the entire system. [16]

---

14 The mandate of the G-30 committee is to further improvements to the risk management efficiency and competitiveness of the Canadian securities processing infrastructure. For further information on the Year 2000 readiness of the Canadian securities processing industry, see the Special Year 2000 edition (September 1997) of *G-30 News & Views*.
15 CDS acts as the central clearinghouse for transaction information and processing.
16 See Chris Stringer, "Securities Settlement and Processing: Year 2000 Readiness" in *G-30 News and Views* (September 1997).

5

Year 2000 Disclosure Requirements

It should be noted that the information contained in this chapter has been undergoing rapid change. Readers are advised to review the current state of disclosure requirements with their legal advisor.[1]

5.1 CONTINUOUS DISCLOSURE OBLIGATIONS OF PUBLIC COMPANIES IN THE UNITED STATES

The disclosure provisions of the securities legislation and filing requirements applicable to public companies are intended to provide information that will enable the investing public to make informed investment or voting decisions. The United States Securities and Exchange Commission ("SEC") took an early lead in addressing Year 2000 disclosure requirements of public companies. The SEC Report advised that when Year 2000 issues are material to investors, they must be addressed in filings with the Commission.[2] The SEC also addressed the issue in an important follow up Staff Legal Bulletin whose purpose was to remind public operating companies, investment advisers, and investment companies to consider their disclosure obligations relating to anticipated costs, problems and uncertainties associated with the Year 2000 issue.[3]

---

1 It should also be noted that companies in certain industries may be subject to additional disclosure requirements that are specific to those industries. Examples may include broker dealers and non-bank transfer agents. Such entities may be required to file reports with the SEC disclosing costs and plans for making any necessary Year 2000 conversions.

2 SEC Report, Section 6(4).

3 Bulletin No. 5, October 8, 1997 (subsequently revised on January 12, 1998). It should be noted that the Staff Legal Bulletin represents the Divisions staff's views; it is not a rule, regulation or statement of the SEC. Furthermore, the SEC has not approved or disapproved of its content.

The Staff Legal Bulletin, issued by the Divisions of Corporation Finance and Investment, states:

> Many companies must undertake major projects to address the Year 2000 issue. Each company's potential costs and uncertainties will depend on a number of factors, including its software and hardware and the nature of its industry. Companies also must coordinate with other entities with which they electronically interact, both domestically and globally, including suppliers, customers, creditors, borrowers, and financial service organizations. If a company does not successfully address its Year 2000 issues, it may face material adverse consequences. Companies should review, on an ongoing basis, whether they need to disclose anticipated costs, problems and uncertainties associated with Year 2000 consequences, particularly in their filings with the Commission.

Public companies may have to disclose the above mentioned information in filings made with the Commission because it is required by the specific form or report. Disclosure may also be necessary if, in addition to the information that the company is specifically required to disclose, the disclosure rules require disclosure of any additional material information necessary to make the required disclosure not misleading.[4]

The Staff Legal Bulletin advises companies to include disclosure in their "Management's Discussion and Analysis of Financial Condition and Results of Operations" if:

- the cost of addressing the Year 2000 issue is a material event or uncertainty that would cause reported financial information not to be necessarily indicative of future operating results or financial condition; or
- the costs or the consequences of incomplete or untimely resolution of their Year 2000 issue represent a known material event or uncertainty that is reasonably likely to affect their future financial results, or cause their reported financial information not to be necessarily indicative of future operating results or future financial condition.

Finally, the Staff Legal Bulletin provides:

---

4 See *Securities Act of 1933*, 15 U.S.C. Rule 408, *Securities Exchange Act of 1934*, 15 U.S.C. Rule 12b-20, and *Exchange Act* Rule 14a-9. It is also necessary to consider the anti-fraud provisions of the *Securities Act of 1933* (17(a)) and the *Securities Exchange Act of 1934* (section 10(b) and 10b 5) that apply to statements and omissions both in filings with the Commission and also outside of such filings.

♦ if Year 2000 issues materially affect a company's products, services, or competitive conditions, companies may need to disclose this in their "Description of Business." In determining whether to include disclosure, companies are advised to consider the effects of the Year 2000 issue on each of their reportable industry segments;

♦ a company's Year 2000 costs or consequences may reach a level of importance that prompts it to consider filing a Form 8-K (report of significant events).

The SEC Staff Legal Bulletin was revised on January 12, 1998 to provide more specific guidance due to the importance of the Year 2000 issue and because of uncertainty expressed by some members of the accounting and legal professions regarding what should be disclosed. The revised version states:

> If a company has not made an assessment of its Year 2000 issues or has not determined whether it has material Year 2000 issues, the staff believes that disclosure of this known uncertainty is required. In addition, the staff believes that the determination as to whether a company's Year 2000 issues should be disclosed should be based on whether the Year 2000 issues are material to a company's business, operations, or financial condition, without regard to countervailing circumstances (such as Year 2000 remediation programs or contingency plans). If the Year 2000 issues are determined to be material, without regard to countervailing circumstances, the nature and potential impact of the Year 2000 issues as well as the countervailing circumstances should be disclosed.

The disclosure required by the foregoing must be reasonably specific and meaningful, rather than standard "boiler plate."

Year 2000 disclosures required for compliance with securities law disclosure purposes should generally be presented as part of Management's Discussion and Analysis. Disclosure in notes to a company's audited financial statements should generally be avoided as such disclosure must be verifiable by auditors. This requirement places constraints on what can and cannot be stated in the notes to financial statements. It has also been suggested that non-commercial entities, including non-public companies, not-for-profit organizations, government entities, and others should assess whether disclosures about the Year 2000 problem would be useful to their stakeholders.[5]

---

5 American Institute of Certified Public Accountants, "The Year 2000 Issue—Current Accounting and Auditing Guidance" (October 31, 1997).

5.2 CONTINUOUS DISCLOSURE OBLIGATIONS OF ISSUERS IN CANADA

Issuers in Canada are subject to various obligations, which arise from securities legislation and policies adopted by securities regulators, to provide continuous disclosure of material facts and material changes. If material, a company's Year 2000 issues and/or remedial plans may need to be disclosed pursuant to such general disclosure obligations. Specific Year 2000 disclosure obligations may also be applicable.

(a) General Obligations

(i) Securities Act Requirements

Securities legislation in many jurisdictions create an obligation for issuers to issue a statement when a material change occurs in the affairs of a reporting issuer.[6] For instance, see section 75(1) of the *Ontario Securities Act* and section 118(1) of the *Alberta Securities Act*.[7]

(ii) National Policy No. 40

Issuers whose securities are publicly traded in Canada, including reporting issuers or the equivalent in any Canadian jurisdiction, must also consider the disclosure requirement set out in National Policy Statement No. 40.[8] The Policy does not replace the disclosure requirements set out in the provincial securities statutes but is supplementary to compliance with the relevant provincial statute.

---

6 "Material change," when used in relation to the affairs of an issuer, means "a change in the business, operations or capital of the issuer that would reasonably be expected to have a significant effect on the market price or value of any of the securities of the issuer and includes a decision to implement such a change made by the board of directors of the issuer or by senior management of the issuer who believe that confirmation of the decision by the board of directors is probable." [*Securities Act* (Ontario), section 1]

7 Ontario's *Securities Act*, R.S.O. 1990, c. S.6; Alberta's *Securities Act*, R.S.A. 1980, c. 5-6.

8 In some cases, certain policies mentioned in this chapter may have been adopted into rules in a particular jurisdiction.

Pursuant to the Policy, an issuer is required to disclose material information concerning its business and affairs forthwith upon the information becoming known to management, or in the case of information previously known, forthwith upon it becoming apparent that the information is material. Immediate disclosure of all such material information through the news media is required.[9]

Although the Policy does not specifically address Year 2000 issues, it would appear that in some circumstances, such information may constitute material information and may, therefore, need to be disclosed.

(iii) Ontario Securities Commission Policy Statement No. 5.10—Management's Discussion and Analysis of Financial Condition and Results of Operations

Additional disclosure obligations are set out in OSC Policy Statement No. 5.10—"Annual Information Form and Management's Discussion and Analysis of Financial Condition and Results of Operations" (the "Policy Statement"). The Policy Statement was issued because financial information prescribed under the *Securities Act* (Ontario) was not felt sufficient by itself to inform the market adequately about the financial condition and prospects of an issuer. The primary objective of Policy Statement No. 5.10 is to enhance investor understanding of the issuer's business by providing supplemental analysis and background material to allow a fuller understanding of the nature of an issuer, its operations and known prospects for the future.

According to the Policy Statement, "additional disclosure and analysis beyond the financial statements is necessary to provide an adequate basis for assessment of an Issuer's recent history and outlook for the future." The General Statement under Part III of the Policy Statement provides:[10]

> MD&A is a supplemental analysis and explanation which accompanies but does not form part of the financial statements. MD&A provides management with the opportunity to explain in narrative form its current financial situation

---

9 "Material information" is defined as "any information relating to the business and affairs of an issuer that results in or would reasonably be expected to result in a significant change in the market price or value of any of the issuer's securities." Material information consists of both material facts and material changes relating to the business and affairs of an issuer.

10 Note that "MD&A" refers to the Management Discussion and Analysis section of a company's annual report.

and future prospects. MD&A is intended to give the investor the ability to look at the Issuer through the eyes of management by providing both a historical and prospective analysis of the business of the Issuer.

Known material trends, commitments, events or uncertainties that are reasonably expected to have a material impact on the Issuer's business, financial condition or results of operations are to be disclosed.

It advises Issuers to:

Discuss and analyze risks, events and uncertainties that would cause reported financial information not necessarily to be indicative of future operating results or of future financial conditions. This would include descriptions and amounts of (A) matters that would have an impact on future operations and have not had an impact in the past, and (B) matters that have had an impact on reported operations and are not expected to have an impact on future operations.[11]

A MD&A Guide published by the Office of the Chief Accountant elaborates on the Policy Statement. It states that the nature of the disclosure of management's assessment of recent performance and future prospects turns on its "materiality." For the purposes of the Policy and the preparation of the MD&A:

An item of information, or an aggregation of items, is material if it is probable that its omission or misstatement would influence or change a decision.

This concept is broader than that embodied in the definition of "material change" or "material fact" in the *Securities Act* (Ontario), but is consistent with the financial reporting notion of materiality contained in the CICA Handbook.

The Guide also discusses forward-looking disclosure. It states that the Policy contemplates, both explicitly and implicitly, that MD&A should not be confined to historical or static analysis or disclosure:

Required disclosure is based on presently known trends, commitments, events, and uncertainties that are reasonably expected to materially affect the issuer. A disclosure duty exists where a trend, commitment, event or uncertainty is both presently known to management and reasonably expected to have a material impact on the issuer's business, financial condition or results of operations. . .

Issuers are encouraged, but not required, to supply other forward-looking information. Optional forward-looking disclosure involves anticipating a fu-

---

11 Part III, Specific Instructions, Item 1, (1)(e).

ture trend or event or anticipating a less predictable impact of a known event, trend or uncertainty. The other forward-looking information is to be distinguished from presently known information which is reasonably expected to have a material impact on future operating results, such as future increases in costs of labour or materials, which information is required to be disclosed.

The foregoing requirements, while not specific to Year 2000 issues, may require companies to disclose their exposure to the risks and the steps they are taking to address Year 2000 issues. Where appropriate, companies should also consider incorporating Year 2000 related disclosure in the narrative description of the business portion of the Annual Information Form.

(b) Year 2000 Specific Obligations

(i) Canadian Securities Administrators

In January 1998, the disclosure of Year 2000 issues by Canadian issuers was addressed by the Canadian Securities Administrators (the "CSA"). In CSA Staff Notice 44-301 and 51-302 they state:

> Reporting issuers that are required to provide Management's Discussion & Analysis ("MD&A") as a supplement to their financial statements are required to disclose in the MD&A information on risks and uncertainties facing the issuer. These disclosures, which should emphasize risks and uncertainties likely to be factors within the next two financial years, are required to the extent they are necessary for an understanding of the issuer's financial condition, changes in financial condition and results of operations. In addition, reporting issuers are required to discuss and analyze in their MD&A risks, events and uncertainties that would cause reported financial information not necessarily to be indicative of future operating results or future financial condition.

> Staff believe the Year 2000 issue gives rise to uncertainties that are potentially significant for virtually all reporting issuers. Further, in some circumstances, the uncertainties may be considered to cause reported financial information not to be indicative of future operating results or of future financial condition. Accordingly, all reporting issuers should assess carefully the nature and extent of information about the Year 2000 issue that needs to be disclosed to meet the requirements of securities legislation.

> In making this assessment, staff expect that senior management and the Board of Directors of a reporting issuer would consider matters such as the following:

- the scope of activities undertaken to date to evaluate the extent of potential problems by identifying operating and information systems and equipment used by the reporting issuer that may require remedial action;
- the scope of activities undertaken to date to assess the reporting issuer's vulnerability to the state of readiness for the Year 2000 of third parties, including suppliers, customers, lenders and borrowers;
- the scope of the reporting issuer's action plan defining the steps necessary to minimize its exposure to risk as a result of the Year 2000 issue, including identification of those systems that will be replaced and those systems that will be modified;
- the availability of sufficient appropriate resources, both internal and external, to carry out the necessary remedial actions within a time frame that allows for completion and testing prior to January 1, 2000;
- the progress made in relation to each phase of the reporting issuer's action plan, including whether activities are proceeding on schedule and the status of testing of remedial actions taken;
- the extent of risks and uncertainties that may prevent successful completion of any aspect of the reporting issuer's action plan, including an assessment of the potential consequences of failure and whether contingency plans exist to provide for this eventuality.

In staff's view, narrative disclosure explaining the risk and uncertainties arising from the Year 2000 issue and how those risks and uncertainties are being managed should include, at a minimum:

- a discussion of the reporting issuer's vulnerability to the Year 2000 issue, taking into account its dependence on information technology the complexity of its systems and the extent of its interaction with third parties;
- a description of the reporting issuer's evaluation of its situation and the plans made to deal with critical systems within the remaining time available;
- a discussion of the status of implementation of the reporting issuer's remediation plans and the expected timing of completion, including testing and implementation; and
- information about associated costs, both incurred to date and expected to be incurred in the future, including a description of the accounting treatment afforded such costs.

Staff believe reporting issuers that are not required to provide MD&A should consider providing information about the Year 2000 issue as part of other information that accompanies annual financial statements.

The nature of the Year 2000 issue and the short time frame within which it must be addressed are such that staff believe reporting issuers should consider updating annual MD&A disclosure in subsequent interim financial reports. This will contribute to ensuring that participants in capital markets are made aware of significant information on a more timely basis than would otherwise be the case.

Although the CSA Notice discusses disclosure obligations in the context of MD&A, securities regulators such as the OSC are expected to require similar disclosure from entities that are not required to file MD&A (such as mutual fund companies) and will likely be reviewing all filings (including offering memorandums, amalgamation/takeover agreements, and other filings) to determine if the Year 2000 disclosure issue is being adequately addressed.

(ii) Ontario Securities Commission

The OSC has sent a letter to all registrants under its direct supervision, including mutual fund dealers, securities dealers, scholarship fund dealers, limited market dealers, and advisors, to raise attention to the Year 2000 issue and to set out their disclosure requirements.

(iii) Task Force Year 2000

Task Force Year 2000 recognized the importance of Year 2000 disclosure by publicly held companies. In its report released in February 1998, the Task Force reiterated the need to include a discussion in the risks and uncertainties section of the Management Discussion and Analysis ("MD&A") in annual reports on how a company is addressing the Year 2000 problem. The Task Force stated that such a discussion would need to reflect the fact that the directors of a corporation have made Year 2000 preparedness a priority.

The Task Force advised securities commissions to assure themselves that companies under their jurisdiction are, in fact, reporting on Year 2000 issues in their MD&A and that these disclosures are adequate. It recommended that all securities commissions, during 1998 and 1999, review a 20 per cent representative sample (at a minimum) of annual reports of the companies they regulate to determine if such disclosure is being made. The Task Force also recommended that all securities commissions, either as a matter of regulatory mandate or administrative policy, should promote Year 2000 preparedness as a consideration in the due diligence process associated with mergers and acquisitions.[12]

---

12 Task Force Year 2000 Recommendation 3. However, it should be noted that not all merger and acquisition transactions are reviewable by securities regulators.

(iv) Stock Exchange Requirements

An issuer with securities listed on one or more stock exchanges must also comply with the requirements of the relevant exchanges concerning timely disclosure.[13] Stock exchanges may also adopt rules that specifically address Year 2000 disclosure. For instance, TSE By-law No. 685, *A By-law with Respect to Disclosure by Listed Issuers Regarding Year 2000*, amending the General By-law of the Toronto Stock Exchange[14] provides:

> Disclosure Regarding Year 2000—Every Issuer having securities listed on the Exchange shall make disclosure of material information concerning systems issues and related business implications and uncertainties for the issuer resulting from the year 2000 century change, and any remedial actions the issuer is taking in this regard. Such disclosure shall be made in all annual reports mailed to shareholders by the Issuer from April 1, 1998 to December 31, 1999.

A letter sent by the TSE to listed companies in early February 1998, included copies of the SEC Staff Legal Bulletin and the CSA Notice. The letter advised companies that, in interpreting the application of the TSE by-law, companies should look to the guidelines in these notices and in the publications of any other applicable regulatory bodies. The letter also stated that if an issuer determines that there are no material Year 2000 implications to disclose, this fact should be stated in the annual report.

The TSE by-law therefore appears to require disclosure by each listed company of material information concerning its Year 2000 issues and the remedial steps being taken. Interestingly, an issuer that concludes that it does not have any material Year 2000 issues apparently must still report this finding to show that it has addressed the issue. The OSC is expected to adopt a similar position.

5.3 CONTINUOUS DISCLOSURE—EXAMPLES

Equifax is an example of multinational company that has addressed the Year 2000 issue in its annual report. The Management Discussion and

---

13 An example is the Toronto Stock Exchange's Policy Statement on Timely Disclosure (October 1990). The TSE Policy Statement was the basis for National Policy 40 and, therefore, the two are substantially the same.

14 Passed and enacted on January 6, 1998. See also Policy I-16 adopted by the Montréal Exchange, which imposes Year 2000 disclosure requirements for companies listed on the Montréal Exchange.

Analysis portion of Equifax's 1996 Annual Report contained a list of important factors that could cause actual results to differ materially from these expressed in the forward-looking statements. One such factor listed was "the inability of the Company to accurately estimate the cost of systems preparation for Year 2000 compliance." Equifax also provided a breakdown of its projected Year 2000-related expenses on a per share basis.

The Year 2000 issue was addressed in the 1996 Annual Report of Air Products & Chemicals, Inc., another United States-based Fortune 500 company, which stated:

> The company recognizes the need to ensure its operations will not be adversely impacted by Year 2000 software failures. Software failures due to processing errors potentially arising from calculations using the Year 2000 date are a known risk. The company is addressing this risk to the availability and integrity of financial systems and the reliability of operational systems. The company has established processes for evaluating and managing the risks and costs associated with this problem. The computing portfolio was identified and an initial assessment has been completed. The cost of achieving Year 2000 compliance is estimated to be approximately [US] $10 million over the cost of normal software upgrades and replacements and will be incurred through fiscal 1999.

The Year 2000 issue has also been addressed by a number of companies in Form 10K filings [United States regulatory filings with the SEC]. In such filings made in 1996, some companies stated that they were currently in the process of evaluating their systems and had not yet quantified the costs of resources that would be required to deal with the problem. Some included warnings that if the corrective actions are not completed on time, the Year 2000 problem could have a material impact on the operations of the company. Others highlighted the interdependent nature of computer systems and pointed out that the company could be adversely affected in the year 2000 depending on whether or not other unaffiliated entities address the Year 2000 issue successfully.[15]

Some Canadian companies, including a number of the chartered banks, (e.g., Royal Bank of Canada) started to add Year 2000 disclosure information in their annual reports as of the Fall of 1997. Other companies can be expected to follow in 1998 and 1999 in order to comply with guidelines and requirements issued by regulators and auditors.

Disclosure issues have also been considered by companies outside North America. For instance, Telstra, an Australian company, warned potential

---

15 See <http://www.y2k.com/disclosu.htm>.

shareholders regarding possible negative consequences that may arise due to the Year 2000 problem. A Public Offer Document, released in early October 1997, stated that there were no assurances that the company's $500 million program to address the Year 2000 problem would be successful, or that the date change from 1999 to 2000 would not materially affect its operations and financial results. The Public Offer Document stressed that Telstra's operations could also be affected by the ability of third parties to manage the effect of the Year 2000 problem to their operations.[16]

Even certain governments have felt the need to include a note regarding the effect of the Year 2000 problem. For instance, the State of Florida included the following note to its Financial Statements for the Fiscal Year that ended June 30, 1996:

> State Government Information Technology—The State of Florida currently has initiatives underway to address the potential impact the Year 2000 Problem will have on the information technology of the State. This problem is referred to by various names including "Y2K," "Turn of the Century Problem," "The Millennium Bug," and "Year 2000 Problem." This is the result of many of the State's existing information technology applications having a two-digit indicator but not a century indicator. Unless corrected before January 1, 2000, many computer applications will either stop working or, worse, begin producing erroneous results on that date. State agencies are currently working with the State's Information Resource Commission to develop methods to correct this problem before the year 2000. Although cost estimates vary from agency to agency, it is clear that substantial resources, in terms of millions of dollars and manpower, will be needed to resolve this issue over the next several years. The Information Resource Commission has reported preliminary estimates of Year 2000 Problem costs and related issues for the 1997-98 and 1998-99 fiscal years which may range from [US] $90 to $120 million.[17]

As previously noted, many of the above examples of disclosure are from 1996 and more comprehensive and specific disclosure will likely be required in 1998 and 1999 as the time remaining grows shorter.

5.4 PROSPECTUS REQUIREMENTS

The Canadian Securities Administrators, in Staff Notice 41-301 and 51-302 state:

---

16 See AFR Net Services at <http://www.afr.com/au/content/971014/inform/inform2.html>.

17 State of Florida—Notes to the Financial Statements for the Fiscal Year ended June 30, 1996, Note 8

Reporting issuers that make an offering of securities by way of prospectus are required under securities legislation to provide full, true and plain disclosure of all material facts relating to the securities issued or proposed to be distributed. A "material fact" is a fact that significantly affects, or would reasonably be expected to have a significant effect on, the market price or value of the securities issued or proposed to be distributed.

Staff believe the Year 2000 issue is potentially significant to virtually all reporting issuers contemplating the issuance of securities by way of prospectus. Accordingly, reporting issuers should give careful consideration to the Year 2000 issue when assessing the nature and extent of information that needs to be disclosed in a prospectus to meet the requirements of securities legislation. Staff expect that, in making this assessment, a reporting issuer would consider matters such as those discussed above under "Continuous Disclosure Obligations."

A prospectus for the issue of securities may need to contain such information as investors and their professional advisers would reasonably require and expect in order to make an informed assessment of the company. Where the Year 2000 problem is likely to impact materially on a company's financial position or prospects, a company will need to disclose its strategy for dealing with the relevant risks and costs.

These issues should be considered in a due diligence review prior to the issuance of a prospectus to determine whether disclosure is required. The disclosure requirements in other jurisdictions where a company's stocks are traded also need to be considered.

A company planning to issue a prospectus may also want to consider listing the Year 2000 problem as one of the risk factors. For instance, it may include a statement such as either of the following:

The widespread use of computer programs and equipment containing embedded logic that relies on two-digit fields to store the year component of dates to perform calculations and decision-making functions may cause computer systems to malfunction, either in, or in some cases, prior to the year 2000. The Company has implemented a program to address this issue. However, due to the interdependent nature of computer systems, there is a risk that the Company may be adversely impacted depending on whether it or other entities not affiliated with the Company address this issue successfully.[18]

Or:

---

18 Adopted from Morgan Stanley Group, Inc., Form 10K for Fiscal Year 1996.

The Company has conducted a comprehensive review of its computer systems to identify the systems that could be affected by the "Year 2000" issue and is developing an implementation plan to resolve the issue... The Company presently believes that, with modifications to existing software and converting to new software, the Year 2000 problem will not pose significant operational problems for the Company's computer systems as so modified and converted. However, if such modifications and conversions are not completed timely, the Year 2000 problem may have a material impact on the operations of the Company.[19]

Securities regulators are also expected to impose similar Year 2000 disclosure obligations in respect of registrations of mutual funds.

5.5 LEGISLATIVE INITIATIVES

More onerous disclosure requirements may also be imposed by Year 2000 specific legislation. A recent legislative proposal in the United States is the *Year 2000 Computer Remediation and Shareholder (CRASH) Protection Act of 1997*, which was introduced in the Senate[20] by Senator Bill Bennett (R-Utah). The Bill would require publicly traded corporations to make specific disclosures in their initial offering statements and quarterly reports regarding the Year 2000 readiness of their computer systems and their ability to manage the business risks associated with possible computer system problems after January 1, 2000.

The Bill recognizes the concern that the failure of computer systems to operate correctly after January 1, 2000 threatens the interest of consumers and investors, the financial results of corporations, and the continued soundness of the global economy. Without clear and specific disclosure requirements, it is believed that corporations, fearing competitive disadvantage, will resist making specific disclosures about the Year 2000 readiness of their computer systems, the costs of remediation and their ability to manage the business risks associated with Year 2000-related problems.

The bill would require issuers to provide:[21]

---

19 Highlands Insurance Group, Inc., Form 10K for Fiscal Year 1996.
20 105th Congress, 1st Session, Bill S.1518. Introduced on November 10, 1997 and referred to the Committee on Banking, Housing and Urban Affairs.
21 s. 3.

- ♦ a description of the progress of the issuer in completing the five recognized phases of Year 2000 remediation[22] (*i.e.*, awareness, assessment, renovation, validation, and implementation), by division, department, or other appropriate business unit of the issuer;
- ♦ a summary of costs incurred by the issuer in connection with any remediation effort and an estimate of additional costs that the issuer expects to incur in connection with future remediation efforts;
- ♦ an estimate of anticipated litigation costs and liability outlays associated with the defence of legal actions against the issuer (or the directors or officers of the issuer) as a result of Year 2000 computer system problems, including breach of contract, tort, shareholder class action, and product liability actions;
- ♦ information relating to the existence of any insurance policies of the issuer that cover specific Year 2000 computer system problems, as well as the defence of legal actions against the issuer (and the officers and directors of the issuer) in connection with those problems; and
- ♦ information relating to any contingency plans developed by the issuer to ensure continued operation of the essential business functions of the issuer in the event of a Year 2000 computer system problem by the issuer itself or by a vendor, partner, or other affiliate of the issuer.

A Year 2000 disclosure bill was also under consideration in the United Kingdom. The Companies (Millenium Computer Compliance) Bill would have required all companies to report annually on the progress being made towards Year 2000 compliance.

---

22 Remediation is the name given to the process of a company assessing and addressing its Year 2000 problems.

6

Financial Reporting and Auditing Issues

6.1 FINANCIAL REPORTING CONSIDERATIONS

The Canadian Institute of Chartered Accountants ("CICA") has recently taken an active role in dealing with auditing and financial reporting issues related to the Year 2000 problem. The issue was addressed in detail in the January 1998 edition of CICA's *Risk Alert* publication. This special edition of *Risk Alert* clarifies the auditor's role with respect to the effects of the Year 2000 problem and provides guidance on communications with clients in connection with the Year 2000 problem.[1]

CICA's *Risk Alert* alerts Canadian auditors to Year 2000 issues beyond the two-digit date field issue. It identifies other important Year 2000 issues for auditors such as:

♦ possible impact on systems prior to the year 2000;
♦ the use of "99" in the date field to represent something other than a date in the year 1999;
♦ the failure of some systems to recognize the year 2000 as a leap year; and
♦ the need to consider other organizations with which the client is inter-dependent (both in terms of electronic interactions as well as inabilities to deliver goods or services).

A good overview of how the Year 2000 problem affects auditors in the United States can be found in a publication of the American Institute of Certified Public Accountants ("AICPA") titled *The Year 2000 Issue—*

---

1 Further information is available from CICA's Web site at: <http://www.cica.ca/>.

Current Accounting and Auditing Guidance ("AICPA Year 2000 Guidance").[2] The publication includes:

♦ a summary of accounting, disclosure and auditing standards;
♦ a description of the responsibilities of various parties;
♦ a clarification of the auditor's role;
♦ a guidance on communications with clients;
♦ a description of disclosure considerations; and
♦ advice on practice management matters.

CICA, in conjunction with AICPA, has produced a guide, *Potential Implications of Year 2000*, which contains a good discussion of the Year 2000 problem and accounting implications. The guide is available on CICA's Web site or from CICA.

(a) Accounting for the Costs

The Year 2000 problem raises a number of issues related to financial reporting. The first issue concerns the manner of accounting for the costs of addressing the Year 2000 problem. In the United States, the issue was addressed by the Emerging Issues Task Force ("EITF") of the Financial Accounting Standards Board in EITF Issue No. 96-14, *Accounting for the Costs Associated with Modifying Computer Software for the Year 2000*. The consensus reached by the EITF was that external and internal costs specifically associated with modifying software used internally by a company to address Year 2000 problems should be charged as a current period expense as it is incurred. In Canada, the issue was addressed in CICA's Emerging Issues Committee Abstract of Issue Discussed, EIC-80, *Accounting for the Costs of Modifying Internal Use Computer Software for Year 2000 Compliance*. According to CICA, costs incurred to modify internal-use computer software for Year 2000 compliance can be treated as current or capital, depending on the facts.

Where a company incurs expenses to repair or debug a non-compliant system, such expenditures will likely be treated as a current period expense (*i.e.*, deductible from income in the fiscal year in which they are incurred). This is particularly true if the system is merely restored to its original condition to perform the same applications for its originally assessed useful life.

---

2 Published October 31, 1997. Available at <http://www.aicpa.org/members/y2000/intro.htm>.

However, where a company decides to deal with a non-compliant system by either (i) replacing the system with a new compliant system,[3] or (ii) improving or enhancing an existing system by extending the system's originally assessed life or increasing its functionality, such expenditures are typically to be amortized over a number of years (and added to the appropriate Capital Cost Allowance class, for Canadian tax purposes). Purchases of new software or other assets whose purpose is to ensure Year 2000 compliance of existing software are treated similarly.

(b) Revenues, Losses and Contingencies

The second issue concerns the recognition of revenues and losses. The Year 2000 problem may have an impact on customer acceptance, cancellation privileges and customer support, and therefore may have an effect on the timing of revenue recognition. The Year 2000 problem may also create product warranty and product return issues for suppliers of computer products and services, as well as suppliers of other products that contain software.[4] AICPA advises such suppliers to consider FASB Statement of Financial Accounting Standards No. 5 ("FAS No. 5"), *Accounting for Contingencies* if there are product-warranty or product-defect liability issues and FASB Statement No. 48, *Revenue Recognition When Right of Return Exists,* in respect of the product return issue.

Financial Accounting Standards No. 5 defines a contingency as an existing condition, situation, or set of circumstances involving uncertainty as to possible gain or loss contingency. When a loss contingency exists, the loss may range from probable to reasonably possible to remote. According to FAS No. 5, an accrual is required if the loss is probable and can be reasonably estimated. If the contingency is not probable, or cannot be estimated, disclosure should be made when there is at least a reasonable possibility that a loss or additional loss may have been incurred. The disclosure should indicate the nature of the contingency and should give an estimate of the possible loss, or range of loss, or state that such an estimate cannot be made. A pending failure of a company's computer system in the year 2000 may constitute a contingency that would require consideration by companies and their auditors as one that would fall under the accounting and disclosure requirements of FAS No. 5.

---

3 If an existing non-compliant system is replaced with a compliant system, the unamortized cost of the old system must be removed from the company's assets and charged as a loss to income.

4 See the AICPA publication at page 7.

Another issue that must be considered is the potential impairment of inventories and of fixed assets of non-compliant hardware or software. The Year 2000 problem can also affect the estimated useful lives of such fixed assets (*i.e.*, it may reduce the applicable period for amortization).[5]

If a company expects that it may not complete its Year 2000 efforts in time, it may need to include a note to that effect in its financial statements. If the amount of the loss can be reasonably estimated, a charge against earnings for the estimated loss may be required.[6] The financial impact of other Year 2000 issues mentioned above must also be adequately addressed.

The Canadian Institute of Chartered Accountants provides similar advice. It advises Canadian auditors to consider a number of recognition, measurement and disclosure considerations resulting from the effects of the Year 2000 problem, including:[7]

♦ data processing errors affecting the completeness of assets and liabilities because certain transactions may not be recognized due to an unrecognized date;
♦ data processing errors affecting the computation of estimates (for example, bad debt allowances based on aged accounts receivables);
♦ categorization of software modification costs as assets or expenses;
♦ effect of the Year 2000 problem on other estimates (for example, in the case of a software vendor, warranty provisions to provide for a software vendor's absorption of the software's Year 2000 conversion costs required by its maintenance agreements);
♦ impairment of assets (for example, "write downs" and amortization policies of capital assets such as computer hardware that is not Year 2000 compliant and is intended to be scrapped, or capital assets or inventories containing software that is not Year 2000 compliant);

---

5 References to applicable guidelines are listed in the AICPA publication.

6 First, the company has to conclude that it is likely that a *future event* will confirm that an asset *had been impaired or a liability incurred* at the date of the financial statements (see CICA Handbook paragraph 3290.12). Many accountants and auditors argue that the Year 2000 issue *per se* has not impaired any assets or created any liabilities prior to January 1, 2000. That is, even if a company's systems are not Year 2000 compliant now, it takes a very complex series of events for that problem to lead to a significant loss to the company. Furthermore, management and auditors have no experience evaluating this particular contingency. Therefore, most management and their auditors will likely conclude that it is not "likely" that a contingent loss should be accrued prior to January 1, 2000. Hence the importance of disclosure of the uncertainty created by the Year 2000 issue.

7 CICA, *Risk Alert* (January 1998) at 8.

♦ measurement uncertainty (for example, when it is reasonably possible that the recognized amount of loans receivable from companies that are not Year 2000 compliant could change by a material amount in the near term);

♦ commitments (for example, costs contracted to complete Year 2000 conversions); and

♦ contingencies (for example, a software vendor and installer whose recent installations may not be Year 2000 compliant).

(c) Auditor Checklists

Some of the large accounting/auditing firms have developed lists of Year 2000 compliance questions for use by their auditors. For instance, KPMG utilizes a six page questionnaire with 47 questions.

6.2 AUDITING CONSIDERATIONS

(a) Securities and Exchange Commission Report

Auditing considerations related to the Year 2000 problem were discussed in the SEC Report. The following are extracts from the SEC Report.[8]

> The Codification of Statements on Auditing Standards ("Codification"), issued by the American Institute of Certified Public Accountants, contains procedures that an auditor must carry out in the normal course of an examination of a company's financial statements. Included in these procedures are several steps which should alert the auditor to the Year 2000 problem.
>
> AU Section 319.23 provides:
>
>> "During the course of an audit, the auditor may become aware of matters relating to the internal control structure that may be of interest to the audit committee. The matters that this section requires for reporting to the audit committee are referred to as reportable conditions. Specifically, these are matters coming to the auditor's attention that, in his judgment, should be communicated to the audit committee because they represent significant deficiencies in the design or operation of the internal control structure, which could adversely affect the organization's ability to record, process, summarize, and report financial data consistent with the assertions of management in the financial statements."

---

8 SEC Report, Section 6(3)(1).

The Codification does not specifically address the Year 2000 problem, nor would application of the sections of the Codification cited above necessarily have required identification of the lack of preparation for the Year 2000 as a reportable condition at the conclusion of calendar year audits for 1996. However, auditing firms generally are aware that issuers must begin assessment and remediation of their financial reporting systems now in order to be prepared for the Year 2000.

The SEC has been informed by an international audit firm that as a matter of policy, the firm required a warning about the Year 2000 problem in management letters that were issued to their clients at the conclusion of the 1996 audit. The firm indicated that it is essential that the seriousness of the problem be communicated to audit committees, or those who have responsibility for oversight of the financial reporting process if there is no audit committee. The staff believes other firms are taking a similar approach."

(b) American Institute of Certified Public Accountants Position

United States auditors can seek guidance on Year 2000 issues relevant to the conduct of an audit from an interpretation of AU section 311, *Planning and Supervision* (the "Interpretation"), which was issued by AICPA's Audit Issues Task Force ("AITF") and reproduced in the AICPA Year 2000 Guidance.[9]

According to AICPA, in an audit of financial statements conducted in accordance with generally accepted auditing standards, the auditor has a responsibility to plan and perform the audit so as to obtain reasonable assurance about whether the financial statements are free of material misstatement, whether caused by error or by fraud. The auditor's responsibility relates to the detection of material misstatement of the financial statements being audited, whether caused by the Year 2000 problem or by some other cause. However, an auditor does not have a responsibility to detect current or future effects of the Year 2000 problem on operational issues that do not affect the company's ability to prepare financial statements in accordance with generally accepted accounting principles or another comprehensive basis of accounting.[10]

The Interpretation recognizes that the planning for an audit of financial statements may be affected by the existence of the Year 2000 problem. When an auditor is considering the methods used by the company to process

---

9 AICPA, *Professional Standards*, vol. 1, AU section 9311.38—9311.47.
10 AICPA Year 2000 Guidance at page 14.

accounting information, the auditor may determine that it is necessary to consider whether data processing errors caused by the Year 2000 problem could result in a material misstatement of the financial statements being audited. The results of this consideration may affect the auditor's assessment of control risk, testing of internal control and substantive procedures.

Another important issue addressed in the Interpretation is the responsibility of an auditor who may become aware that, in some period after the period being audited, a Year 2000 problem could adversely affect the company's ability to record, process, summarize and report financial data, or more generally, that the company's system, which is currently correctly processing data, may not function correctly if used to process data in the year 2000. According to the Interpretation, this "potential significant internal control deficiency," which would not occur until the year 2000, is not a reportable condition prior to such time. This deficiency becomes a reportable condition only when, in the auditor's judgment, it could adversely affect the company's ability "to record, process, summarize and report financial data consistent with the assertions of management in the financial statements."[11]

(c) Canadian Institute of Chartered Accountants Position

CICA has taken the position that the auditor's responsibility relates to the detection of material misstatements in the financial statements being audited, whether caused by the Year 2000 problem or some other cause. The Year 2000 problem does not create any new responsibilities for the financial statement auditor. CICA places responsibility for assessing the impact of the Year 2000 problem and remediating its effects entirely on management. It states that the auditor does not have a responsibility to detect the current or future effects of problems on business operating systems that do not affect the company's ability to prepare financial statements in accordance with Generally Accepted Accounting Principles ("GAAP"), including those problems caused by the Year 2000 problem.

However, in obtaining an understanding of the accounting process used by a company, the auditor may determine that it is necessary to consider whether date processing errors caused by the Year 2000 problem could result in a material misstatement in the financial statements under audit. Any identified control weakness resulting from the Year 2000 problem that

---

11 AICPA Year 2000 Guidance at page 15.

would not prevent or detect a material misstatement in the financial statements being audited would be communicated to the client's audit committee.

In the conduct of an audit, an auditor may also identify other conditions arising from the Year 2000 problem that may be of interest to management in discharging its duties. While not required by generally accepted auditing standards, as part of overall client service, the auditor may want to inform management about the issue, and encourage management to assess its impact and take appropriate remedial steps. CICA suggests that an auditor may wish to note in his or her management letter if the client is not adequately addressing the Year 2000 problem or is not meeting its Year 2000 compliance project timetables.

(d) Added Risk Due to System Changes

CICA has commented that in dealing with the Year 2000 problem, many companies will modify their systems and/or install new systems. These changes increase the risk of material misstatement in the financial statements because:

♦ modified and new systems may contain new defects unrelated to the Year 2000 problem;
♦ new systems may not function as intended; and
♦ controls may be inadequate during periods when systems are modified or when new systems are being installed (the likelihood of unauthorized activity is also increased).

Auditors are advised to consider the effect of these factors in their audit plans and that such system changes may require the performance of additional tests of controls.

(e) Clarifying the Auditor's Responsibilities

The Interpretation advises auditors to clarify for clients that an audit conducted in accordance with generally accepted auditing standards cannot be relied upon to disclose information about the potential effects on the client of the Year 2000 problem.[12] Nevertheless, the Interpretation recog-

---

[12] Only in exceptionally rare cases will an auditor, auditing 1998 financial statements, conclude that, at that point in time, there is overwhelming evidence available that

nizes that the auditor may identify matters that in his or her judgement, are not reportable conditions but that the auditor nonetheless may choose to communicate.[13] For instance, the auditor may wish to communicate information obtained regarding the company's understanding of Year 2000 issues, and the progress of its Year 2000 compliance to senior management and the audit committee. However, auditors are cautioned not to imply that they are providing assurance on Year 2000 compliance.

The net effect of the position taken by AICPA appears to be that auditors may (and are encouraged) to raise Year 2000 issues. However, AICPA appears to be taking care to avoid making the identification and disclosure of Year 2000 problems a requirement (unless these can result in a material misstatement of the financial statements being audited). Some auditors may take steps beyond these minimum requirements to identify and disclose significant Year 2000 problems in order to reduce the risk of potential lawsuits.

CICA provides similar advice. It recommends avoiding misunderstandings about the auditor's responsibilities with respect to the Year 2000 problem and states that the auditor may find it necessary to specifically set forth his or her responsibilities under current auditing standards in communications with the client during audits leading up to the year 2000. It recommends that auditors consider incorporating such communications in the engagement letter, management letters, correspondence, discussions with management and the audit committee, brochures, pamphlets, newsletters, and articles. CICA also provides sample wording that may be used in the engagement letter, communication with audit committees and the management letter.

(f) Certification of Compliance

CICA cautions auditors to be extremely cautious about being associated with assertions that clients' systems are Year 2000 complaint or guarantees

---

indicates that there is substantial doubt that the company will not continue as a going concern as a result of Year 2000 problems. In these circumstances, an auditor would provide a qualified opinion only if the company does not disclose this situation in its 1998 financial statements. It should be noted that "going-concern" considerations have traditionally been assessed one year from the opinion date by Canadian auditors and one year from the balance sheet date by auditors in the United States.

13 AICPA Year 2000 Guidance at page 15.

that systems will become compliant by a specified date.[14] According to CICA and AICPA, an auditor is not responsible for and is not in a position to be able to evaluate the completeness or adequacy of management's assessment of the company's Year 2000 risk or its remediation plans. Due to the pervasive impact that the Year 2000 problem could have on the company, it is not possible for management to assert, or the auditor to verify, that the company has or will achieve Year 2000 compliance or that its remediation efforts will be successful. Accordingly, the position of both CICA and AICPA is that an audit conducted in accordance with generally accepted auditing standards is not designed to, and does not, provide any assurance that Year 2000 issues that may exist will be identified, or report on the adequacy of the company's Year 2000 remediation plans regarding operational or financial systems, or whether the Company is or will become Year 2000 compliant on a timely basis. This position is expected to be forcefully articulated, both in Canada and in the United States, in forthcoming guidance to auditors.

With respect to disclosures in the financial statements of information regarding the effects of the Year 2000 problem, the auditor is required to obtain sufficient appropriate audit evidence in respect of that disclosure. When information about a client's exposure to risks and uncertainties caused by the effects of the Year 2000 problem is disclosed in Management's Discussion and Analysis, the auditor is required to consider whether that information is consistent with the financial statement disclosure.

(g) Other Initiatives

In early February 1998, CICA sent members a package of materials related to the Year 2000 issue that included:

♦ *Guidance for Directors—the Millennium Bug*;[15]
♦ *Executive Summary—Potential Implications of Year 2000*. This publication sets out the highlights of a study conducted jointly with AICPA to provide information to organizations and their public accountants on

---

14 It should be noted that certain types of special purpose audits may be useful to help address some very specific Year 2000 compliance issues; for instance, a "S5900" report on controls at a service organization (over a past period) or a "S5800" report on compliance with contractual obligations (over a past period).

15 CICA, Control and Governance—Special Edition, February 1998. Also available from CICA's Web site. This document is intended to provide guidance to boards of directors in discharging their responsibility for oversight of how management deals with the Year 2000 problem.

the potential problems for mission critical financial and operating systems;

♦ *Summary of other CICA Year 2000 Project initiatives*;
♦ *Connections*.

Appendix "A" of *Guidance for Directors* contains sample questions that directors should ask management about the millennium bug. Some of the questions may also be suitable for inclusion in inquiry letters that may be sent by suppliers and other stakeholders (such as lenders, investment analysts, and others) who need to understand the status of a particular company's efforts in addressing the Year 2000 problem.

Other CICA initiatives include:

♦ CICA's Auditing Standards Board has released an Assurance and Related Services Guideline, *The Year 2000 Issue—Considerations for Audit Planning and Communication of Matters*.
♦ An Accounting Guideline on the disclosure aspect of the Year 2000 issue is currently targeted for release in July 1998. If the principles proposed for this Guideline are approved by the Accounting Standards Board, the Guideline would virtually mandate that every Canadian company disclose the uncertainty associated with the Year 2000 issue in its financial statements. This Guideline may also discuss the company's disclosure obligations if the potential impact of the Year 2000 issue raises substantial doubt about the viability of a company to continue as a going concern.
♦ An Assurance and Related Services Guideline to provide guidance on the audit procedures that would generally be required to audit the disclosures required by the Accounting Guideline is targeted for release in June 1998.
♦ An Assurance and Related Services Guideline that would provide guidance on the Year 2000 issue for auditors of service organizations (such as companies that outsource data processing activities, trust companies that hold investments for pension plans and depositories such as Canadian Depository for Securities) who have been engaged to report on the service organization's internal controls is targeted for release in June 1998.
♦ A "Best Practices" Year 2000 Guide. The objective of the guide is to provide "best-practices" information to members in public practice for dealing with Year 2000 engagements.

AICPA is currently working on an auditing interpretation of Statement on Auditing Standards No. 59—*The Auditor's Consideration of an Entity's*

Ability to Continue as a Going Concern—that will provide guidance to American auditors regarding when the potential impact of the Year 2000 issue raises substantial doubt about the viability of a company to continue as a going concern (targeted for release in June 1998). AICPA has also released an auditing interpretation of Statement on Auditing Standards No. 70—*Reports on the Processing of Transactions by Service Organizations*—that provides guidance on the Year 2000 issue to auditors of service organizations.

(h) Other Responsibilities

An auditor may have a responsibility to clients that goes beyond what professional standards require. Many clients expect their auditors to communicate issues of importance to the company at the appropriate level of management and to the audit committee (even if such issues are beyond the scope of the audit). In order to reduce the potential for disputes that may arise due to a gap between a client's expectation and what auditors intend to deliver, many auditors are providing clients with written information on the responsibility they intend to assume in respect of Year 2000 issues (as discussed above). Other steps include completion of Year 2000 questionnaires for all audit clients and distribution of information regarding the Year 2000 problem, with proposed solutions, to CEOs and the client audit committees.

6.3 MANAGEMENT DISCLOSURE OF YEAR 2000 ISSUES

A key part of the financial reporting aspects of the Year 2000 issue relates to disclosure in Management's Discussion & Analysis ("MD&A"), which appears in the annual reports of public companies. Most auditors believe that it would be preferable for companies to discuss the Year 2000 issues in MD&A, rather than in the notes to the financial statements. MD&A provides a more flexible format for the company to discuss the issue candidly, and to make forward-looking comments about their plans to deal with it. In contrast, any disclosure about Year 2000 that appears in the financial statements must be auditable, which places constraints on what can and cannot be disclosed.

MD&A disclosure regarding the Year 2000 problem should include:[16]

---

16 Doug Pirie, "Will Auditors Opine on Year 2000 Readiness—What Can You Expect from Your Auditor?" *The Year 2000 Computer Problem*, Insight Information Inc., (Toronto,

- a short description of the generic reasons for the Year 2000 problem;
- a description of the status of the company's Year 2000 projects;
- a description of any risks and uncertainties, as well as any contingency plans;
- an estimate of the expected total cost and timing, or a statement that these have not yet been determined; and
- a description of the accounting treatment being used.

The status of a company's Year 2000 project could address whether:

- the company has completed an assessment of the impact of the Year 2000 issue;
- a plan of action has been developed/put into action;
- resources have been dedicated;
- the remediation work has been completed;
- testing has been completed.

A company's potential costs and uncertainties will depend on a number of factors, including:

- the software and hardware used by the company;
- the nature of the industry in which the company is operating;
- the extent of electronic interaction of the company with suppliers, customers and other companies;
- the degree of dependancy on external suppliers (including non-IT suppliers);
- the degree of dependency on foreign customers and suppliers located in countries that have been slow to address the Year 2000 problem.

Companies in the United Kingdom should review requirements imposed by the Accounting Standards Board. The Board's Urgent Issues Taskforce Abstract 20 requires directors to make specific and detailed disclosures of the potential impact of the century date change on their business and operations, and the company's general plans for addressing the potential issues that arise. This requirement applies in respect of all accounting periods ending on or after March 23, 1998.

February 19, 1998).

6.4 AUDITOR INDEPENDENCE

In addition to performing audits of financial statements, many audit firms provide their clients with many types of non-auditing services. Many auditing firms are offering assistance in identifying and correcting Year 2000 problems.

Providing these services can raise a concern that, in certain circumstances, it may impair the audit firm's independence with respect to the audit of that client's financial statements. This issue may be of concern to securities regulators. For instance, the SEC Report stated the following:[17]

> The independence of accountants who audit the financial statements included in filings with the Commission is crucial to the credibility of financial reporting and, in turn, the capital formation process. Enhanced public confidence in the reliability of issuers' financial statements provided by the performance of independent audits encourages investment in public companies. This sense of confidence depends on reasonable investors perceiving auditors as independent professionals who have neither mutual nor conflicting interests with their clients and who exercise objective and impartial judgment on all issues brought to their attention.
>
> The Federal securities laws recognize the importance of independent audits by requiring, or permitting the Commission to require, that financial statements filed with the Commission by public companies, investment companies, broker/dealers, public utilities, investment advisers, and others, be certified (or audited) by independent public accountants, and by granting the Commission the authority to define the term "independent."
>
> Although specific guidance regarding Year 2000 is not set forth in the Commission's independence regulations, the independence issues can be addressed using existing guidance applicable to auditing firms providing other non-audit services. The staff generally does not object to an auditor's provision of non-audit services to SEC audit clients unless provision of services results in one of the following conflicts for the auditor:
>
> - The dependence of the auditor on fees from non-audit services,
> - The auditor supplanting the role of management in making decisions about a particular problem, and
> - Self-review by the auditor, including the effect on objectivity of auditing the product of systems designed or modified by the auditor.
>
> Based on the aforementioned guidance, an auditor's independence may be impaired by the provision of non-audit services by the auditor. Consequently, an independence issue may arise if the auditor of the registrant's financial statements designs or modifies programs to correct the Year 2000 problem.

---

17 SEC Report, Section 6(3)(2).

The SEC's position would only apply to a Canadian auditor of an SEC registrant. Canadian regulators do not appear to have expressed a similar concern.

6.5 TAX CONSIDERATIONS

The tax treatment for Year 2000 expenditures as described above appears in section 6.2(a) to have been accepted by Revenue Canada, the Internal Revenue Service[18] (United States) and Inland Revenue (United Kingdom). However, companies may wish to consult with their tax advisor to confirm the applicability of the above in their particular jurisdiction, and to see if a Year 2000 expenditure can be structured in a special way to maximize tax benefits.

Sales tax and withholding taxes issues should also be considered. Sales taxes may differ between services and tangible goods. Payments in respect of services that are made to Year 2000 solution providers located in foreign countries may be subject to withholding tax.

In an interpretation letter dated November 21, 1997, Revenue Canada indicated that the cost of remedying Year 2000 problems may either be considered as a current expense or a capital expenditure depending on the facts. Costs incurred to address Year 2000 problems will be considered a current expense if the software is merely being restored to its original condition so that it may continue to be used for the balance of its originally assessed useful life. However, the costs will be considered a capital expenditure if the work can be characterized as an enhancement, including any work that extends the use of the software beyond its originally assessed useful life.

In the fall of 1997, Canadian Industry Minister John Manley had indicated that there will not likely be any special tax breaks for costs incurred to fix Year 2000 problems. One of the recommendations of Canada's Task Force Year 2000 was that the federal government consider introducing revenue-

---

18 The IRS has announced that it will accept a taxpayer's treatment of costs incurred to address its Year 2000 problems if the taxpayer treats the costs in accordance with Rev. Proc. 69-21.

neutral tax encouragement measures with a primary focus on small and medium-sized enterprises ("SMEs") as soon as possible.

On October 21, 1997, the Internal Revenue Services in the United States published the guidelines it will follow when examining the tax returns of taxpayers that incur software costs in connection with Year 2000 remediation projects and that no special treatment should be expected.[19] However, the IRS subsequently announced a revenue-neutral initiative—special amortization rules for Year 2000 preparedness expenses—providing greater financial flexibility for affected firms.

Once again, companies may wish to consult with their tax advisor regarding the exact nature of any special Year 2000-related tax incentives.

---

19 The IRS guidelines confirmed that Year 2000 costs fall within the purview of Rev. Proc. 97-21 and that Year 2000 costs will only qualify for a research tax credit in extraordinary circumstances. IRS Rev. Proc. 97-50.

7

Corporate Governance and the Liability of Directors and Officers

To avoid unwelcomed legal action, Canada's Task Force Year 2000 urged business leaders and owners to promptly seek legal advice to help assess the legal implications of Year 2000 problems for their business. The Task Force advised firms to be cognizant of the legal duties, obligations and potential liabilities that may arise from a lack of Year 2000 preparedness. As a matter of corporate governance, firms were advised to first determine how and to what extent their business is subject to specific commercial, professional, industrial, and regulatory obligations before a comprehensive remediation plan can be designed and implemented. The Task Force recommended that the Year 2000 management team work closely with its professional advisors and consultants to ensure that the identified obligations are satisfied and exposure to legal liabilities is minimized.

Task Force Year 2000 suggests reviewing and assessing legal rights, obligations and liabilities, including risk management issues such as an assessment of insurance coverage and contractual indemnities.

7.1 DUTIES AND RESPONSIBILITIES OF DIRECTORS AND OFFICERS

(a) Duty of Care

General duties and responsibilities are placed upon directors by the statutes under which their company is incorporated. Obligations may also be established by legislation governing the industry in which a company operates or the various activities conducted.[1] Other obligations may also arise from common law or securities legislation.

Directors and officers have certain fiduciary responsibilities in respect of their companies including the duty of care. The precise formulation of the duty of care varies depending on the jurisdiction. However, in most jurisdictions, the duty of care is satisfied if a director or officer has in good faith, acted on an informed basis, in the honest belief that his or her decisions are in the best interest of the company.

In Canada, actions and decisions of directors and officers of companies incorporated under federal legislation must be considered based on the following standard:

> Every director and officer of a corporation in exercising his powers and discharging his duties shall exercise the care, diligence and skill that a reasonably prudent person would exercise in comparable circumstances.[2]

An example of equivalent legislation in one United States jurisdiction is Section 309(a) of the *California Corporations Code*,[3] which provides:

> A director shall perform the duties of a director . . . in good faith, in a manner that such director believes to be in the best interests of the corporation and its shareholders and with such care, including reasonable inquiry, as an ordinary prudent person in a like position would use under similar circumstances.

The duty of care requires that a director or officer exercise reasonable diligence in managing or supervising the management of the company.[4] If circumstances surrounding a decision or the oversight of the corporation's affairs include the potential for liability of the corporation, then prudent behaviour may require that a process or procedure be put in place to avoid

---

1 For instance, see section 166 of the *Insurance Companies Act*, S.C. 1991, c. 47. Other obligations may be imposed upon the company and/or the directors by statutes that relate to operation of the company, including statutes that address employment, environmental, occupational health and safety, income tax, record keeping, securities and similar aspects of a company's operation.

2 *Canada Business Corporations Act*, R.S.C. 1985, c. C-44, s. 122(b), [hereinafter "CBCA"); Ontario's *Business Corporations Act*, R.S.O. 1990, c. B.16, s.134(b) [hereinafter "OBCA"]. Statutes governing corporations in other jurisdictions contain similar provisions.

3 West's Ann. Cal. Corp. Code Title 1.

4 The standard of care may be higher if the company acts as a trustee for third parties. In such cases, the company should consider the extent to which Year 2000 problems may harm the beneficiaries and the potential liability of the company in that respect.

liability. The Year 2000 problem has been extensively publicized and it would be difficult for directors and officers to claim ignorance of the problem.

Prudent management of a company likely means that directors and officers have a duty to investigate the Year 2000 problem and deal with the problem to reduce to the extent possible the likelihood of a loss. This means that they must ensure not only that their company's systems are ready for the millennium, but also that their company will not be adversely affected by key suppliers, some of whom may not be taking adequate steps to become prepared for the next millennium.

Directors and officers must generally take the type of action that a prudent person would take to protect his or her own assets in comparable circumstances. The minimum standard is an objective one. However, the experience and role of a particular director or officer may raise the standard to be applied. Professionals, including lawyers and accountants, are expected to recognize problems within their areas of expertise and should be able to ask in depth questions about such matters. Directors and officers who fail to take reasonable action to protect the long term interests of their company may be held liable.

(b) Reliance on Others

Directors and officers are entitled to reasonably rely on expert advisers.[5] Directors may also rely in good faith on reports made by officers and employees who are more directly involved with an issue. In some cases, directors who reasonably rely upon the expertise of others may be protected from liability by statute (although such protection may not extend to officers).[6] Of course, directors and officers should take reasonable steps to confirm the expertise of such advisors.

An essential component of the duty of care is the duty of due inquiry.[7] The duty of care requires that directors and officers make their decisions on an informed basis following reasonable diligence in gathering and evaluating all material information. They must inquire further if they have any suspicions about the accuracy or completeness of the information given by their

---

5 *CBCA*, s. 123(4); *OBCA*, s. 135(4); s. 309(b) of the *California Corporation Code*.

6 See s. 309(c) of the *California Corporation Code*.

7 Certain corporate legislation, such as the *California Corporation Code* referred to previously, include an explicit requirement to exercise reasonable inquiry.

advisers. A director should document all the information sought and received in order to establish compliance with the duty of due inquiry.

Directors are entitled to delegate certain responsibilities to officers and senior management. However, they may not abdicate responsibility entirely.[8] Due to the importance of the Year 2000 problem, careful monitoring is required.[9] Directors must develop high level business strategies, and select and supervise the persons responsible for implementation. Directors also have obligations to ensure that adequate disclosure is made to shareholders and regulators. Failure to meet these obligations can expose directors to personal liability, distinct from that which may be imposed on the corporation.

(c) Business Judgment Rule

Directors, officers and management are entitled to exercise judgment. Courts recognize that risk-taking may be part of the management of the firm and the enhancement of value to shareholders. Courts do not require that such persons make perfect decisions as long as due care is exercised in the decision-making process and the decision maker forms a reasonable belief that the decision serves the best interest of the corporation.

Courts will typically apply what is known as the "business judgment rule" to decisions taken by corporate management.[10] A typical formulation of the rule involves five prerequisites:[11]

♦ a business decision;

---

8 See the report of The Toronto Stock Exchange Committee on Corporate Governance in Canada, released December 1994.

9 With respect to federally regulated financial institutions in the United States, the Federal Financial Institutions Examination Council ("FFIEC") has stated that in order to be fully informed and to provide effective direction, management must provide the board with status reports, at least quarterly, on the financial institution's Year 2000 efforts. See Federal Financial Institutions Examination Council, "Safety and Soundness Guidelines Concerning the Year 2000 Business Risk" (December 17, 1997) at <http://www. ffiec.gov/federal.htm>.

10 "It is a presumption that in making a business decision that the directors of a corporation acted on an informed basis, in good faith and in the honest belief that the action taken was in the best interest of the company." *Aronson* v. *Lewis*, 473 A.2d 805, 812 (Del. 1984). The business judgment rule is based on a recognition that corporate management is better equipped to make decisions regarding their business.

11 William E. Knepper, *Liability of Corporate Officers and Directors* (Charlottesville, VA: Michie, 1988) section 1.13.

- disinterestedness;
- due care, which is an informed decision following a reasonable effort to become familiar with the relevant and available facts;
- a reasonable belief that the best interests of the corporation and its stockholders are being served; and
- good faith.

United States courts apply the "business judgment rule" when those conditions have been established, unless it can be shown that the directors acted with a primary objective of achieving some illegitimate purpose or that the decision taken is contrary to their statutory obligations. Canadian courts have not recognized a specific "business judgment rule" and may not always give it the same weight as courts in the United States. However, there is a general reluctance to hold management to have failed in its duty of care on the basis of a decision made in good faith even if it turns out to be an incorrect decision.

In order to avail itself of the business judgment rule, corporate management needs to be able to demonstrate that it took steps to acquire the necessary information, asked questions and considered the relevant issues. The business judgment rule cannot be invoked where there was an absence of a conscious decision or where corporate management failed to act at all. In the case of major initiatives, directors and officers should consider insisting on being presented with comprehensive documentation and analysis.

(d) Steps to Reduce Potential for Liability

In some circumstances, a due diligence defence may be available to the corporation and for directors and officers if they are subject to potential liability. The measure of due diligence will depend on the applicable regulatory statute, the corporation, and the situation. Implementation of a reasonable Year 2000 compliance program may assist in the establishment of such a defence. In relation to the Year 2000 problem, the following steps are recommended to reduce the potential liability of directors and officers:

- Take steps to gain a better understanding of the Year 2000 problem. Attend seminars on managing the risks associated with the Year 2000 problem and, where possible, ask for briefings from professional advisors including legal counsel.
- Initiate the company's Year 2000 project as soon as possible. In those cases where the company does not become ready on time, the liability

of directors and officers may be reduced if they act reasonably and diligently compared to their colleagues in comparable businesses.

♦ Develop a comprehensive Year 2000 compliance plan that sets priorities and that contains strict deadlines. This plan should also specify the resources needed, accountability structures, and the procedure for reporting and monitoring the achievement of the different phases of the plan. Directors may need to go beyond simply relying on a plan put together by management. It may be advisable to have outside experts— technical and legal—review the plan.

♦ Allocate sufficient resources to the company's Year 2000 compliance efforts.[12] As well, directors and officers should ensure that financial plans reasonably reflect the anticipated cost of the company's Year 2000 compliance efforts.

♦ Create an effective response team to address to the Year 2000 problem. This team should include people with technical, financial, legal and management capabilities. One of the team's first tasks must be to do a technical audit and a legal audit of all the systems that may be affected by the Year 2000 problem. This team should report on a regular basis to the directors and officers.

♦ Conduct due diligence to determine whether dates promised by suppliers for Year 2000 fixes are reasonable, obtain sufficient information from suppliers on how they intend to address Year 2000 issues, and monitor their progress.

♦ Ensure that licence, maintenance, outsourcing and other key agreements are reviewed to ascertain whether the supplier is responsible for ensuring Year 2000 compliance.

♦ Investigate the Year 2000 compliance status of key customers, suppliers and business partners. A company may be Year 2000 compliant but may nevertheless be adversely affected by a Year 2000 problem if any other company in its "value chain" is not Year 2000 compliant.

♦ Ensure the company's insurance policies are reviewed by a specialist to confirm the scope of protection provided.

♦ Ensure fair disclosure is made in financial and regulatory filings.

♦ Ensure the company has adequately addressed the development of contingency plans.[13] Ensure the company has a contingency plan to deal with any Year 2000 problems that may arise notwithstanding the com-

---

12 IBM has projected that an average company will need to allocate 42% of its 1998 IT budget to Year 2000 efforts (Presentation to the Conference Board of Canada's Council of Senior Legal Executives, November 7, 1997, by Al Aubry, General Manager, Transformation 2000, IBM).

13 It would be prudent to assume that no one will get everything 100% right. There will undoubtedly be some residual risk of some systems failing. Contingency plans should be put in place to deal with such risks.

pany's efforts. According to the FFIEC, institutions should develop contingency plans for all vendors that service mission critical applications and establish a trigger date for implementing alternative solutions should the vendor not complete its corrections on time.

♦ Review the company's document retention program.
♦ Educate themselves about the Year 2000 problem.

For defensive litigation purposes, it would also be advisable for directors and officers to be able to demonstrate (i) that the company sought and obtained advice from external experts in the design of its Year 2000 compliance program; and (ii) that the scope of the company's Year 2000 compliance program and the associated effort expended in addressing its Year 2000 issues are comparable to what others in the industry are doing.

Although it is not completely certain that the adoption of these measures will avoid personal liability for directors and officers, they will demonstrate that reasonable efforts were taken and that directors and officers acted diligently and prudently, and may assist in exonerating them from liability.

7.2 DISCLOSURE OBLIGATIONS AND COMPLIANCE

Companies that reasonably expect to incur significant costs to make their systems Year 2000 compliant, or that face potential liability from system failures, may be required to disclose such information in annual reports, continuous disclosure documents, and other filings with regulatory authorities. Failure to disclose information about losses that are known, or that can be determined based on due diligence, may subject the organization and its officers and directors to fines or other liability.

Banks, venture capitalists and other investors are increasingly likely to inquire about a company's Year 2000 compliance before making significant loans to or equity investments in the company. Companies that have not implemented a Year 2000 compliance program will have a difficult time persuading these stakeholders that they are taking reasonable steps to address this serious risk.

7.3 LIABILITY FOR TRADING SECURITIES BASED ON UNDISCLOSED YEAR 2000-RELATED INFORMATION

Directors, officers and other parties that are in a special relationship with a reporting issuer may incur liability if they buy or sell securities of the reporting issuer with knowledge of a material fact or material change that has not been generally disclosed.[14]

A serious Year 2000 problem or a decision to spend a significant amount of money to address the problem can constitute a material fact, and in certain circumstances, discovery of a serious Year 2000-related problem may constitute a material change. Directors, officers and other parties that are in a special relationship with a reporting issuer may, therefore, commit an offence and/or incur liability if they trade securities of that issuer while in possession of material Year 2000 information that has not been publicly disclosed.

---

14 See section 76 of the *Ontario Securities Act* and section 119(2) of the *Alberta Securities Act*, which prohibit such action, and section 134 of the *Ontario Securities Act* and section 171 of the *Alberta Securities Act*, which create an obligation to compensate the seller or purchaser of the securities who does not possess knowledge of the material fact or material change. See also section 131(4) of the *Canada Business Corporations Act*, which imposes civil liability on an insider who trades securities on the basis of specific confidential information, which if generally known, might reasonably be expected to affect materially the value of the security. Similar liability may be incurred pursuant to legislation in the United States.

8

Insurance Issues

8.1 INTRODUCTION

Various types of insurance are used to manage business risks. Common types of coverage include:

♦ property damage (including business interruption)[1]
♦ comprehensive or commercial general liability ("CGL")[2]
♦ directors and officers ("D&O")
♦ professional errors and omissions ("E&O")
♦ fiduciary liability

First-party insurance, such as property insurance, provides an insured with protection for losses that the insured suffers directly, which may or may not result from a wrongful act of another person. Third-party insurance, which includes CGL, D&O and E&O, protects the insured from claims asserted by others that the insured caused them damage. Third-party insurance does not protect the insured against losses that it incurs directly. Both categories of policies should be reviewed to determine if they provide protection against losses arising from Year 2000 problems.

Some specific situations where the insured may be at risk in respect of Year 2000 problems include:

---

1 Business interruption coverage is generally an endorsement added to property coverage for profit lost during recovery from a property loss. It is often tied to a covered loss under a property policy and may not apply if there is no coverage under the property policy. Contingent business interruption is an endorsement designed to provide protection from losses caused by an insurable event to a third party.

2 Related types of policies may include employers' liability and product liability.

- loss of use of, or damage caused by, a product used in the insured's business;[3]
- loss of use of, or damage caused by, a product supplied by the insured to others;
- negligence of the insured in performing Year 2000 services (for instance, contracting to assist its customers in performing Year 2000 conversion work, project management, etc.);
- breach of a Year 2000 warranty relating to services provided by, or products supplied by, an insured;
- losses caused by a failure to fulfill contractual commitments to others; or
- losses due to non-compliant data transmitted to or received from a third party.

Most insurance policies currently in force do not provide explicit coverage for losses resulting from Year 2000 problems. Such losses, depending on the circumstances, may fall within general provisions of certain types of policies. However, depending on the problem, commonly utilized exclusions may negate coverage. There are also differing points of view in respect of whether or not a Year 2000 problem can be considered a fortuitous loss or accident.[4]

Insurance companies have started to examine their potential exposures to Year 2000 problems. Policies are being reviewed. Many insurance companies are taking steps to reduce their exposure to Year 2000 problems through explicit policy exclusions and by refusing to cover high risk parties. Any remaining coverage will likely go to those companies that have instituted a comprehensive Year 2000 compliance program.

This response is in accordance with the recommendations of Canada's Task Force Year 2000. The Task Force recommended that the insurance community (i) provide its corporate clients with early notification of the importance of the Year 2000 issue and of the requirement for a formal Year 2000 action plan, and (ii) make the issuance/renewal of insurance policies contingent on the availability of a formal Year 2000 action plan.[5]

---

3 This example may fall with a property policy. The other examples in the list may fall within various types of third party policies.

4 This goes to the question of whether an insurable loss has occurred.

5 Task Force Year 2000 Recommendation 4.

8.2 CONVENTIONAL POLICIES

(a) General Liability

A CGL policy provides coverage for certain types of injury or damage caused to a third party by the insured's actions or failure to act.

Liability to third parties as a result of the Year 2000 problem can arise in numerous ways. It can arise due to the supply of deficient products or services, or other failure to satisfy contractual duties. A company that supplies a defective product, such as one which fails due to a Year 2000 problem, may face a claim. If a Year 2000 failure causes bodily injury or property damage to third parties, then general liability insurance may provide coverage subject to any applicable exclusions. An employers' liability policy may be applicable if bodily injury results to employees due to a Year 2000 problem, also subject to any applicable exclusions.

(b) Directors and Officers

Directors and officers liability insurance is intended to protect corporate decision makers from lawsuits brought against them personally for wrongful acts (such as negligent business decisions). A "wrongful act" may be defined as an error, omission, act, neglect, error, misstatement, misleading statement, or breach of duty, committed or attempted, or allegedly committed or attempted, by a director or officer acting in his or her capacity as a director or officer.[6] A claim made against a director or officer would likely be based on an allegation that the conduct fell below the standard of reasonably competent, skilful and prudent directors or officers. A company may also obtain coverage to protect itself from the requirement to indemnify directors and officers against claims as set out in the company's bylaws or in a separate agreement.

Claims against directors and officers may be based on an allegation that the director or officer, among other things:

♦ failed to make Year 2000-related disclosures for securities purposes;

---

6 Wrongful acts may also be defined to include any other matter claimed against a director or officer arising from actions taken in that capacity.

♦ approved a merger or acquisition without sufficient due diligence concerning the Year 2000 problem;
♦ failed to ensure that acquisitions made by the corporation were Year 2000 compliant (at a time when the Year 2000 problem was generally known in the industry and the corporation expected to continue using the product past the year 2000);
♦ failed to assess the impact of the Year 2000 problem and its likely effect upon the corporation's existing systems or business operations;
♦ failed to consider and initiate appropriate remedial measures to address the corporation's Year 2000 problems within a time frame that would permit the problems to be corrected or at least minimized;
♦ failed to take necessary or effective action to pursue recovery from suppliers whose Year 2000 non-compliance creates a loss or damages to the corporation; or
♦ was negligent in the selection and monitoring of remediation service providers.[7]

The financial impact of a first party or third party loss may also trigger a secondary suit. If a Year 2000 problem has an impact on a company's share price, shareholders may bring an action against directors and officers.[8] For instance, following a merger in the later 1970s, an airline's computer system was unable to handle the volume of reservations that customers were seeking to make. This lead to a decline in its share price that resulted in a lawsuit by shareholders against the company's directors, alleging that they failed to oversee the airline's information technology system.[9] It should be noted that a claim of this nature could be brought before the Year 2000 and before a company experiences an actual failure of a critical system. An example of a situation that might trigger such a claim is a drop in the company's share price that results from management's failure to demonstrate that it is taking sufficient action to address possible Year 2000 problems.

If directors or officers are sued for failing to properly address their company's Year 2000 problems then a directors and officers policy may be

---

7 Negligence in the selection of a remediation service provider could lead to the loss of control over proprietary software or other intangible assets. Another possibility could be a loss due to the commission of a crime (for example, where a crime is perpetuated while normal security standards are dropped due to the short time available to complete remediation).

8 A decline in share price is the single most common factor leading to claims against directors and officers.

9 "The Year 2000—The Millennium Bug: A Risk Management Assessment" prepared by J&H Marsh & McLennan FINPRO.

called upon to provide coverage. Certain exclusions in a directors and officers policy, particularly a "prior acts exclusion," may be relevant to Year 2000 problems.

Directors and officers liability policies should be reviewed to ensure they cover all persons intended to be covered. The fact that a person's title includes the word "officer" does not mean the person is covered by such insurance. For instance, the Chief Information Officer may not be considered an officer, and is therefore not covered.

(c) Professional Liability (Errors and Omissions)

Professional liability policies provide coverage for errors and omissions committed in the rendering of, or failure to render, professional services. This may include a failure to successfully complete a Year 2000 remediation project or negligence in the design or development of a product or the supply of deficient services.[10] Some issues to consider are:

- ◆ the potential for class actions because an error that is committed may not be restricted to a particular client;
- ◆ policies have aggregate limits that could be used up by claims of other clients;
- ◆ these policies are "claims based" and must remain in effect at the time a claim is made;
- ◆ punitive damages may or may not be covered (for jurisdictions where such damages are available) depending on the specific policy;
- ◆ as the year 2000 approaches, the cost of professional E&O coverage for computer professionals may become very expensive or difficult to obtain.

(d) Property

Property insurance policies may limit coverage to specified named perils (such as fire, theft, etc.). If so, the cause of the loss must constitute a covered

---

10 A policy may provide business liability coverage that covers sums the insured becomes legally liable to pay as compensatory damages because of bodily injury or property damage arising out of the insured business operation. This could conceivably cover a Year 2000 problem that was negligently incorporated in a product developed by the insured and/or negligence arising from a failure by the insured to make proper inquiries related to the Year 2000 compliance of a product supplied by the insured.

peril. It is unlikely that a "named perils" type of policy will be found to include coverage for the Year 2000 problem. However, a "named perils" type of policy is rare for commercial insureds.

Most types of policies are written on an "all risks" basis. Such policies provide coverage for all risks not specifically excluded. "All risk" policies provide very broad coverage and are usually interpreted liberally by courts to provide coverage. Once it is shown that the loss falls within the coverage, the onus is on the insurer to establish that an exclusion applies. Therefore, the onus will likely be on the insurer to show that an exclusion is applicable and that a loss due to a Year 2000 problem should be excluded.

With respect to the property covered, a property policy may cover "business property, including . . . equipment, computer hardware and software." This is typically broad enough to cover other forms of office equipment such as fax machines, PBX systems, etc., which may have embedded logic circuits susceptible to the Year 2000 bug.

In order for business interruption insurance to kick in, the business must be suspended due to direct physical loss or damage to the property caused by or resulting from a peril insured against. In many cases, coverage for business interruption will mirror coverage for property damage. However, some business interruption provisions are broad enough so that the covered peril need not damage or cause the loss of insured property, but need only damage or cause loss of property of the type insured.[11]

Most policies contain an exclusion for any quality in the property that causes it to damage or destroy itself.[12] Insurance coverage may cover damage caused to other insured property but not the cost of repairing the non-compliant property. If property is not damaged and a loss occurs because it does not function as intended, it may not be covered. Alternatively, if a business interruption occurs because computers fail to dispatch inventory, underwriters are not likely to consider the business interruption loss as the result of an insured peril. However, if a fire or explosion occurs because of an unforeseen Year 2000 problem, the resulting loss that consists

---

11 Kirk A. Pasich, "Insurance Coverage for the Year 2000 Problem" *Year 2000 Computer Crises: the Litigation Summit* (November 6-7, 1997) Fulcrum Information Services Inc., San Francisco, California.

12 Opinion is divided whether such an exclusion would be applicable to a Year 2000 type problem.

of physical damage and business interruption would likely be covered, subject to the policy's terms and conditions.[13]

The same logic could be applied to a contingent business interruption exposure. If a company suffers a financial loss because of a supplier's Year 2000 problem (for instance, preventing it from supplying raw materials), a contingent business interruption coverage may not respond. However, if the failure to supply resulted from a fire caused by an unknown Year 2000 problem, the underwriter would be likely to respond more favourably.[14]

Property damage is usually defined in a liability policy as physical injury to or destruction of tangible property including resulting loss of use. The loss of use of computer software or equipment used in a business due to a failure of the software or equipment to operate or due to errors being generated by the software or equipment may potentially be covered.[15] An insured could potentially claim for loss of use of software or equipment acquired from others.

It may be difficult for a policyholder to convince a court that a Year 2000 problem in a software program constitutes physical loss of or damage to tangible property, as would be required under most policies. This will be particularly difficult if the system failure is the result of the program operating as it was designed. The standard wording on most policies would require amendment to cover loss caused by computer viruses and other computer related issues. While the Year 2000 problem might not be construed as a computer virus, it is a defect of the same nature. A prudent policyholder wishing to obtain coverage for the risk would be well advised to expressly include it by name in the policy and make sure coverage is provided for the cost of repair or replacement of both hardware and software.

Some policies contain an Electronic Data Processing endorsement designed to provide coverage for computers. However, even these endorsements normally contain an exclusion for errors in programming that may preclude coverage for Year 2000 problems.

---

13 J&H Marsh & McLennan, "The Year 2000: A Time Odyssey" *Insurable Interests* (Spring 1997) at 3.

14 Ibid.

15 In some policies, the definition of property may explicitly cover data. If not, the definition of property in a policy may not be interpreted to cover data.

Even if coverage is available in respect of a Year 2000 risk, unless the policy also provides contingent time element coverage, the policyholder may not be insured for the many forms of losses that may result. This may include lost business income, extra expense and contingent business income. These types of losses may occur if a supplier's system fails, preventing the policyholder from receiving products or raw materials, or if a customer's system fails, preventing the policyholder from selling their product to their customer.

If a court finds that a Year 2000-related deficiency in a system or product constitutes property damage, a policyholder may still not be entitled to recover unless the defective system or product causes damage to other property (which may be rare).

8.3 POTENTIAL ISSUES RELATING TO COVERAGE

(a) Deciding whether the Year 2000 Problem Constitutes "Damages"

Typically, a general liability policy will cover damage that the insured is required to pay from an occurrence resulting in bodily injury or property damage during the policy period.[16] Property damage is often defined as physical injury to or loss of use of tangible property. Pure economic losses are unlikely to be covered. Money spent on prophylactic measures to prevent damage from occurring (such as reviewing, correcting and testing programs) may not constitute "damages" in most cases.

Many problems expected to arise from the Year 2000 problem are unlikely to involve either direct bodily injury or physical injury to tangible property. Most liability is expected to result from corrupted data, inaccurate results, and from a loss of ability to use non-compliant products. These types and losses are generally expected to be of an economic nature.[17] However, if a computer is rendered useless then an argument might be made that this in itself constitutes a loss of property.

---

16 D&O and E&O policies would respond to a financial loss.

17 This will depend on the industry and the particular activities that the insured is conducting. Some industries, such as airlines and railways, may have a potential for personal injury and property damage on a catastrophic scale.

Insurers may refuse to recognize coverage for a business interruption loss relating to computer equipment unless the computer itself sustains "physical" damage, injury, or loss (such as that arising from something crashing into the computer or a theft of the system). A similar issue arises in respect to damages caused to other parties. However, in many cases, even if a Year 2000 problem does not result in physical damage to tangible property, it will likely result in a loss of use of tangible property (provided it results from a covered "occurrence" as defined in the policy). Property damage is often defined as including such loss of use.

Nevertheless, there will undoubtably be disputes as to whether products that are not Year 2000 compliant will constitute property damage within the meaning of insurance policies, particularly when computer software is involved. However, if a factory explodes as a result of improper maintenance caused by a Year 2000 problem, even if such problem is the result of a Year 2000 problem contained in computer software, any resulting bodily injury or property damage sustained would likely be covered. In this example, the occurrence would be the explosion and the bodily injury and property damage would be the proximate result of the explosion.[18]

(b) Deciding whether the Loss Flows From an "Occurrence"

Insurers do not insure against foreseeable risks, and the year 2000 is foreseeable.[19]

Another issue that must be considered in respect of insurance coverage for Year 2000 problems, particularly in respect of general liability policies, is the requirement that the loss flow from an "occurrence."[20] The occurrence element requires that the damage be neither expected nor intended by the policyholder. To qualify as an occurrence, both the event that causes the injury, as well as the resulting damage, must be unexpected. Some courts have interpreted "expected" to mean substantially certain, practically certain, highly likely or highly probable. An injury can be expected without the insured intending to cause the resulting damage.

---

18 J&H Marsh & McClennan, *supra* at note 13.

19 Malcolm Tarling, Association of British Insurers, quoted in "Insurers claim immunity over millennium" *Computerweekly* (August 28, 1997).

20 While it may be relatively easy to establish that damage was suffered, it will likely be difficult to establish when in time the "occurrence" had occurred. In the case of D&O or E&O policies, coverage will be triggered based on a "wrongful act" rather than on an "occurrence."

Insurers will likely take the position that the use of two-digit fields by an insured party to store the year was an intentional decision made for cost-saving or compatibility purposes, and that in any case, the resulting harm was well recognized and anticipated, particularly leading up to the year 2000.[21] While it may be very difficult for an insured to argue that a Year 2000 problem was not expected, in order to be successful, an insurer may need to demonstrate that the policyholder subjectively intended or expected the resulting injury. Where an insured makes a diligent effort to address its Year 2000 problems but misses something, it may be difficult for the insurer to assert that the insured "expected" the claim.

When the insured knows of a dangerous defect in a manufactured material, or would know if it performed normal inspection, it may be argued that the insured must also do something about both inspection and repair in terms of reasonable efforts to preserve its own property. If it fails to do that, and then the risk is realized, one could say that the loss is not exactly fortuitous or "adventitious."[22] However, it is not clear that knowledge on the part of the insured of the potential or possibility of a Year 2000 problem will be sufficient to eliminate coverage.

An insurer may also have difficulty denying coverage based on the "known loss" doctrine or a "prior act" exclusion if at the time the policy was entered into, the event was only a contingency or risk that may or may not occur within the term of the policy. While the arrival of the year 2000 is inevitable, the resulting damage or imposition of liability may not be certain or inevitable.

A related issue that ties into the section that follows is interpreting what event constitutes the occurrence. For instance, in the case of a non-compliant system, did the occurrence happen on (i) the date the system was installed; (ii) the date the problem was discovered; (iii) various time periods associated with the remediation project; or (iv) the date that damage or injury is suffered?

(c) When Must the Policy be in Effect?

Many types of insurance policies, such as professional liability or directors and officers policies, are written on a "claims-made" basis. Such policies

---

21 The Year 2000 problem has been discussed for more than 25 years and actively discussed in the decade leading up to the year 2000.

22 *Triple Five Corp. v. Simcoe & Erie Group*, [1997] I.L.R. I-3457 (Alta C.A.).

only cover claims made during the policy period (as opposed to providing protection for wrongful acts committed during the policy period even after termination of the policy). Coverage may also be provided for claims arising from wrongful acts committed prior to the commencement of the policy so long as the insured did not know of the possible claim at the commencement of the policy. Any exclusions added to renewals (or a failure to renew a policy) may therefore preclude coverage for events that occur during the period the older version of the policy (*i.e.*, without the exclusions) was in effect. This will likely be an area of significant dispute.

This issue is relevant because many insurers are expected to revise the wording of their policy to specifically exclude coverage for Year 2000 problems. While it is expected that some Year 2000 problems will appear prior to the year 2000, the majority are not expected to appear until after the year 2000.

Some "claims made" policies provide an option that allows an insured, upon payment of a discounted premium, to extend the reporting period for a specified time (for instance, up to 12 months) following cancellation or non-renewal during which the insured can give notice to the insurer of claims made during such extended reporting period for any "wrongful act" committed prior to the end of the policy period. Such a provision may be useful for an insured that is faced with a notification from an insurer of its intention not to renew a policy. It does not appear applicable when an insurer does not refuse to renew, but rather inserts an explicit exclusion for Year 2000 problems.

(d) Disclosure on Renewal

Applications for insurance, such as those for director's and officer's insurance, usually ask the applicant whether they know of a fact or circumstance likely to give rise to a claim. A failure to disclose, or a misrepresentation of a fact or circumstance concerning a Year 2000 problem, in an application for insurance may provide a basis for a subsequent denial of coverage.[23] An insurer may also require an applicant for new insurance to include a warranty statement that is incorporated into the policy.

---

23 Such policies typically contain an exclusions for "wrongful acts" that took place on or before the effective date of the policy if any insured knew or could have reasonably foreseen that such "wrongful act" did or would result in a claim against the insured. This is expected to be another heavily litigated area.

Some insurance renewal applications ask whether material changes have occurred in respect to any information provided in the original application or in the insured's financial statements. Other renewal forms may ask specifically whether an insured is aware of any circumstance that would give rise to a claim. In such cases, an insured should review its Year 2000 compliance status with legal counsel to ascertain whether disclosure is required. In some circumstances, an insured that has reason to believe that its efforts to address the Year 2000 problem may be inadequate and that losses are foreseeable may need to report this to its insurer during the renewal process as a circumstance that might give rise to a claim.

Many insurers are making increasingly detailed inquiries concerning an insured's Year 2000 status and efforts. Unsatisfactory responses are likely to result in further inquiry and action by the insurer to exclude coverage. Some insurers may request insureds to sign a warranty statement as part of a renewal. However, insurance brokers are advising their clients to strongly resist doing so.

(e) Year 2000 Questionnaires

Some insurance companies have sent questionnaires to their policy holders seeking information as to their exposure to the Year 2000 problem.[24] For instance, insurers are sending questionnaires to airlines to determine the efforts they are taking. Some insurers have warned that they would withdraw their coverage for airlines (which would result in planes being grounded) if airlines do not adequately address Year 2000 issues concerning their systems before the year 2000.

An appropriately worded Year 2000 questionnaire can be an important source of information for an insurer assessing a prospective insured's potential exposure to Year 2000 problems. Insurers will want to have such questionnaires drafted carefully because of the potential risk; if there is a subsequent disputed claim, the insured may argue that the insurer waived its rights in certain respects to require full disclosure of all material information related to the Year 2000 problem. Insurers will also want to ensure that any questionnaire is clearly tied to the policy application or renewal (*e.g.* to have binding effect). Although questionnaires may provide some useful information to underwriters, they are not likely to provide a complete picture of an insured's readiness for the year 2000 because most

---

24 Questionnaires can also be used to help educate policy holders.

insureds may not yet be able to confirm their systems are Year 2000 compliant.[25]

A questionnaire titled "Computer/Micro-Controller Inability to Correctly Interpret Dates" has been developed by the Insurance Council of Canada. The questionnaire defines "Year 2000 Compliant" as the "ability of computer hardware, computer software programs and/or embedded micro-chips or micro-controllers to correctly recognize, interpret or process any encoded, abbreviated or encrypted date, time or combined date/time data or date field." The questionnaire seeks to obtain information concerning the extent that a potential applicant may be at risk to the various categories of Year 2000 problems.[26]

Insureds need to be especially careful in responding to information requests from insurance companies. In some cases, a high standard of disclosure may be applicable. It is important that responses to inquiry letters sent by insurers be carefully considered and reviewed to ensure they cannot later be used as a basis for denying coverage.

Insurers should also carefully consider the types of questions being asked on renewal and those asked on any Year 2000 specific questionnaires. It is possible that the information provided by an insured may constitute notice to the insurer pursuant to a "potential claims" provision in a policy.

8.4 COMMON EXCLUSIONS

Existing exclusions must also be reviewed as some exclusions may be broad enough to exclude coverage for certain types of losses stemming from Year 2000 problems. The two most likely exclusions are those dealing with intentional acts and latent defects.

Intentional or criminal acts, which include intentional acts or failure to act by or at the direction of any person who is insured by the policy, may be excluded. Some insurers, particularly in the United States, are sending their policy holders information regarding the Year 2000 problem. Some insurers may be sending such information to improve their ability to rely on exclu-

---

25 Barlow Lyde & Gilbert, "Implications of Y2K for Insurers" *Briefing Note* (February 12, 1998).

26 The categories covered include devices containing embedded chips, exposure to noncompliant products (used or sold), dependencies on external parties, remediation status and contingency planning. Lack of a Year 2000 plan is a "red flag."

sions based on an intentional failure to act, and in order to establish that the insureds were aware of the issue and therefore that any exposures did not result from a fortuitous event. If an insured does act but is unsuccessful (even if due to the negligence of the insured) then it may be difficult for an insurer to rely upon this exclusion.

Also it may be insufficient that the insured was warned that damage may ensue from its actions, or that, once warned, an insured decided to take a calculated risk and proceed. The actual knowledge and intent of the insured will be important.

Most policies exclude coverage for losses caused by latent defects. This exclusion may exclude wear and tear and the cost of repairing faulty or improper material, work quality or design. A Year 2000 problem may fall within any one of these categories, although opinion is divided.

Other exclusions commonly utilized in policies may also be relevant to the Year 2000 issue. Individual insurance policies should be consulted for specific exclusions.

8.5 YEAR 2000 EXCLUSIONS

While it is possible that existing exclusions may be sufficient to exclude liability of an insurer for Year 2000 problems, this conclusion is far from certain. At least some insurers have been advised to adopt specific and explicit exclusions for Year 2000 problems. Insurance companies in the United Kingdom have agreed on standard wording for Year 2000 exclusion clauses.[27] The wording for "All Risks-Material Damage and Business Interruption" provides:[28]

> DAMAGE or CONSEQUENTIAL LOSS directly or indirectly caused by or consisting of or arising from the failure of any computer, data processing equipment or media, microchip, integrated circuit or similar device or any computer software, whether the property of the insured or not, and whether occurring before, during or after the year 2000,
>
> (i)   to correctly recognize any date as its true calendar date;

---

27 "Insurers take steps to avoid 'millennium bug' payments" *BBC News* (November 10, 1997), <http://news.bbc.co.uk>.

28 See *Computerweekly*, November 13, 1997 at <http://www.computerweekly.co.uk>, which contains copies of exclusions for other types of policies.

(ii) to capture, save or retain, and/or correctly to manipulate, interpret or process any data or information or command or instruction as a result of treating any date otherwise than as its true calendar date;

(iii) to capture, save, retain or correctly to process any data as a result of the operation of any command which has been programmed into any computer software, being a command which causes the loss of data or the inability to capture, save or correctly process such data on or after any date;

but this shall not exclude subsequent DAMAGE or CONSEQUENTIAL LOSS not otherwise excluded, which itself results from a Defined Peril.

Model exclusions for use in liability, professional indemnity, directors and officers, and other policies have also been developed by the Association of British Insurers.

The Insurance Services Office, Inc. ("ISO"), which provides standard insurance policy forms and underwriting information for American insurers, has developed endorsements to policies to exclude the Year 2000 problem. ISO's exclusion provides:

This insurance does not apply to any injury or damage directly or indirectly arising out of:

1. Any actual or alleged failure, partial failure, malfunction or inadequacy of:
   a. Any of the following (whether owned by you or by others):
      (1) computer hardware;
      (2) computer software, including, but not limited to, applications and operating systems;
      (3) computer networks;
      (4) microprocessors (computer chips);
      (5) any electronic equipment or components containing or utilizing any of the above; or
   b. Any other products, services or functions that directly or indirectly utilize or rely upon, in any manner, any of the items listed in paragraph 1.a. of this endorsement.

   due to inability of the products, services or functions described in 1.a. and 1.b. to correctly recognize, distinguish, interpret, process, accept or handle data or information related to the year or due to the failure to program, input or update data or information which incorporates the year.

2. Any advice, consultation, design, delay, evaluation, inspection, installation, maintenance, omission, repair or supervision done by you or for you to determine, rectify or test for any potential or actual problem, failure or malfunction arising out of data or information with respect to the year.

The Insurance Bureau of Canada has also developed model wording and endorsements that can be used to include or exclude various types of losses that may arise due to Year 2000 problems. Coverage is excluded in respect of any bodily injury, property damage or personal injury arising out of the failure of any:

a. electronic data processing equipment, or other equipment, including micro-chips embedded therein;
b. computer program;
c. software;
d. media;
e. data;
f. memory storage system;
g. memory storage device;
h. real time clock;
i. date calculator; or
j. any other related component, system, process or device, to correctly read, recognize, interpret or process any encoded, abbreviated or encrypted date, time or combined date/time data or date field.

Such failure shall include any error in original or modified data entry or programming.[29]

Aside from adding Year 2000 exclusions to new policies, insurance companies are also amending existing policies to exclude Year 2000 risks from coverage and are reviewing such policies for ambiguities that could be exploited by policyholders to obtain coverage for losses arising from Year 2000 problems. However, even without a specific Year 2000 exclusion clause, most insurers will likely take the position that the Year 2000 problem is not an insurable risk.

An insured presented with a Year 2000 exclusion on a renewal should shop around and attempt to find a policy with no such exclusion or the most limited exclusion. If a decision is made to switch insurers, care must be exercised in filling out applications in order to avoid assertions of misrepresentation by the insurers in the event that a claim is subsequently made.

An insured that is notified that a Year 2000 exclusion is to be added to a policy upon renewal should consider whether circumstances exist to allow it to provide notice to the insurer, prior to the expiration of the original

---

29 An exception may be provided for loss or damage caused directly by fire or an explosion of natural, coal or manufactured gas.

policy without the Year 2000 exclusion, of a claim or any facts or circumstances that may reasonably be expected to give rise to a claim for which coverage would be afforded by the policy. An existing policy may provide coverage for such a future claim as long as the insured gives notice of the potential claim within the term of the existing policy. However, a certain level of specificity is likely to be required.

Some insureds are providing a "laundry list" of potential claims near the end of the policy period, particularly if a Year 2000 exclusion is being added to the renewal. While the effectiveness of such an approach is not certain, such notice may be sufficient to satisfy the requirements of some policies. Of course, an insured should first review the language of its particular policy and seek the advise of its professional advisors. If used inappropriately, such an approach can result in a loss of coverage upon renewal.

Insurance industry analysts expect insurance companies to inform their clients, before policies are renewed in 1998, that Year 2000 related risks will be excluded from coverage. However, in some cases, the addition of Year 2000 exclusions at a time after the start of 1998 may be too late. A policy written in 1998 will provide coverage during at least part of 1999 and problems in many types of systems are expected to start appearing in 1999.

8.6 YEAR 2000 SPECIFIC POLICIES

Insurance coverage for Year 2000 problems could be a valuable component of a comprehensive risk management strategy. Several insurance companies are marketing insurance products that explicitly cover Year 2000 losses. These include J&H Marsh and McLennan's "2000 Secure" product and American Insurance Group Inc.'s "Millennium" product.[30] Travellers Property Casualty Corp. have also announced that they plan to offer some form of Year 2000 coverage. These types of policies are best suited for large companies that are taking proper steps to address their Year 2000 problems but that wish to obtain additional protection. Year 2000 specific insurance coverage, and the associated audit that must be performed in order to

---

30 An article in the March 3, 1998 issue of *Computerweekly* stated that AIG had six confirmed clients and was receiving about 25 applications a month for its risk-sharing policy. However, other reports suggest that very few Year 2000 specific policies have been sold.

qualify, may provide comfort to interested parties such as investors, share-holders, bankers, regulators and the capital markets.

(a) Coverage

The Millennium and 2000 Secure products mentioned above take an "all risk" approach. They provide business interruption and legal liability coverage in the event that Year 2000 conversion efforts by the insured or a third party should fail. The *direct* business interruption component covers loss of profits for business interruption resulting from unsuccessful conversion by the insured of its own systems. The *contingent* business interruption component covers loss of profits and extra expense for business interruption of the insured due to an unsuccessful or incompatible conversion by a third party that results in the failure or interruption of a third-party system or data transmission capability. The third party liability component includes errors and omissions, and directors and officers insurance, and covers an insured's legal liability resulting from its own or a third party's conversion efforts. The 2000 Secure policy also provides a "hot site expense" component that can reimburse the insured for the use of a qualified service bureau to process specified back-office functions as well as the cost of on-site corrective work.[31]

(b) Premiums

The 2000 Secure policy is available with aggregate limits of liability of up to $200 million and runs until January 1, 2001. Premiums are expected to vary between 2-8% of the policy's limit on liability and will depend on the risk profile of the applicant, the limit of liability elected, and the level of risk the applicant chooses to retain as a deductible or self-insured retention. The AIG policy collects premiums totalling 65-85% of the coverage amount but returns a large portion if there are no claims.[32] The 2000 Secure policy offers true risk transfer whereas the Millennium policy is a "finite risk" product.

---

31 This summary and the remainder of this chapter is provided for informational purposes. Please confirm the exact scope of any Year 2000 specific policy you may wish to obtain with your broker or insurer. It should also be noted that as the year 2000 approaches, some or all of the brokers offering Year 2000 specific policies may discontinue offering such coverage.

32 See Andrew M. Reidy and Robert L. Carter, "...But Insurance Policies Could Provide Coverage", *National Law Journal* (Monday, November 3, 1997) at B12.

(c) Underwriting Requirements

The 2000 Secure policy requires the insured to provide a corrective plan, permit technical and legal audits and regular progress reports. Pre-underwriting requirements for both products are similar and require the applicant to demonstrate:

- a Year 2000 compliance plan was approved by the board of directors and has commenced;
- the compliance plan allows sufficient time for testing well in advance of the year 2000;
- the applicant has budgeted for expenses associated with its Year 2000 compliance plan in its 1998 and 1999 budgets;
- the applicant has reviewed the extent to which its major suppliers are Year 2000 compliant; and
- the applicant has established a contingency plan in the event its efforts to prevent a Year 2000 failure should fail.

Other Year 2000 specific policies will also likely include close scrutiny of what the policyholder has done to address the Year 2000 problem and mitigate potential loses.

(d) Exclusions

Year 2000 specific policies, like other all risk products, contain limitations and exclusions. For instance, the 2000 Secure policy contains various exclusions, including:

- willful non-compliance with the insured's Year 2000 compliance plan;
- Year 2000 problems caused by hardware or software that the insured intentionally or recklessly withheld from identification in its inventory;
- any "slow down" in EDP functions resulting from the use of data, hardware or software that is Year 2000 compliant or otherwise part of the insured's Year 2000 compliance plan;
- Year 2000 problems related to BIOS chips in non-computer equipment (*i.e.*, any problems with equipment containing embedded logic);
- intellectual property infringement (liability component);
- contractual liability, in the case of service providers only (liability component);
- EDP problems that are not Year 2000 problems (non-liability components); and

♦ legal restrictions on the use of software, hardware or firmware (non-liability components).

(e) Other Considerations

A company that contracts for a Year 2000 policy should ensure that all relevant parties are included under the coverage. This would typically include the named insured and any subsidiary specifically listed in the declarations. For at least certain components of the policy, an insured will want to confirm coverage for past, present and future directors, officers, partners and employees of the named insured and listed subsidiaries, while acting within the scope of their duties.

8.7 CONCLUSIONS

A company's risk managers should keep themselves informed of new developments in Year 2000 coverage and review their plan to preserve maximum coverage for Year 2000-related claims. It is also suggested that aggregate limits applicable to various policies be re-examined in light of possible exposure due to Year 2000-related problems.

Clearly the Year 2000 problem raises complicated questions relating to the existence and adequacy of coverage under a company's liability and property insurance policies. The services of a knowledgeable and skilled broker should be retained to review a company's existing coverage and the options available. Consultation with legal counsel is also recommended where applicable.

9

Employment Issues

9.1 INTRODUCTION

> Local and international competition for Year 2000 practitioners is cut-throat. Corporate compensation policies and practices must be reviewed now to create the flexibility needed to retain and replace key Year 2000 professionals.[1]

> Businesses hungry for technicians to fix their computer problems are devouring the labour pool, making programming talent hard to find. They have now turned to snatching workers away from government jobs, offering bonuses and higher salaries.[2]

As the year 2000 approaches, many categories of computer professionals, already in heavy demand, are expected to become more difficult to recruit and retain. According to a report on the implications of the Year 2000 problem prepared by the Congressional Research Services in the United States, leading research in the field indicates that the number of available persons with skills to address the Year 2000 problem will diminish as a result of increased demand. Year 2000 project managers are becoming an especially hot commodity. The difficulty in obtaining the expertise and skill required to deal with the problem may lead to improper recruiting practices and legal disputes.

Increased competition and anticipated shortages of Year 2000 specialists are prompting many companies to create special classes of employees who receive compensation and perks not enjoyed by workers in other areas. Compensation for project managers and COBOL programmers increased 25% in the second half of 1997 and is expected to keep increasing.[3]

---

1 ITAC's Challenge 2000: Executive Guide to Year 2000 Computing Solutions.
2 "States Won't Fully Meet Deadline" *USA Today* (December 17, 1997) at 10A.
3 While there is a significant demand for programmers experienced in COBOL and FORTRAN, the Year 2000 problem is not language specific and may be encountered in programs written in any computer programming language.

One aspect of the demand for Year 2000 specialists is that it is expected to be limited in duration. Flexibility in employment arrangements and compensation schemes will be necessary to allow downward adjustments to market levels after the expected peak in demand. Some employers are addressing this issue by paying a "realistic" base salary and high bonuses so that compensation can be more easily reduced after the Year 2000. Care must be taken, however, when reducing compensation as this may result in a constructive dismissal, at common law. Obtaining the employee's agreement now to a reduction in compensation "down the road" may reduce this risk.

The following are additional employment-related issues that should be considered:

♦ Recruiters for foreign companies that are late in commencing their Year 2000 efforts will likely target North America for experienced talent;
♦ Companies will need to ensure that any Year 2000 staff execute appropriate agreements that cover assignment of intellectual property rights and non-disclosure obligations. Furthermore, companies should ensure that appropriate exit procedures are followed for departing employees;
♦ A company that anticipates hiring staff for a short term to work on its Year 2000 project should confirm that the contents of any employee handbook or policies that are not intended to apply to such short-term workers will not in fact apply;
♦ Contracts of key staff should be amended, where possible, to make it more difficult for such persons to leave. Without contractual restrictions, many employers may have little choice other than to match large sign-up bonuses that can be expected to be offered to certain categories of staff as late starters scramble to address their Year 2000 problems. However, any such amendment may need to be tied to a promotion or pay increase, and voluntarily accepted by the employee, to avoid a claim that it constituted constructive dismissal. Also, like any restrictive covenant, these provisions must be carefully drafted to increase the prospect that they will be enforced;
♦ In some companies, the most important resource may be a long-term employee with knowledge of an older application. Many older applications were poorly documented on paper and most of the company's knowledge about the application may be contained in the head of one or two individuals. However, employees in this category were frequently targeted by downsizing initiatives in the late 1980s and early 1990s, and may no longer be available;

◆ Companies also need to be concerned about whether the Year 2000 solution providers they engage will be able to hold on to their own employees.

9.2 RECRUITMENT AND RETENTION PERKS FOR YEAR 2000 STAFF

One solution to attracting programmers is to pay high compensation. However, this may create a clash and alienate other employees. It also won't do much to retain valuable programmers in the longer term unless compensation continues to increase.

Performance bonuses are an option. However, it may be difficult to devise an appropriate method of measuring performance. Retention or completion bonuses payable over time provided the employee remains with the company (also known as "golden handcuffs") may be the most useful tool to encourage valuable employees to stick around and can be an important element of a well designed Year 2000 compensation package.

Special working conditions can also be a useful inducement for some individuals. Many computer professionals prefer to work at home or at odd hours. Others may want greater independence or special reporting relationships. To the extent that those unique circumstances can be accommodated within the organization, then they may prove important in the overall compensation package.

Certain components of the employment package may need to be customized for the needs of certain categories of employees. For instance, older programmers may be especially interested in a guarantee of early retirement, while younger programmers may be looking for a post-Year 2000 career path or guarantee of continued employment.

Companies are reminded to review the provisions of any applicable collective agreements and consider whether any such agreements may impose restrictions or limitations on the company's ability to offer special terms to its Year 2000 staff.

9.3 USE OF CONTRACT STAFF

Where additional staff must be hired, whether to work on the Year 2000 project or to replace employees who are transferred to the Year 2000 project, the company will be faced with deciding whether to bring on the additional staff as "employees" or as independent contractors or consultants. In some cases, these individuals will themselves want to be engaged as contractors or consultants for tax purposes or other reasons.

Whether an individual is truly an independent contractor or employee is determined by the substance of the relationship rather than its form. Many employers are surprised to learn that an individual who has for many years been considered an independent contractor, is in reality, an employee. This finding can have significant repercussions on the employer, including liability for wrongful dismissal and unpaid withholdings and penalties under various statutes, including tax legislation. It is critical that a company wishing to enter into such an arrangement first consult with an employment law specialist.

One of the issues that will need to be addressed is whether engaging such staff as "contract staff" rather than as "employees" will result in a breach of licence agreements applicable to any software such individuals will be using or modifying. This is because some software licence agreements contain provisions that restrict access or use only to "employees" of the licensee. This issue is discussed in greater detail in Chapter 10.

Another important issue that should be considered is the potential difference in liability that may be created by one arrangement as opposed to another. Persons who provide services to a company as a contractor rather than as an employee, while potentially enjoying certain tax advantages and/or higher income levels, may be at a higher risk of liability for a claim that the work they performed was deficient and as a result damages were suffered by the corporation.[4] Likewise, a computer professional employed by a supplier may have obligations to his or her employer's customer that are independent of those owed by his or her employer. Persons in these positions would be well advised to ensure that their responsibilities, and

---

4 Providing services as a contractor became increasingly popular after recent downsizing, particularly in the information technology sector. Corporations may also prefer engaging the services of project managers, consultants and programmers to perform Year 2000-related work, pursuant to such arrangements as they may be less disruptive on internal compensation scales and may be easier to terminate following completion of Year 2000 remediation work.

appropriate limitations on liability (and where applicable, indemnities) are documented in a written contract for services.

A skilled employee may be liable to indemnify his or her employer for any legal damages that the employer must pay as a result of the employee's negligence. Such liability may be imposed if the employment contract contains an express or implied term of indemnification for losses caused by the acts or defaults of the employee, or if the employee professes to possess some skill upon which the employer relies.[5] However, courts, at least in Ontario, appear to be reluctant to find an employee liable to the employer unless the negligence results in the employer becoming vicariously liable to a third party. Nevertheless, employees working on critical components of an employer's Year 2000 project may want to consider negotiating for contractual limitations on their liability and for appropriate indemnities.

9.4 SAFETY ISSUES

An employer may be under a duty to provide its employees and others with a safe work environment. This duty may arise from common law. Additional obligations may also be imposed by statute, breach of which may constitute a quasi-criminal offence.

In some circumstances, an employer may be under a duty to carry out a risk assessment covering the conduct of their business in order to ensure the health and safety of its employees. Appropriate action would need to be taken to address any issues that are identified including any critical safety equipment that may contain embedded systems that are not Year 2000 compliant.

9.5 USE OF FOREIGN PROGRAMMERS

Companies encountering shortages of qualified personnel, especially CO-BOL programmers, may want to review the option of acquiring work permits for programmers to be brought in from foreign countries.

In response to the growing shortage of computer professionals, particularly those with Year 2000-related skills, Canada's Task Force Year 2000 recommended that governments should adopt immigration laws, regulations

---

5 For example, if the employee misrepresented his or her qualifications or experience to the company.

and policies to create a specific category of temporary employment authorization permitting persons with specialized Year 2000 skills and experience to work in Canada exempt from the employment validation process; thereby permitting foreign workers to secure such temporary employment authorization directly at the port of entry.[6]

For some companies, the solution to the problem of recruiting and retaining programmers is to send some of their Year 2000 conversion work offshore to locations where salaries are lower and there are more qualified persons available to do the work. Although salaries for off-shore programmers have been rising (from about US$12 per hour to about US$25 to $35 as of early 1998), these salaries may be as low as half of comparable rates in North America. North American rates are also expected to increase by as much as 10% per quarter until the Year 2000.[7]

In some cases, time zone differences can allow foreign programmers with network access to North American systems to work during hours when offices are closed here. Popular destinations include India, Ireland, Israel, China, the Philippines and countries in Eastern Europe such as the Ukraine. Destinations that can offer a combination of high skill level and minimal language barriers are particularly attractive.

6 Task Force Year 2000 Recommendation 14.

7 Claire Tristram, "Offshore Rescue?" *Information Week* (October 27, 1997) at 117.

10

Third-Party Licensed Software Issues

10.1 LICENCE AGREEMENT RESTRICTIONS

Software that is found to contain Year-2000 related problems will need to be modified in order to allow continued uninterrupted use. Where such software was developed internally within the company, generally the company will be free to modify such software as it wishes. However, when software is licensed from another party, the licensee only acquires the rights granted in the licence agreement and will be subject to any restrictions contained therein.

Most licence agreements contain an explicit prohibition on the modification of the licensed software, or the creation of a derivative work, by any person other than the licensor. Many also prohibit the licensee from disassembling, decompiling, translating, converting or reverse engineering the software.

Even where a licensee may be provided with certain limited rights to make modifications, such right may be subject to certain conditions and restrictions. For instance, a licence agreement may contain a restriction that permits only employees of the licensee to make any modifications to the software. Even without an explicit restriction, other provisions in the licence agreement such as those dealing with non-disclosure, may effectively permit only "employees" of the licensee to make modifications to the software.[1]

If a licensee utilizes the services of a contractor to assist with Year 2000 conversion initiatives in respect of software that is licensed subject to such

---

1 For instance, the licence agreement may provide that the software is the trade secret of the licensor and that the licensee agrees not to disclose or provide a copy of the software to any person except its employees.

restrictions, or if the licensee itself makes modifications where the making of such modifications is prohibited by the licence agreement, then a breach of the licence agreement will occur. Many licence agreements provide that upon any breach of the licence agreement the licensor may terminate the licence to use the software.

Even where a licence agreement permits the making of modifications by a licensee or its agents, the licence agreement may provide that any modifications made by the licensee will be owned by the licensor with the licensee only acquiring a licence to use such modifications for its internal business purposes.[2] The licensee may be obligated to provide the licensor with notice of and copies of any modifications developed by the licensee. The licensor may then be free to distribute copies of such modifications to other licensees, including competitors of the licensee who developed the modifications.

10.2 COPYRIGHT LAW ISSUES

In some cases the licence agreement may be silent with respect to the issue of modification of the software by the licensee. Software programs are protected by copyright and even without an explicit prohibition, the making of modifications[3] or the creation of a derivative work (*i.e.*, a new program that is based on an existing program) is generally reserved to the owner of copyright unless the licence agreement provides otherwise.

Section 3(1) of the *Copyright Act*[4] (Canada) provides that 'copyright' means "the sole right to produce or reproduce the work or any substantial part thereof in any material form." Section 3(1)(a) provides that copyright includes the "sole right to produce . . . any translation of the work." Section 27(1) provides that "copyright in a work shall be deemed to be infringed by any person who, without the consent of the owner of the copyright, does anything that, by this Act, only the owner of the copyright has the right to do." The United States *Copyright Act*[5] contains comparable provisions.

---

2 Such a restriction may prevent a number of licensees from cooperatively funding the development of modifications. Different licensees may also be prevented from sharing modifications by the application of confidentiality provisions contained in the licence agreement.

3 The making of modifications may be restricted indirectly, by for instance the *Copyright Act* (Canada) which reserves the right to make reproductions to the owner of copyright. As the modification of a work must typically involve the creation of at least one reproduction, particularly in the case of computer software, the reproduction right in such cases can also be used to prohibit the making of modifications.

4 R.S.C. 1985, c. C-42.

5 17 U.S.C. See section 116, which sets out the exclusive rights reserved to owners of

There have been numerous court decisions that have held that a licence that includes a right to use does not include the right to prepare a modified version of the program. However, many of these dealt with translation of a program from one computer language to another and they did not address necessary and minor modifications to correct errors inherent in the program, such as Year 2000 problems.[6] It is therefore possible that in certain circumstances, such as where a computer program is sold without any restrictions governing its use, or where it is licensed but the licence agreement is silent in respect to the making of modifications by the licensee, a right may be implied to make minor modifications for such purpose, particularly where the modified copy of the software program is to be used by the licensee only.

Also, in some cases where the licence agreement is silent on the issue of the making of modifications by the licensee, certain statutory exemptions may be applicable. For instance, section 27(1) of the *Copyright Act* (Canada) provides an exemption for:

> the making by a person who owns a copy of a computer program, which copy is authorized by the owner of the copyright, of a single reproduction of the copy by adapting, modifying or converting the computer program or translating it into another computer language if the person proves that:
>
> (i)   the reproduction is essential for the compatibility of the computer program with a particular computer,
> (ii) the reproduction is solely for the person's own use, and
> (iii) the reproduction is destroyed forthwith when the person ceases to be the owner of the copy of the computer program.

Similarly, in the United States, section 117(1) of the *Copyright Act*[7] provides that it is not an infringement for the owner of a copy of a computer program to make or authorize the making of another copy or adaption of that program provided that such new copy or adaption is created as an essential step in the use of a computer program in conjunction with a machine and that it is used in no other manner.

Case law in the United States has established that this right of adaption includes the right to make modifications and enhancements as long as these are made for the purchaser's internal use and not distributed to third parties.

---

copyright, and which includes the right to make reproductions and the right to prepare a derivative work.

6 See *Sookman Computer Law: Acquiring and Protecting Computer Technology*, (Toronto: Carswell, 1992-Release 1) at section 3.7(e).

7 17 U.S.C., section 117.

The making of minor modifications to eliminate Year 2000 deficiencies would therefore likely not be held to constitute an infringement of copyright.

One significant problem in relying on the above-mentioned provisions is that they refer to an "owner" of a copy of a computer program and it is not clear whether they would apply where the computer program is licensed and the licensee is merely given the right to use the computer program but where there is no transfer of ownership rights.

The issue of moral rights may also need to be addressed. For instance, section 14.1(1) of the *Copyright Act* (Canada) provides "The author of a work has, subject to section 28.2, the right to the integrity of the work..." Section 28.2(1) provides that "the author's right to the integrity of a work is infringed only if the work is, to the prejudice of the honour or reputation of the author, (a) distorted, mutilated or otherwise modified..." However, it is not likely that a modification made to address Year 2000 deficiencies would be found to constitute prejudice to the honour or reputation of the author.

Other than creating liability for infringement of copyright, unauthorized modification of third-party software may also void existing representations and warranties relating to the software program, including on-going maintenance obligations on the part of the licensor.

If the licence agreement does not include an explicit right of the licensee to make modifications or is silent on this issue, the licensee should seek the licensor's permission to modify the software. If the licensor refuses to provide permission to the licensee to modify the software and does not provide reasonable and credible assurances that it will take the necessary steps to make the software Year 2000 compliant, the licensee should assess any available defences to a copyright infringement claim by the licensor and seek legal advice on how to proceed.

10.3 Testing Issues

Conducting Year 2000 testing on a production system can severely corrupt or destroy valuable data, or cause other problems such as the premature expiration of licensed software programs that contain built-in time limits. Therefore, for many companies, testing will require setting up an isolated, dedicated test environment on which conditions prior to, during and after the change of century can be simulated, including the leap year condition in the year 2000.

In order to facilitate such testing, additional equipment may need to be acquired. In such cases it will be necessary to ensure that additional licences or appropriate consents are acquired in respect of any software that may need to be installed on such equipment.[8] Some companies are offering special discounted prices for licensees that wish to acquire a second copy of the software for testing purposes.

Some software programs may also contain date protection facilities that require the licensee to obtain new licence numbers annually in order to allow such programs to continue functioning. In such cases, special licence numbers may be required from suppliers to allow such programs to be tested on computer hardware whose clocks are set forward for Year 2000 testing purposes.

10.4 OWNERSHIP OF MODIFICATIONS

An important issue that must be considered in regard to any initiative to modify existing software programs, whether such modifications are performed by internal staff or third-party conversion service providers, is the ownership rights in the converted programs.

The general rule is that the author or creator of a work, which can be a new program or modifications to an existing program, is the first owner of copyright in that work. An exception is where the author of a program is in the employment of another person under a contract of service or apprenticeship and the work is made in the course of his or her employment—in such a situation, in the absence of any agreement to the contrary, the first owner of copyright is the employer and not the employee.[9]

Where an independent contractor is hired to develop a computer program, absent a signed written agreement to the contrary, the independent contractor, and not the person paying for the development of the program, will ordinarily be its owner. This is particularly true in Canada where the applicable provision focuses on whether the author was an employee.

---

8 A user may have only been granted the right to operate one copy of the software and may be restricted to use of the software only on a specific computer.

9 *Copyright Act*, section 13(3). The United States *Copyright Act* contains a comparable provision—see 17 U.S.C., section 201(b).

However, even under the "work-for-hire" doctrine applicable in the United States, which is broader in scope and will apply to certain forms of relationships that may not constitute a traditional employer-employee relationship,[10] the contractor may retain rights to modifications developed to address Year 2000 issues.

Even where the employer becomes the first owner of copyright or is otherwise assigned the copyright, the author may retain certain limited rights of fair dealing in relation to the program and certain moral rights such as the right to integrity of the work, and where reasonable, the right to be associated with the work as its author by name. It is therefore important for a company wishing to have Year 2000 conversion work performed to set out contractually that it will be the owner of copyright in the work and to obtain a waiver of moral rights from all programmers that are engaged to perform modifications to an existing program or the development of a new program.

It should be noted that no assignment of copyright is valid unless it is in writing and signed by the owner of the right or by his or her duly authorized agent.[11] While certain exceptions to the writing requirement have been recognized, customers should insist on a signed written assignment where Year 2000 conversion work is to be performed by someone other than an employee.

---

10 A work-for-hire includes some works that are specially commissioned or ordered, but may be limited by statute.
11 *Copyright Act* (Canada), section 13(4). The United States *Copyright Act* contains a comparable provision—see 17 U.S.C. section 204.

11

General Contractual Obligations and Limitations

Many organizations are reviewing their key acquisition, maintenance and other agreements as part of an overall Year 2000 compliance program. This is being done to assess each party's responsibilities in respect of addressing Year 2000 related problems. This chapter considers some of the potential sources that may create an obligation to correct a Year 2000 problem as well as common limitations and exclusions that may be applicable.

11.1 LIABILITY OF SUPPLIERS FOR YEAR 2000 PROBLEMS

(a) Explicit Year 2000 Compliance Warranties

An agreement may contain an explicit Year 2000 warranty, although the wording of such a warranty may not always be as comprehensive as may be desirable from the perspective of the customer.

It is becoming increasingly difficult to obtain comprehensive Year 2000 warranties. Many suppliers have become more cautious and are offering warranties that are much more limited in scope. Some suppliers are also adopting a position that treats the Year 2000 issue as a product specification rather than as a warranty.

A detailed discussion of Year 2000 warranties is contained in Chapter 12.

(b) Other Explicit Warranties

Even where a contract may lack an explicit warranty covering Year 2000 issues, an obligation to correct Year 2000 problems may arise from other obligations assumed by the supplier in the contract. For instance, a contract for the acquisition of a product or the licensing of software may contain a warranty that the product or software will comply with certain functional, technical and/or performance specifications.[1] The specification may cover a date-related function that specifically anticipates processing of dates after 1999.

For instance, in *Atlaz v. Software Business Technologies*,[2] Atlaz alleged that SBT sold its software pursuant to an express warranty under which SBT warranted that the product would "operate in substantial conformity with its written specifications for a period of . . . five years after the date of licence . . ." (and would therefore cover any product sold after 1995 into the Year 2000). However, Atlaz found numerous examples where Year 2000 deficiencies contained in versions of SBT Pro Series software prior to version 3.2I would cause the software to fail to operate in substantial conformity with its written specifications.

Examples of Year 2000 deficiencies, as alleged by Atlaz, include:

♦ maximum due days in the Accounts Payables Module were specified to be "999", although the system will not function properly if dates after December 31, 1999 are entered;
♦ finance charge calculations based on a date that extends into the Year 2000 will be incorrect as will aging of customer accounts;
♦ selection of a date in the year 2000 as part of a date range for data to be displayed or printed would cause the system to either reject the selection or to create an incorrect report;
♦ any sorting by date field will be defective.

A warranty to correct errors, defects, deficiencies or other bugs in the software may or may not apply to require a supplier to correct Year 2000 problems. The supplier would likely argue that a Year 2000 problem is not a bug or deficiency but rather was an intentional design limitation. Such an argument may have greater credibility in the case of older software that was

---

1 Similar warranties may be contained in maintenance agreements. Likewise, a contract in respect of the provision of computer services may contain a warranty that such services will be provided or performed in conformance with certain specifications.
2 *Supra*, at Chapter 2, note 23.

written when computer memory was very expensive, and the year 2000 was far in the future, or in the case of software that was written to specifications provided by the customer that explicitly required the use of non-compliant dates.[3] Such an argument would likely have much less credibility if made in respect of software written in recent years (in fact, memory prices had come down significantly by the late 1970s and this would likely counter an argument that use of two-digit year fields was done intentionally for reasons of cost). However, unless the agreement contemplated annual licence fees and/or on-going maintenance to be provided by the supplier, any such warranty to make corrections may be limited in duration to a specified period following delivery or acceptance.

Software agreements should be reviewed for the presence of a warranty that the software will not contain any disabling code. These types of warranties were originally intended to deter a supplier from inserting protection routines that would prevent the software from operating on other than a specified serialized computer system or from operating after a certain date (and therefore ensuring that the customer would require regular updates to permit uninterrupted use of the software). Depending on the language utilized, a Year 2000 problem may result in a breach of a warranty that "the software will not contain any clock, counter or other limiting or disabling code, design or routine that would cause the software to be rendered incapable of performance after the lapse of a certain period of time."

Any warranties dealing with computer viruses should also be reviewed. Depending on the language, such a warranty may be broad enough to include certain manifestations of the Year 2000 problem. For instance, non-compliant data may "infect" another system. Non-compliant code might constitute a "trojan horse" or a "time bomb."

Agreements should also be reviewed to ascertain whether they contain a warranty that all work performed by the supplier will be of a certain quality. For instance an agreement may provide:

> Supplier warrants that all work performed by Supplier shall be performed in a professional and workmanlike manner by skilled and competent personnel in a timely manner in accordance with standards generally accepted in the industry.

---

3 This may have been done to address compatibility issues with other applications or systems.

Courts may interpret these types of warranties broadly enough to require any programming work performed in recent years to properly account for the year 2000. Such a warranty may also be breached if a consultant or other advisor assisting in the acquisition of a computer system or product fails to adequately consider Year 2000 issues.

(c) Pre-Contractual Representations and Secondary Sources of Documentation

A customer may also be able to rely upon representations made by a supplier or its staff prior to the signing of a contract or at the time of sale. These may include pre-contractual oral representations (although more difficult to prove) as well as those contained in numerous types of secondary sources of documentation, even if not incorporated into the actual signed contract. For instance, in *Atlaz v. Software Business Technologies*,[4] Atlaz alleged that SBT described its accounting software package as "the world's most widely installed, high-end Windows accounting software, designed to meet the needs of business today and into the next century."

Examples of secondary sources of documents include:

- Request for Proposals ("RFPs") issued by the customer, including specific requirements contained therein;
- Supplier's Response to the RFP;
- Product manuals and documentation;
- Supplier's sales and marketing materials, including advertisements, catalogues, brochures and quotations;
- Correspondence between the parties, including e-mail; and
- Memorandums of Understanding ("MOUs") and Letters of Intent ("LOIs").

In some cases, oral statements made at the time of sale, or written statements contained in the above categories of documents, may be found to constitute express warranties.

Suppliers who wish to reduce the risk that a customer will be able to rely on a representation made outside of the agreement may add a "disclaimer notice" on such materials that states that the information contained is subject to change, does not constitute a warranty and that the supplier does

---

4 *Supra*, at Chapter 2, note 23.

not intend to be bound by the contents of such documents unless specifically incorporated into the executed contract.

It is also common for suppliers to incorporate what is commonly referred to as an "entire agreement" or "integration clause" into their contracts. The purpose of such a provision is to exclude any representations made prior to the execution of the agreement or contained in documents that are not specifically incorporated into the agreement.

(d) Implied Warranties and Conditions

Unless excluded by the agreement, implied warranties and conditions of merchantability and fitness for purpose may be applicable. Depending on the severity of the Year 2000 problems inherent in a particular product, one or both of these implied warranties and conditions may be breached. However, these implied warranties and conditions are excluded in most types of agreements related to the supply or licensing of information technology.

It is also possible that a term relating to durability of a product or a minimum useful life may be implied. Computer products, like other products, can be assumed to have a limited useful life. It would not be unreasonable to expect that a major computer application would be capable of continued use for at least a minimum reasonable period of time. The type of application and its cost of acquisition may be factors that would be considered in determining what minimum expected life might be reasonable. In many cases, it may be found reasonable to expect that a significant software acquisition will have a useful life of at least five to ten years.

A term may therefore be implied in the sales contract or licence agreement that the product (which may be software, hardware or non-computer equipment) will be capable of operation for a certain reasonable period of time. If both parties contemplated that the product would continue working past the year 1999, then a failure to do so may constitute a breach of contract.

11.2 CONTRACTUAL LIMITS ON SUPPLIER'S LIABILITY

A well drafted agreement (from the supplier's perspective) typically imposes various limits for any breaches of the agreement. The following are some of the common provisions found in agreements, particularly those relating to the supply of information technology products or services, which may exclude or limit a supplier's liability. This section should be helpful in analysing rights under existing agreements or in negotiating new agreements. With respect to new agreements, customers will want to negotiate changes, where possible, to these types of provisions.

(a) Limitation on Warranty Period

It is common to include a limited warranty in respect of a product that is sold or licensed or in respect of a service that is provided by a supplier. However, such warranties commonly have a limited duration. Warranty periods between 30 days and 1 year are typical.

The following are examples of warranty provisions of the kind that may be found in a contract for the supply of computer-related goods and services, and which contain a limitation on the warranty period:

Product Warranty
For a warranty period of one (1) year after acceptance of the [product] (the "Warranty Period"), the [product] shall have the features and shall perform in accordance with the Specifications.

Service Warranty
[Supplier] warrants that its [consulting] services will be of a quality conforming to generally accepted industry standards and practices. This warranty shall be valid for 90 days from completion of the services. In order to receive the remedies for any breach of the warranty set out in this Agreement, the deficiencies in the [consulting] services must be reported to [Supplier], in writing, within ninety (90) days of completion of the Services.

However, a product or software warranty may be extended in duration if the customer contracts with the supplier for ongoing maintenance and support services.

(b) Exclusive Remedy (Repair or Replace) Provisions

Many agreements include a provision that provides that if the product or service does not meet the requirements then the supplier, at its option, will repair or replace the product or re-perform the service. This type of provision is known as an exclusive remedy provision. The following is an example:

> Customer's exclusive remedy, and Supplier's entire liability, for a breach of the warranty set forth in this Agreement shall be that to the extent practicable, Supplier shall re-perform the Services which did not meet the standards set forth in section [X], failing which Supplier shall provide service credits in respect of the portion of such Services which failed to conform to such warranty.

If included in the agreement, an exclusive remedy provision can significantly limit the usefulness of any express Year 2000 warranties because a supplier may escape liability for the losses incurred by the customer with the only obligation being to correct the problem within a reasonable period of time.

If a customer must accept the inclusion of an exclusive remedy provision, it would be desirable to negotiate that it will not apply to Year 2000 problems that are not corrected prior to the year 2000 or Year 2000 problems that may arise prior to the year 2000 if not corrected within a reasonable period (specified in the agreement) after they are reported to the supplier. However, even this may be difficult to obtain from many suppliers.

(c) Disclaimer of Other and Implied Warranties

Most standard form computer-related agreements will provide that the customer waives all implied warranties and conditions (including the implied warranties and conditions of merchantability and of fitness for purpose).

The following is an example of a comprehensive warranty disclaimer provision of the kind that may be found in a contract for the acquisition of computer-related goods and services:

> The warranties provided in this Agreement are exclusive and are in lieu of any other understandings, representations, warranties, covenants, conditions, promises, guarantees or agreements, express or implied, statutory or otherwise, or arising from a course of dealing or usage of trade, relating to the Services, including but not limited to any warranty or condition of merchantability or fitness or adequacy for any

particular purpose or use, or of quality, productiveness, capacity or accuracy.

The warranty disclaimer provision may go even further and provide:

No representation or other affirmation of fact, including without limitation, statements regarding capacity, quality, suitability for use or performance, whether made by [Supplier's] employees or otherwise, shall be deemed to be a warranty by Supplier for any purpose or give rise to any liability of Supplier whatsoever.

(d) Exclusion of Indirect and Consequential Damages

Many commercial agreements contain an exclusion of liability for indirect, consequential or similar types of damages. The following provision is a typical example:

Supplier shall not in any event be liable for any indirect, incidental, special or consequential damages occurring out of or in connection with the delivery, use or performance, or failure of the [Products/Services], or arising from any breach of this Agreement (including fundamental breach) or from the negligence of Supplier [or its representatives], even if Supplier has been advised of the possibility of such damages.

(e) Limitation (or Cap) on Total Liability

Many types of commercial agreements will include a cap on the total liability of the supplier or of both parties. The following is an example:

Supplier's liability to Customer for all losses, damages, claims, demands or causes of action whether based on contract (including fundamental breach), tort (including negligence) or otherwise arising out of or resulting from this Agreement shall not in the aggregate exceed the lesser of [X] Dollars ($X) or the total charges paid by Customer to Supplier for the [Services/ Deliverables] during the six (6) month period preceding the event giving rise to the first claim made by Customer against Supplier, regardless of the number of claims.

In some cases, the supplier's maximum potential liability may be further reduced by any amounts paid by the supplier to third party suppliers (such as licensors of Year 2000 tools) or other subcontractors, and/or expenses incurred by the supplier in the performance of the services.

In some cases, the cap on total liability may be further reduced to the amounts paid in respect of the specific products or services that caused the loss or damage. For instance:

> The remedies available to Customer shall be limited to actual damages not to exceed the amount of [Licence/Consulting/Maintenance Fees] (exclusive of expense reimbursements) actually paid by Customer to Supplier with respect to the specific [Products/Services] which directly caused the loss or damage.

Therefore, notwithstanding the inclusion of a Year 2000 warranty, the remedies that a customer may be able to obtain may be significantly limited so as not to exceed the fees paid by the customer.

(f) Subtle Revisions to Documentation/Specifications

Any warranty or support obligation of a supplier may be limited to the conformance of a product or software with documentation provided by the supplier. For instance, a warranty may provide that the product will perform in accordance with the specifications set forth in the documentation.

However, the agreement may provide supplier with a right to revise the documentation from time to time (and therefore potentially alter the scope of its warranty or support obligations). The following is an example of such a provision in a contract for the acquisition of computer-related goods and services that would permit the supplier to change the specifications applicable to a product:

> Supplier may at any time add, delete or change the specifications with respect to products comprising Supplier's product line and system.

A customer should resist the incorporation into the agreement of this type of provision or negotiate an added clause that "in no case shall such change reduce the functionality or performance of the product."

(g) Exclusion of Third-Party Components from Scope of Supplier Warranty

Any warranty provided by a supplier may be restricted to products developed, manufactured or produced by the supplier. The warranty provision may explicitly exclude any third party software or other components from the application of the warranty.

In many cases, a third party component (such as an Oracle or Sybase relational database management system) may constitute a significant component of a "system" that is acquired by the customer. In such a case, a failure or deficiency in the third party component can result in a failure of the system as a whole. Accordingly, a clause excluding any third-party components from the scope of any supplier warranties may leave the customer with little recourse.

In some cases, the agreement may provide that the customer's only rights will be those set forth in any warranties provided by the third party suppliers (to the extent that the benefit of such warranties may be assigned to the customer). For example:

> With respect to any third party software (developed and owned by parties other than Supplier) used by Customer in conjunction with the [Supplier's products], Supplier transfers and assigns to Customer, if and to the extent transferable and assignable, all warranties and indemnities granted to Supplier, if any, by the manufacturer of such third party software and Supplier shall have no other obligation to Customer in respect of such third party software.

(h) Customer Responsibilities

Some agreements may specify obligations that must be performed by the customer. For instance, an agreement may provide that:

> Customer shall provide such cooperation, information and assistance as may be reasonably requested by Supplier to enable Supplier to provide the Services. Customer shall also be responsible for providing the specific deliverables or for achieving the specific results or objectives which are described in a Schedule, to enable Supplier to provide the Services to Customer. Customer shall make available its personnel

with such skills and expertise as may be reasonably necessary to coordinate and assist Supplier in the provision of the Services.

The following is an example of a provision of the kind that may be found in a commercial agreement that excuses the supplier to the extent its failure or delay is due to a failure or delay by the customer or by its agents in performing their responsibilities or obligations:

> Supplier shall be relieved of any failure, liability or delay in performing the Services or other obligations to the extent that such failure or delay is caused by any failure or delay by Customer or its agents in performing their responsibilities as set out in this Agreement.

A supplier that has included such provisions in an agreement and which subsequently falls behind schedule (for instance, in completing any Year 2000 remediation work) may rely on certain delays attributable to the customer's staff in order to excuse its own defaults or delays.

(i) *Force Majeure* (Act of God) Provision

A *force majeure* provision is usually intended to excuse a party that fails to perform its obligations under the agreement where such non-performance is due to an act of God or other event beyond a party's reasonable control. For instance:

> Except as expressly provided otherwise in the Agreement, dates and times by which a party is required to render performance shall be postponed to the extent and for the period of time that such party is prevented from performing due to riots, storms, floods, explosions, earthquakes, acts of God, acts of any governmental authority, war or any other unforeseen cause or causes which are beyond the reasonable control of such party.

The Year 2000 problem would not appear to constitute a cause that is beyond the reasonable control of a party to remedy, particularly if the party has advance notice of a problem or potential problem in its product. However, a "supplier-oriented" *force majeure* provision may provide some latitude to a supplier that fails to meet deadlines specified in the agreement. For instance:

> Supplier shall not be liable to Customer for any delay or failure to perform its obligations hereunder due to strikes, labour disruptions, riots, storms, floods, explosions, earthquakes, acts of God, acts of any governmental authority, war, failure or delay of any third party supplier, unavailability or shortages of materials or labour, equipment failures, or without limitation, any other cause or causes which are beyond the reasonable control of Supplier.

The Year 2000 problem is a known problem and would not normally constitute the type of event commonly contemplated by a *force majeure* provision. However, to reduce the potential for disputes, customers may want to state in any agreement that any delay or default caused by any Year 2000 problem does not constitute a *"force majeure"* event. Furthermore, customers should reject references to events such as labour shortages as constituting a *force majeure* event.

(j) Entire Agreement Clause

The following is an example of an "entire agreement" or "integration" provision of the kind that may be found in a commercial contract.

> This Agreement constitutes the entire agreement between the parties hereto pertaining to the subject matter hereof and supersedes all prior agreements, understandings, representations, negotiations and discussions, whether oral or written, of the parties hereto, and there are no warranties, representations or conditions between the parties hereto in connection with the subject matter hereof except as specifically set forth herein. For further clarification, Customer acknowledges and agrees that it is not relying upon any representation in any advertising, marketing material, catalogues or similar materials provided by Supplier.

Such a provision may exclude any representations or warranties not contained in the agreement itself or otherwise incorporated by reference into the agreement.

(k) Limitation Period on Claims

The following is an example of a contractual limitation period in an agreement for the acquisition of computer-related goods and services:

With the exception of payment obligations or an action to protect proprietary rights, no action arising out of this Agreement, regardless of its form shall be brought by either party against the other one (1) year following the date on which the cause of action arose.

In some cases, the limitation period is specified to commence from the date of delivery or acceptance of the products or services. These contractual limitation periods, where included in agreements, typically range from one to three years, with two years being the most common. A shortened limitation period generally benefits the supplier since certain claims may not be discovered until long after acceptance of the product or service. Customers should seek to avoid such a provision or seek to have the limitation period commence not on the date on which the cause of action arises (or if applicable, the date of delivery or acceptance), but rather on the date on which it is discovered or should reasonably have been discovered by the party seeking to commence the action.

It should be noted that some jurisdictions may provide a minimum period for commencing a lawsuit that cannot be shortened by contract.

Statutory limitation periods must also be considered. In most cases, a claim must be brought within a specified number of years after the date the plaintiff knew or ought to have known of the facts that gave rise to the claim. If no legal claim is made within this period then the action becomes "statute barred." Limitation periods may serve to extinguish the liability of a supplier of software that was licensed or a product that was sold outside the applicable limitation period where the supplier is not under ongoing maintenance obligations. See Chapter 2 for a more detailed discussion of limitation periods.

An interesting issue in respect of Year 2000-related claims is when the limitation period will be considered as having started to run. In many cases, a system that only utilizes two digits to store the year portion of a date may still be Year 2000 complaint (for instance, if the internal logic is set up to treat numbers less than a specific number, such as 50, as falling in the next century). It may therefore not be obvious to a customer if a particular product is or is not Year 2000 compliant simply by virtue of whether or not it utilizes four digits to store the year. Courts will have to decide whether in such cases the limitation period began to run at the time of delivery of a product or at the time a particular user acquired knowledge of a Year 2000 problem in the product, and therefore could be said to have understood that a claim may lie against the supplier of such a non-compliant system.

Some vendors have gone public, actively contacting customers and advising them that some of their older products may fail to function properly after the year 1999. Such notification may result in the commencement of the limitation period and may be particularly important where the agreement provided for a short limitation period.

(l) Termination and Survival

Some agreements for computer-related goods and services may permit termination of the agreement by the supplier (or either party) upon notice. For instance, it is common for a maintenance agreement to contain a provision whereby it is renewed automatically at the end of each year of the agreement unless it is terminated by notice provided from one party to another within a specified period prior to the end of any year. Some suppliers may attempt to terminate such agreements before the year 2000.

With respect to new agreements, customers will want the supplier to agree to offer maintenance for a specified minimum period, at least until after the time any Year 2000 problems are expected to arise.

11.3 DEALING WITH CONTRACTUAL LIMITATIONS AND EXCLUSIONS

In some cases, the limitation and exclusion clauses discussed in the previous section may be held to be unenforceable by a court. The grounds for avoiding such provisions may be categorized as follows:

◆ subsequent amendment
◆ collateral contract
◆ deficiencies in specific clauses
◆ challenges to the enforceability of the agreement
◆ claims under negligence
◆ other issues

(a) Subsequent Amendment

The original agreement applicable to the supply of a particular product may be amended or replaced by the execution of an amending agreement or a new agreement to replace the original agreement. An amendment to an agreement may also be made by other means, such as by a schedule executed subsequent to the original transaction that may change provisions in the original agreement. The limitations or exclusions in the amending or new agreement may be more favourable to the customer.

An interesting issue concerning shrink-wrap software is that there may be a separate sales transaction with the retailer that contains express or implied terms that may be applicable to the software. A customer who acquires software under such an arrangement may argue that the retailer's agreement displaces the shrink-wrap licence agreement, and therefore the exclusions, disclaimers and limitations contained in the shrink-wrap licence agreement are not applicable.

(b) Collateral Contract

Unfavourable limitation and exclusion clauses may also be overcome if it can be shown that there was a collateral contract that subsists apart from the original agreement. For instance, the supplier may have assumed an obligation to correct errors and deficiencies as part of a separate maintenance and support agreement. While it is likely that such an agreement may contain the same or comparable limitations and exclusions as the original agreement, the maintenance and support agreement may renew periodically, which may at least assist with any potential problems as to a limitation period.

The increasing complexity of software programs and other high technology products has resulted in many customers contracting to obtain various consulting and implementation services. More recently, such services are increasingly being included within the scope of the agreement to supply the applicable product and may therefore be covered by the same limitations and exclusions. However, this was not always the case, and such services may have been acquired pursuant to a separate agreement with different warranties, limitations or exclusions. It is also possible that consulting and implementation services, or the development of custom modifications, may have been performed without written agreement or on the basis of a customer's purchase order. If there were deficiencies in the performance of such services, which may include a failure to adequately address Year 2000 issues, then the supplier may be liable and may not be entitled to benefit from limitation and exclusion clauses contained in the "main" agreement.

Another possibility is that additional products may have been acquired subsequent to the original transaction and their acquisition may not fall within the scope of the original agreement. For instance, the product being acquired may consist of software to be installed on a specific serialized CPU. If additional quantities or different versions of the product are acquired subsequently then, depending on the provisions contained in the original agreement, the disclaimers and exclusions in the original agreement may not apply to the subsequent transactions.

Another issue that should be considered is whether purchase orders and/or other order or shipping documents were utilized. It is common for large customers to issue purchase orders in the normal course of any acquisition. Such purchase orders commonly contain pre-printed terms and conditions (favourable to the customer) that are likely to conflict with those contained in the signed agreement. A purchase order may contain an explicit Year 2000 warranty or may contain terms that negate certain exclusions or limitations on liability contained in the signed agreement. Where a purchase order is issued subsequent to the execution of the agreement (and this would typically be the case), and the supplier ships the products listed on the purchase order without giving notice that it is not agreeing to the terms contained in the purchase order, then an issue may arise with respect to the "battle of the forms."

A customer would argue that the purchase order did not fall within the scope of an entire agreement provision or was a subsequent amendment of the original agreement, and that the supplier indicated its agreement by shipping the goods that were specified in the purchase order. Such an argument may be even stronger where the purchase order lists new products or services not contemplated by the original agreement.

(c) Deficiencies in Specific Clauses

Provisions that impose limitations on the supplier's liability or that exclude liability for certain types of damages may contain deficiencies that may preclude their enforceability in certain circumstances. These include:

♦ a disclaimer provision that disclaims implied *warranties* but does not disclaim implied *conditions* (this is a Canadian issue and commonly occurs when language for a disclaimer provision is copied from an agreement drafted for use in the United States);

- a limitation of liability provision that mentions liability arising from a breach of contract but fails to mention fundamental breach;
- a provision that excludes certain types of damages but which does not specifically mention claims in tort (including negligence);
- a limitation or exclusion provision that fails to meet applicable requirements relating to conspicuousness[5] (*i.e.*, so that the other party is given reasonable notice) or which is otherwise unclear or ambiguous; and
- the presence of other language in the contract that is inconsistent with the limitation or exclusion provision.

Clear and unambiguous language is required to negate any implied conditions. The disclaimer may be required to specifically refer to the implied condition of merchantability and the implied condition of fitness for purpose.[6] Furthermore, a limitation or exemption clause may be found unenforceable unless the other party is given prominent notice at the time of contracting.

The same result is applicable under the *Uniform Commercial Code* (the "UCC") in the United States. For instance, the implementation of section 2-316 of the UCC in many American states permits vendors to disclaim implied warranties, particularly in business transactions. However, the disclaimer must be conspicuous[7] and must meet certain requirements. Blanket disclaimers of implied warranties through the use of phrases such as "as is" or "with all faults" or comparable language may also be permitted. Warranty disclaimers in the United States must also comply with the requirements of the *Magnusson-Moss Warranty Act*.

There is also a possibility that disclaimers of implied warranties may be held to be unconscionable under section 2-302 of the *Uniform Commercial Code*. That provision allows a court to refuse to enforce a contract or provision found to have been unconscionable when the contract was made.[8] While to date this argument has been largely unsuccessful, a court may be willing to accept such an argument in an appropriate case (for instance, where software is acquired by an uninformed consumer in the late 1990s under a very limited warranty).

---

5 Conspicuousness is often achieved by highlighting the exclusions in heavier print or using upper- case characters.

6 In the United States and Canada, where the warranty of merchantability is excluded in writing, the language of exclusions must include the word "merchantability" and must be conspicuous.

7 See UCC section 1-201(10) for a definition of "conspicuous."

8 The test is one of unfair surprise or oppression at the time of contracting.

A related issue arises from UCC section 2-719(3), which provides that consequential damages may be limited unless such limitation is unconscionable. This may require an evaluation of the negotiation process, each party's bargaining power, whether the agreement was a contract of adhesion, and other factors. Limitation provisions may also be unenforceable if they are ambiguous (see section 2-718), are found to have failed their essential purpose, or are induced by fraud.

In construing an exemption clause, the court will likely attempt to construe the clause strictly and limit its effect to the narrow meaning of the words employed. An exemption clause must also clearly cover the exact circumstances that have arisen in order to afford protection to the party claiming the benefit of the clause. It is generally to be construed against the party in whose favour the clause is drafted. This is particularly the case where the clause is found in a standard printed form of contract, frequently termed a contract of adhesion, which is presented by one party to the other as the basis of their transaction.[9]

(d) Challenges to the Enforceability of the Agreement

Limitations and exclusions contained in an agreement can also be overcome by attacking the enforceability of the agreement itself. A customer may argue that the parties did not agree to the terms of an agreement particularly where the agreement was not signed by both parties. This can occur when a subsequent amendment is sent by a supplier but not acknowledged by the customer or in the case of agreements where the customer's assent is to be indicated by conduct (*i.e.*, shrink-wrap licence agreements). While to date there has been some recognition of shrink-wrap licence agreements (and by analogy, Web-wrap or click-through agreements), renewed attacks on the enforceability of such agreements may be expected as customers seek to overcome limitations and exclusions.

Even if such agreements are generally held to be enforceable, they may nevertheless be unenforceable in certain circumstances, such as where a customer may reject such a contract by returning the software to the place of purchase but where the retailer has policies that do not allow returns of software (particularly if the outer packaging has been opened).

---

9 *Sookman Computer Law: Acquiring and Protecting Computer Technology*, (Toronto: Carswell, 1992-Release 1) section 2.18(k).

In applicable cases, the enforceability of an agreement may be challenged, or a claim may be made based on causes of action outside the agreement (and beyond the scope of the limitation clauses), by showing that the supplier, or its staff, had engaged in fraudulent representations or negligent misrepresentations to induce the customer to enter into the agreement. For instance, in *Atlaz* the plaintiff claimed "fraud and deceit" based on allegations that prior to the supply of the software statements and representations in sales materials and elsewhere were made by the defendants:

> ... defendants were in a superior position to know true facts regarding the SBT Pro software packages and the Year 2000 problem those software packages contained and either knew or recklessly disregarded the same. Defendants owed a duty to disclose the true facts to plaintiff and the class members but failed or refused to do so, choosing instead to fraudulently conceal the true facts from the public.[10]

(e) Claims under Negligence

In appropriate circumstances, negligence claims may exist against the supplier's supplier (for instance, in product liability). A claim may also be made against a retailer for selling a product containing Year 2000 deficiencies if a duty of care can be found to exist to test or obtain reasonable assurances from its suppliers.

Finally, an agreement may protect a supplier but leave its staff exposed, particularly staff that are retained by a supplier on a contractual basis as opposed to "employees." For instance, a supplier may contract with an independent consultant to provide implementation or other services to its customer. Actions against such individuals for negligent performance of their responsibilities or negligent advice may be available to a customer who has suffered damages and is limited in its ability to seek redress from its supplier.

(f) Other Issues

In a number of cases relating to the acquisition of computer technology, the courts have recognized the effective inducements of promotional literature, letters and oral statements made by the supplier's representative and have treated them as express warranties, in some instances, even where the

---

10 *Supra*, at Chapter 2, note 23.

contract between the parties has contained an integration clause excluding such warranties.[11] Specific representations may also be admissible under one or more of the exceptions to the "parol evidence rule." It is therefore important to interview staff involved in the acquisition process and document their recollections of negotiations (and inventory other documents in their possession) as soon as possible.

Even where pre-contractual representations are successfully excluded through iron-clad provisions in the agreement, civil liability under various laws (for instance, the Canadian *Competition Act*) may still be applicable in the event such representations can be found to constitute misleading or false advertising, or unfair business practices. Consumer protection legislation in some jurisdictions may also extend liability for representations or promises (including those made prior to a sale) relating to the sale or to the quality, quantity, condition, performance or efficacy of a consumer product, or relating to its use or maintenance.

In appropriate circumstances, a court may find the breaches of the express warranties to be so fundamental that it will not give effect to certain contractual exclusions or limitations, including an exclusion of consequential damages.[12] Alternatively, a court may find that a Year 2000 deficiency is serious enough to constitute a fundamental breach of the agreement or that there has been a failure of the essential purpose of the transaction, and that the agreement should be set aside.

The doctrine of fundamental breach applies where a particular breach of the contract by one party is or are such as to go to the root of the contract so as to entitle the other party to treat such breach as a repudiation of the whole contract. The breach must have the effect of depriving the other party of substantially the whole benefit that it was intended to obtain from the contract. If a fundamental breach is found to have occurred, the party that was injured has the option of either affirming the contract and treating the breach as a breach of warranty, or of treating the contract as being at an end.

---

11 *Sookman Computer Law: Acquiring and Protecting Computer Technology* (Toronto: Carswell, 1992-Release 1) section 2.18(c); a representation made prior to the written agreement, whether oral or written, can create an express warranty. See *Sharrad, McGee & Co. v. Suz's Software, Inc.*, 100 N.C. App. 428, 396 S.E. 2d 815 (1990); see also U.C.C. section 213. The term "warranty" does not have to be used, nor is it necessary that the seller have the specific intent to create a warranty.

12 *RBX Industries Inc. v. Lab-Con Inc.*, 772 F. 2d (9th Cir. 1985).

Where a Year 2000 problem prevents a customer from obtaining close to the entire benefit of a contract, then such a customer may argue that fundamental breach has occurred. An example might be the acquisition of a computer system, or a product containing embedded logic, in the late 90s, where such system or product would be expected to have a long expected useful life but is made useless due to a Year 2000 problem that the supplier is unable or willing to correct. It should be noted, however, that it may not be the case in all jurisdictions that a fundamental breach will necessarily result in a court refusing to enforce any exclusionary provisions.[13]

Finally, under the UCC, if the "repair or replacement" remedy is interpreted as a promise, the failure to repair or replace may amount to a second breach of the contract, with a corresponding entitlement to damages or other remedies under the UCC, including revocation.

---

13 For instance, in *Hunter Engineering Co. v. Syncrude Canada Ltd.* (1989), 57 D.L.R. (4th) 321, [1989] 1 S.C.R. 426 (S.C.C.), the Supreme Court of Canada held that clauses that purport to limit or exclude liability are *prima facie* enforceable but the Court was divided as to the circumstances in which such a clause should be set aside. Wilson J. found that where there had been a fundamental breach, an exclusionary clause would be enforced where it was fair and reasonable to do so; Dickson C.J.C., however, found that such a clause should be enforced except where it would be unconscionable to do so. See also *Fraser Jewellers (1982) Ltd. v. Dominion Electronic Protection Co. et al.* (1997), 34 O.R. (3d) 1 (C.A.).

12

Year 2000 Warranties
(for Acquisitions)

This chapter examines the typical components of Year 2000 warranties. It also incorporates extracts from Year 2000 warranties (October 1, 1997 versions) adopted by the Government of Canada following 14 months of negotiations with ITAC.[1]

It should be noted that many customers may not have sufficient bargaining power to obtain a Year 2000 warranty that covers all the issues discussed in this chapter.

12.1 APPLICATION

The scope of the goods and services to be covered by the Year 2000 warranty should be considered. Customers will want to ensure that the warranty covers all goods and services being acquired and any required interoperability with other systems. Suppliers may wish to limit the scope of a Year 2000 warranty to a subset of the components to be provided. For instance, where a system is to be provided that incorporates a combination of "licensed software" developed by the supplier and components provided by a third party (for instance, a run-time library that provides certain functions or a database management system such as those licensed by Oracle or Sybase), the supplier may propose a Year 2000 warranty in respect only of the "licensed software."

---

[1] Four versions were adopted to cover the acquisition of (i) goods, (ii) services, (iii) systems integration and (iv) facility management/outsourcing. These will be referred to in this chapter individually as the "Year 2000 Warranty" or collectively as the "Year 2000 Warranties."

Such suppliers may also agree, to the extent possible, to assign to the customer the benefit of any warranties that they receive from other suppliers of any third party components that are incorporated into their product. However, from the customer's perspective, they are contracting for the acquisition of a "system" that will meet certain functional, technical and performance specifications, and the presence of a Year 2000 problem in any component of the system may have the same adverse consequences. Customers will therefore desire a warranty that the system as a whole will be Year 2000 complaint.

Suppliers may argue that they cannot ascertain the Year 2000 compliance of third party components incorporated into their products. The counter-argument is that if suppliers are willing to market their product on the basis of the system as a whole corresponding to certain specifications, then the Year 2000 compliance issue should not be treated differently. In any case, such suppliers will typically be in a better bargaining position to obtain reasonable Year 2000 warranties from their suppliers than would their customers.

Another area where suppliers may attempt to provide a Year 2000 warranty that is narrower in scope than that desired by their customers is in a contract for the acquisition of computer hardware. For instance, the supplier may attempt to limit the scope of a Year 2000 warranty to the processor component only. A customer should seek to obtain a warranty that is broad enough to include the operating system and any associated applications being licensed in conjunction with the processor.

Customers should also note that some suppliers are providing Year 2000 warranties on new acquisitions but not retroactively for past purchases. Such warranties may also only be applicable to specific products that are designated by the supplier (for instance, those designated as Year 2000 ready).

The following are examples of the scope portion of Year 2000 warranties for various types of products and services.

(a) Goods (Individual Products and Combination)

The Government of Canada Year 2000 Warranty for goods provides as follows:

[The Contractor warrants that] 1) all hardware, software and/or firmware products delivered individually or 2) hardware, software and firmware products delivered in combination as an integrated system under this Contract, as the case may be . . .

(b) Integrated System

The wording used by the Government of Canada Year 2000 Warranty for systems integration provides as follows:

The Contractor warrants that all hardware, software and firmware products delivered or developed and any deliverables resulting from the services provided, as an integrated system . . .

(c) Exchange of Data

The following is sample language that defines the scope of a Year 2000 warranty to cover systems that exchange data with a customer's computer system:

Supplier warrants that any computer systems that interface or exchange data with any Customer system through electronic data interchange ("EDI") or other electronic means, including any systems feeding Supplier's systems such as those of other suppliers utilized by Supplier . . .

(d) Provision of Services

The Government of Canada Year 2000 Warranty for services provides:

The Contractor warrants that the deliverables resulting from the services provided under this Contract . . .

(e) Outsourcing

The Government of Canada Year 2000 Warranty for facilities management/outsourcing provides:

The Contractor warrants that all hardware, software and firmware products which may be delivered to Canada and/or utilized by the Contractor to perform services under this Contract . . .

12.2 APPLICATION TO SUBCONTRACTORS

Some customers are asking for Year 2000 warranties that extend to subcontractors. The Government of Canada Year 2000 Warranties provide, in part:

> The obligations contained herein apply to the products delivered by the Contractor and its Subcontractor(s) involved in the performance of this Contract.

However, many suppliers are reluctant to provide Year 2000 warranties that extend to products or services provided by third parties. Some members of ITAC were opposed to the agreement by ITAC to include this component in the Government of Canada Year 2000 Warranties.

12.3 WARRANTY

The following are some specific elements of a Year 2000 warranty with respect to the compliance of a product (*i.e.*, so as to be Year 2000 compliant):

> . . . shall manage and manipulate data involving dates, including single century formulas and multi-century formulas, and will not generate incorrect values or invalid results involving such dates.

> . . . will accommodate a four digit field for the year in all date data fields and will accurately determine chronological dates and accurately perform all calculations and data manipulations based upon such dates, including leap year calculations . . .

> . . . will correctly recognize and process records containing dates both before and after January 1, 2000, including leap years, without variation in performance . . .

In order to also potentially address any use of the year 1999 as an indicator rather than as a valid date, some warranties also add that:

> no value for current date will cause any interruption in the operation of the [system]

or

the [system] does not use date fields as indicators or for purposes other than to store valid dates[2]

The Government of Canada Year 2000 Warranty for goods provides, in part:

> shall meet the Contractual requirement so as to accurately and automatically process any and all date and date-related data including, but not limited to calculating, comparing, and sequencing and that such date-related processing will take into consideration leap year calculations when used in accordance with the documentation provided by the Contractor and accepted by Canada.

Some warranties may state that a product or service is Year 2000 compliant. In some cases, customers need to ensure that the supplier's definition of "Year 2000 compliant" is the same as the customer's. For instance, some customers may require that certain testing be conducted before a critical system can be designated as Year 2000 compliant. An unsophisticated supplier may designate a system as compliant following verification that programming code utilizes four-digit year fields without further investigation to confirm compliance.

In the event that a product or service being acquired is not yet Year 2000 compliant, then the wording of the above warranty would need to be adapted to reflect the delay until a Year 2000 compliant version of the product will be provided to the customer.

Some Year 2000 warranties may refer to specific tests that were conducted by the supplier to test their product for Year 2000 compliance. While this can be helpful, customers should not accept a reference to such testing in lieu of a Year 2000 warranty as they may not be in as good a position as the supplier to know if such testing is sufficient to uncover all Year 2000 problems. For instance, testing based on advancing the date in a logical partition running on a system may not reveal Year 2000 problems that may appear when the hardware itself encounters a date of 2000 or beyond.

Another issue concerns the ability of some systems to utilize dates in a four-digit year format as well as in two-digit shortcuts for the year (with the system converting and internally storing the appropriate date in four-digit format). In some cases, customers will want the supplier to also warrant that their system will correctly translate these two-digit shortcuts

---

2 Many systems will require a value for any date field. As a result, a supplier providing a Year 2000 warranty may want to alternatively state that "other than default values, no date fields contain non-date data."

to and from their four-digit equivalents. However, since there are no industry standards applicable to such translations, the warranty should set out how such translations will be made.[3] For instance, if appropriate for both customer and supplier, it could provide that any two-digit shortcuts for the year that are between "00" and "49" will correspond to the years "2000" through "2049" (values of "50" and above will correspond to dates in the 1900s).

Some systems manipulate and store all dates using only two digits for the year. In such cases it is important to ensure that the applicable Year 2000 warranties do not require support for four-digit dates. A warranty should however be provided that where any date element is represented without a century, the correct century shall be unambiguous for all manipulations involving that element. In other words, that clear rules exist that describe the two-digit year ranges that are to correspond to dates in the 2000s and those that are to correspond to dates in the 1900s.

It should also be noted that some suppliers may propose warranties for Year 2000 compliance as of January 1, 2000. Such a warranty would not give a right or remedy to a customer where the product fails to recognize a forward date (of January 1, 2000 or beyond) at a time on or before December 31, 1999. The language for such a warranty may commence with:

> After December 31, 1999, the [Product] will accurately process date data . . .

Finally, the wording utilized by some suppliers provides that the supplier "certifies" or "warrants" compliance. A warranty is a legal promise, which if not complied with, entitles the recipient to claim damages arising from the failure to comply with the warranty. Customers should attempt to negotiate Year 2000 warranties that require the supplier to "represent and warrant" compliance in order to enhance their ability to obtain equitable remedies, including recision where appropriate, as well as legal remedies such as damages.

---

3 Specifically, the warranty should set out which year will be used as the pivot year. Some applications may have pivot years that are as close as 2009.

12.4 CONFORMANCE TO CONTRACTUAL REQUIREMENTS/SPECIFICATIONS

A customer may also want the supplier to warrant that date processing issues will not prevent the product from conforming to other requirements set out in the Agreement.

> Supplier also warrants that date-related processing will not, in any way, prevent hardware, software or firmware from conforming to the requirements of the Agreement, prior to, during, or after the year 2000.

It should be noted that the modification of existing software to properly recognize and process Year 2000 dates may increase processing times. A customer will want to ensure that upon meeting any obligation to make software Year 2000 compliant, the supplier will also be required to ensure that such modified software will continue to meet any required performance specifications.

12.5 CONDITIONS AND EXCLUSIONS

Suppliers may attempt to exclude liability for any other Year 2000 problem that falls outside the scope of the explicit Year 2000 warranty. The customer should consider reasonable conditions and exclusions but should be careful not to accept those that will unreasonably dilute the value of the Year 2000 warranty.

The following may be reasonable:

> ... when used in accordance with the documentation provided by the Supplier [and accepted by Customer] ...

> ... and provided that all hardware, software and firmware products used with the [deliverables] properly exchange accurate date and date-related data with them.

> The Year 2000 Warranty shall not apply where a modification has been made to a deliverable provided under the Agreement by a party other than Supplier, its subcontractor or a party approved in writing by either of them.

It may also be reasonable to require the customer to give prompt notice of any Year 2000 problem upon learning of the existence of such a problem.

However, customers should avoid agreeing to a condition that the supplier's obligations or liability will only arise if the Year 2000 problem is "solely caused" by the supplier's product. There may be situations where the problem is the result of more than one cause and where a sharing of responsibility may be reasonable.

It may also be reasonable for customers to agree that they will be responsible for ensuring that all software other than that provided by the supplier, that is operated on the hardware or used in conjunction with the system being acquired, will be Year 2000 compliant. However, customers will not want to agree to this as a condition to the supplier's obligations under the Year 2000 warranty. It is also questionable whether such an exclusion should apply to third party products recommended by the supplier.

Customers may also be expected to perform certain tests to confirm the Year 2000 compliance of a product being obtained. However, customers will not want to make the performance of such testing a condition precedent to the supplier's obligations under the Year 2000 warranty.

Finally, some suppliers have attempted to make their obligations relating to Year 2000 compliance conditional on the customer continuing to contact with the supplier for support and maintenance service. Customers may argue that such a condition is not reasonable as the Year 2000 warranty is intended to address a potential defect in the product at the time of delivery. However, this is a business decision that the parties will need to negotiate.

12.6 DEMONSTRATION AND VERIFICATION OF COMPLIANCE

Compilation is a process of translating a computer program through the use of another program called a compiler from a form that may be understood by a human reader into a form that can be more efficiently processed by a computer system. Some compilers are not Year 2000 compliant, notwithstanding the apparent use of four digits to represent the year in dates and may, for instance, automatically insert "19" in front of the year obtained from the hardware. As a result, any program that was compiled using such a non-compliant compiler will experience date problems in the year 2000 notwithstanding that an examination of the program may reveal that the program itself was written to be fully Year 2000 compliant.

The only way to truly ensure that a system is Year 2000 compliant is to conduct comprehensive testing. Many computer programs, including those written in COBOL, must be "compiled." While it is important for a customer to ensure that agreements contain an appropriate Year 2000 warranty, a customer may also want the right to confirm that a product critical to its operations actually is compliant. Accordingly, a customer may want to incorporate the following language in a Year 2000 warranty:

> Customer may, [at no additional cost,] require Supplier [prior to performance of the services,][at time of acceptance of any such hardware, software and firmware products] to demonstrate compliance and/or compliance techniques and test procedures it intends to follow in order to comply with all of its obligations pursuant to the Year 2000 Warranty.

Demonstration and verification obligations are particularly important if a product is not Year 2000 compliant at the time of acquisition. An obligation of the supplier to demonstrate compliance may also be important in the case of regulated entities that are being advised by their regulators to confirm suppliers' claims of compliance. In such cases a customer should request a right to re-perform an acceptance test following delivery of a Year 2000 compliant version of the product and should also consider providing a right of early termination (and the right to obtain a refund) where compliance cannot be adequately demonstrated by the supplier on or before a specific date.

12.7 DISCLAIMERS OF WARRANTIES AND LIMITATIONS ON LIABILITY

(a) Warranty Disclaimer Clauses

Nearly all agreements for computer-related products and services contain warranty disclaimer clauses. The effect of such provisions is to exclude any warranties not specifically set out in the agreement, including any implied warranties and conditions contained in sale of goods legislation. A customer will want to ensure that any warranty disclaimer provision contained in the agreement will not in any way limit an explicit Year 2000 warranty and should therefore consider the addition of a provision similar to the following:

> The Year 2000 Warranty is separate and discrete from any other warranties specified in the Agreement, and is not subject to any disclaimer of warranty which may be specified in the Agreement [and its appendices, schedules, annexes] and any other document incorporated into the Agreement by reference.

(b) Limitation on Liability Provisions

Agreements for computer-related products and services also typically contain limitation of liability provisions. The purpose of such clauses is typically to limit the liability of the supplier:

(a) to direct damages only (and exclude liability for indirect, incidental or consequential damages); and

(b) to incorporate a cap on the liability of the supplier, to the amounts paid to the supplier under the agreement.

A customer may want to negotiate that any limitation of liability provisions contained in the agreement will not be applicable to a breach of an explicit Year 2000 warranty where such breach was intentional or reckless on the part of the supplier or where the supplier does not remedy a Year 2000 problem within a reasonable time of receiving notice from the customer.

Suppliers may generally resist a provision that states that a breach of the Year 2000 warranty will not be subject to any limitation on the supplier's liability that is contained in the agreement and will seek to incorporate a provision similar to the following:

> The Year 2000 Warranty is subject to any limitation on the Supplier's liability specified in the Agreement.

In some cases, a compromise approach may be to agree that a breach of a Year 2000 warranty will be subject to a separate cap on total liability, which might be expressed as a fixed dollar amount or a percentage (greater than 100%) of the cap on total liability otherwise applicable to other breaches of the agreement.

(c) Exclusive Remedy Provisions

Customers will want to negotiate appropriate amendments to any exclusive remedy provision that may be contained in the agreement. Depending on the language, an exclusive remedy provision may limit a supplier's obligation to correct a Year 2000 problem until after a problem has actually occurred and prevent the customer from obtaining any compensation for damages that are suffered. Customers will want an exclusive remedy provision to require rectification by the supplier of any problem within a specified time period, failing which the customer will be entitled to seek damages.

12.8 REMEDY

Customers will want an undertaking from the supplier that it will provide Year 2000 compliant upgrades that will correct any Year 2000 problems that are discovered in the products or services being supplied. The following is an example:

> Supplier shall provide Customer, free of charge, with any new versions, upgrades, or other releases of the [Software] which are necessary to meet the requirements of this warranty or to correct any breach of this warranty, and shall provide such number of copies corresponding to the number of copies of the [Software] provided for in this Agreement.

Customers will also want a prompt escalation protocol for any repair obligation being assumed by the supplier. This may also include a requirement that the supplier provide the services of a minimum number of persons, on a dedicated basis, to resolve the problem.

Customers in a strong negotiating position will also want the supplier to accept liability for all damages that result from Year 2000 deficiencies in the products or services being supplied. Such customers may request provisions that provide:

> Supplier shall be liable for all damages which result from a breach of this warranty.

or alternatively,

> Supplier shall promptly repair and replace any [system] that does not meet the requirements of this section and shall pay all losses, damages, costs and expenses incurred by Customer and any of its customers as a result of any breach of this representation and warranty.

In contrast, Suppliers will want their obligation to correct Year 2000 problems to be the customer's exclusive remedy and their sole liability.

Other alternatives in respect of remedies that customers may wish to consider include:

♦ liquidated damages (the amount of which will increase according to the period of time that the supplier requires to correct the problem);
♦ a requirement that the supplier reimburse the customer for any costs incurred performing operations manually or through a third-party service provider;
♦ where a problem cannot be resolved within a specified time period, a requirement that the supplier provide alternative compliant technology until resolution;
♦ a requirement to hold back a portion of any fees payable until sometime in the year 2000 (for instance, at the end of the first calendar quarter).

Where a copy of the source code for software acquired from a third party is to be placed in escrow, a customer should also negotiate a contractual right of access to the source code for the purpose of rectifying a Year 2000 problem that is not addressed by the supplier within a reasonable period. One method to accomplish this is to make Year 2000 non-compliance a "trigger event" or an "event of default" for the purpose of the escrow agreement.

12.9 DURATION OF YEAR 2000 WARRANTY

Suppliers may want to limit the availability of a Year 2000 warranty to the normal warranty period set out in the agreement or to a specific period following delivery or implementation. This will be unacceptable to most customers who will want the warranty to cover the period of time that it may take for the consequences of a Year 2000 problem to become apparent.

The Year 2000 Warranty adopted by the Government of Canada provides:

> The warranties contained herein shall have a term extending either:

a) to June 30, 2000, or,

b) for a period of six months following acceptance of the hardware, software and/or firmware, whichever is the later date.

An alternative would be to provide:

The Year 2000 Warranty shall continue for a period of three (3) years after the acceptance of the [services] [system], or such longer period of time that the Supplier is providing any services for the support or maintenance of the [system].

In any case, it would also be desirable to provide:

The Year 2000 Warranty shall survive the termination of this Agreement.

or reference the survival of this warranty in the appropriate section in the agreement that deals with survival of specific provisions upon expiration or termination of the agreement. However, some suppliers will want any Year 2000 warranty to terminate with any termination of the applicable agreement.

13

Negotiating Year 2000 Compliance

13.1 WHAT TO DO ABOUT NEW AGREEMENTS

Between now and the year 2000, companies will continue to acquire new software, hardware and other equipment. In some cases these are being acquired to replace older products that are not Year 2000 compliant. However, such companies should not trade one problem for another problem.

Customers should try to obtain an explicit representation and warranty that products and services are Year 2000 compliant in all new contracts.[1] Customers should also add Year 2000 warranties to purchase orders, "standard terms" incorporated into acquisition or other agreements, and in any request for proposals ("RFPs") that are issued. While some of these documents may not themselves represent binding contractual commitments,[2] they may provide additional protection in some circumstances.

Other recommendations for customers in respect of new acquisitions include:

♦ ensuring that confidentiality provisions allow the exchange of information with other users concerning Year 2000 compliance of programs;

---

1 In the case of services, this would include a representation and warranty, as applicable, that (a) the deliverables created from the services are Year 2000 compliant; and (b) that the ability of the supplier to perform its obligations under the agreement (*i.e.*, continue to deliver the services) will not be disrupted due to a Year 2000 problem.

2 Disputes concerning enforceability are likely to arise, particularly if inconsistent terms are utilized by the other parties in their forms and/or if the terms contained in such secondary documents are inconsistent with a negotiated and executed agreement between the parties. This leads to what is commonly referred to as a battle of the forms.

- specifying that Year 2000 non-compliance is an event of default that gives the licensee a right to access any source code that is placed in escrow;
- including a right of the licensee to modify the software for Year 2000 compliance;
- clarifying that Year 2000 non-compliance is not a *force majeure* event;
- extending the term of any Year 2000 warranty until the year 2001 or other appropriate date;
- ensuring that the full history of pre-contractual discussions is documented;
- ensuring that any new agreement cannot be terminated by the supplier prior to the year 2000 and that the supplier cannot otherwise abandon its products or responsibility for making Year 2000 corrections;[3] and
- ensuring that support contracts contain appropriate Year 2000 warranties and that the customer has the right to extend such contracts past the year 2000.

13.2 WHAT TO DO ABOUT EXISTING AGREEMENTS

There are three basic alternatives for dealing with the Year 2000 problem. An organization can convert, rewrite or replace an application that is not Year 2000 compatible. In some cases, a fourth alternative is to eliminate an application that is no longer required.

In the case of software licensed from third parties, an organization can replace a non-compliant application or obtain a Year 2000 compliant upgrade from the supplier. Product upgrades for Year 2000 compliance can take a number of different forms:

- There are often many different versions of the same product installed in the supplier's customer base (or in some cases, even within the same customer's operations) at any one time. Suppliers may identify a particular version number for the purposes of Year 2000 compliance and may advise that Year 2000 compliance issues will not be addressed in earlier versions of the product. In such cases, customers may need to upgrade to a more recent release of a product in order to ensure Year 2000 compliance.
- In some cases, supplier's products are compiled with certain interface libraries. Some products may simply need to be re-compiled with the

---

3 Some suppliers are already discontinuing certain products rather than addressing Year 2000 problems of such products.

latest release of interface libraries in order to address Year 2000 compliance issues.

♦ Some products may have been phased out and replaced with newer product lines. In such cases, a supplier may address Year 2000 compliance issues in the replacement products but may elect not to deal with any Year 2000 issues for any products designated as obsolete or discontinued by the supplier. In such cases, customers may be required to change products in order to ensure Year 2000 compliance.

Two important issues must be considered in respect of upgrades:

♦ Newer releases or replacement products may require a change to a more recent hardware/software platform or a system with additional processing, memory or other capacity. A customer may be required to acquire and install new hardware and/or operating system upgrades in order to utilize the Year 2000 compliant release of a product or a replacement product.

♦ Interfaces to customer or third-party systems may need to be considered. Commonly known as Application Programming Interfaces ("APIs"), these may need to be updated. In some cases this may require modifications to any interfacing programs to reflect any updates made to the API. Where an API utilizes a two-digit field for dates, one approach is not to modify the API data format but rather to define a designated date for interpreting the two-digit year field (*i.e.*, any number under 50 will refer to a year between 2000 and 2049). This may still require a change to any customer or third-party system that is interfacing through the API, although the extent of such change may be smaller than would be the case if the data format was being changed.

Users with some degree of leverage are now seeking to amend their existing agreements to include explicit representations and warranties in respect of year 2000 compliance. However, this may be difficult or impossible to do especially in the case of software that is not subject to ongoing maintenance obligations or that was acquired pursuant to a shrink-wrap licence agreement.

Even without an explicit Year 2000 warranty, users may be able to rely on other obligations to compel suppliers to correct Year 2000 problems. For instance, a user may be able to rely on an obligation by the supplier to correct bugs, errors or other deficiencies in the software.[4] The supplier may

---

4 Any testing conducted by users for Year 2000 compliance should be performed as soon as possible in order to provide vendors with adequate notice of any bugs detected.

also have an obligation to maintain the software such that it will perform in compliance with certain specifications or performance criteria. In some cases, these obligations may indirectly require a supplier to address Year 2000 problems.

Customers should contact suppliers with whom they have an ongoing relationship and request that such suppliers confirm the Year 2000 compliance of their products or provide Year 2000 compliant updates. Where suppliers indicate that they are not going to make their products Year 2000 complaint or are not going to provide Year 2000 upgrades prior to the time required by customers, customers must make difficult decisions about whether to repair or replace the non-compliant product. In the event a customer decides to proceed with remediation activities on its own, it would be prudent for the customer to put the supplier on notice regarding any claim the customer believes it may have against the supplier.

The customer should proceed to mitigate damages by using cost-effective means to correct any Year 2000 deficiencies. Any applicable agreements should be reviewed to ascertain which terms facilitate or inhibit remedial actions. In any case, the following contractual issues should be considered before a customer attempts to address Year 2000 problems on its own or by engaging the services of a third party:

♦ A maintenance agreement may contain a provision that specifies that the supplier is not responsible to provide services in the event the product is altered or modified without the supplier's written consent.
♦ An agreement may contain an explicit prohibition on the use of third parties to repair the product. For instance, such a provision might state:

> Customer agrees that it will not engage the services of an outside person, entity or agency to provide any maintenance, support or other services with respect to the [products] or any enhancements, without the prior written consent of Supplier.

♦ Confidentiality provisions may limit access.[5] Consider the following examples:

---

5 However, depending on the circumstances, these types of provisions may be difficult for a supplier to litigate especially where it is not addressing Year 2000 issues itself. A licensee who is sued for breach of such provisions would likely make arguments based on public policy.

> Each party agrees that it will not disclose or otherwise make available to any third party any Confidential Information, or otherwise make use of any Confidential Information, without the prior written consent of the other party.

or alternatively,

> Customer shall limit access to proprietary or confidential material to those employees who require such access for purposes related to Customer's use of the [product] as permitted by this Agreement.

♦ A licence agreement may restrict use of or access to the software to employees of the licensee only.

A written demand should at least be sent to the licensor to reduce the risk that the remediation work undertaken by the customer will be subsequently interpreted as a waiver by the customer of its right to seek reimbursement from the licensor. This and any other consistent actions should be undertaken to preserve any rights the customer may have to obtain reimbursement from the licensor or other potential parties.

One area of concern is that some suppliers may "discontinue" certain non-compliant hardware and/or software products rather than incur the cost of developing Year 2000 upgrades. Customers would then be forced to switch to other product lines, possibly at considerable expense. The applicable agreements would need to be reviewed in order to determine whether the supplier may be precluded from discontinuing any non-compliant product. Some agreements may require the supplier to continue offering support for the original product for a minimum specified period of time.

The form in which a Year 2000 upgrade will be provided may be another issue. One option, in the case of software, is for a supplier to provide a patch that simply addresses Year 2000 deficiencies in an existing version of its software. A second option is to include the Year 2000 corrections as part of a larger enhancement. Some customers are taking the position that any Year 2000 corrections, even if included with other enhancements, should be made available at no charge. A similar position is being taken by some American law firms that have apparently sent suppliers letters stating that such suppliers must provide any Year 2000 upgrade free of charge or risk a class action lawsuit.

Some customers may even prefer to receive Year 2000 corrections without additional enhancements as the latter may require retraining, changes to interfaces, and additional testing. However, suppliers may prefer not to upgrade older versions of software, even if customers are willing to pay extra, due to limited resources.

13.3 WHAT TO DO ABOUT OUTSOURCING ARRANGEMENTS

Many existing outsourcing arrangements, particularly long-term arrangements, may not have contemplated the Year 2000 problem. Suppliers can be expected to strongly resist any suggestion that Year 2000 remediation costs should be absorbed by them as part of any monthly service fee. Outsourcing should therefore not be viewed as a convenient method of shifting the Year 2000 risk to third parties.[6]

Whether a supplier of outsourcing services is responsible for correcting Year 2000 problems in systems transferred as part of a general outsourcing transaction that did not contemplate the Year 2000 issue is not usually clear, and may depend on factors similar to those relevant to support and maintenance agreements. However, a supplier of outsourcing services may have different obligations with respect to systems that the supplier acquired directly (*i.e.*, developed internally or acquired from third parties) to provide services to customers.

The obligation of such a supplier to correct Year 2000 problems may arise from two sources. The first is an obligation in the outsourcing agreement that may require the supplier to correct any "bugs," errors, or deficiencies in systems that are being maintained for a customer. However, it is not clear whether such provisions would be interpreted to extend to an expensive overhaul of an older system. Certain exclusions may also be applicable, such as an exclusion of any obligation to correct defects in customer's proprietary software and third-party software.

The second source may be service level guarantees that require the system being maintained to be operational during certain hours and/or to process a specified number of transactions per unit of time. In either case, a

---

6 The discussion in this section assumes that the outsourcing agreement deals with the operation/maintenance of systems for the customer rather than with the provision of services. Where the outsourcing transaction is structured for the provision of services then the onus will likely be entirely on the outsourcing supplier to ensure Year 2000 compliance.

shut-down of a system due to a Year 2000 problem may prevent the system from performing in compliance with the specified service levels.

Other factors may support supplier responsibility to address Year 2000 problems. These include:

- the supplier may have control of the entire operating environment;
- the non-compliant programs may not have originated with the customer (*i.e.*, were provided by the supplier);
- the outsourcing agreement may lack provisions that deal with change order/special projects;
- the outsourcing agreement may contain a technology refreshment or "keep current" obligation—examples are:

> Supplier shall keep current the equipment, operating system and other technologies used by Supplier in performing the Services in accordance with Schedule A.

or

> The parties anticipate that the Services will evolve and be supplemented, modified, enhanced or replaced over time to keep pace with technological advancements and improvements in the methods of delivering services, and same is not intended to be outside the scope of the Services.

- the outsourcing agreement may contain an obligation of the supplier to undertake lesser, included tasks—for example:

> If any services, functions or responsibilities not specifically described in this Agreement are required for the proper performance and provision of the Services, then they will be deemed to be implied by and included within the scope of the Services. . .

However, other factors may act to negate supplier responsibility. These include:

- the outsourcing agreement may contain provisions that deal with change order/special projects;
- customer may have retained overall control over some or all of the operating environment; and
- non-compliant programs may have been developed or originally acquired by the customer and transferred to the supplier.

Some suppliers may claim that a customer's requirements, either through written specifications or implicitly through the transfer of software to the supplier, specified the use of two digits to represent the year. However, a customer's response to such an argument would be that the use of two digits to represent the year does not in itself need to result in a Year 2000 problem as windowing techniques could be employed (as they are being extensively employed now) to allow for proper recognition and calculation of dates.

In determining whether an outsourcing agreement requires the supplier to address the Year 2000 problem, the specific obligations of the supplier must be considered. Some outsourcing agreements require the supplier to maintain and support the systems that it has acquired from the customer. Other agreements require the supplier only to "operate" the system.

Even where a supplier has agreed to assume an obligation to "maintain and support" the customer system, the provision of such service may be limited to providing either (a) a pool of available resources; or (b) a specified number of individuals allocated to provide services to the customer, with the customer possibly having the right to establish priorities for outstanding tasks. In some cases, suppliers may also be able to rely on a provision that excludes supplier liability where customers have failed to implement hardware or software changes recommended by the supplier.

Another potential difficulty that may be encountered by some customers who attempt to hold suppliers of outsourcing services responsible for correcting Year 2000 problems is that few suppliers of such services have assumed responsibility for making third-party systems work. Many have agreed to only monitor, follow-up, and pursue third-party vendors in order to obtain contracted maintenance services from such vendors.

However, even in situations where a supplier of outsourcing services may not be responsible for correcting Year 2000 problems, depending on the circumstances (including the contractual standard of care and history of dealing between the parties), the supplier may have a responsibility to at least inform customers of the additional work and associated costs that should be undertaken to address potential or actual Year 2000 problems.

It is recommended that parties entering into new outsourcing transactions deal with the Year 2000 issue openly and document their respective responsibilities. Parties with existing outsourcing agreements should initiate a dialogue as soon as possible and negotiate each parties' obligations so that corrective work is not delayed. In many cases, Year 2000 compliance will be treated as a project under the outsourcing agreement.

However, even where the supplier of outsourcing services is retained to address a customer's Year 2000 problems, many such suppliers will be reluctant to give Year 2000 warranties in respect of third-party software or software transferred to the supplier by the customer. Year 2000 warranties may be easier to obtain if the services are to be provided using the supplier's proprietary system.

Customers entering into new outsourcing agreements, or renewing existing agreements, will want to negotiate explicit Year 2000 representations and warranties. Where the supplier is not able to provide such warranties at the commencement of services, and where the customer is limited in its ability to select a supplier that has completed its remediation work and is prepared to provide appropriate representations and warranties, the customer will want to insert certain protections in the agreement. These should at least include the right of the customer to terminate the outsourcing agreement if the supplier has not developed a comprehensive and realistic plan for achieving compliance (which should be well in advance of the year 2000) and demonstrated that it has achieved Year 2000 compliance by specified dates. These dates should be chosen to provide sufficient time to negotiate a new agreement with a new supplier and transfer the customer's operations to the new supplier. If this occurs, the customer will want the non-compliant supplier to reimburse its costs for relocating to another supplier in the event it has grounds to exercise this right.

Customers with existing outsourcing agreements or who plan to enter new outsourcing agreements should ensure that they have the right to keep the contract in force past the year 2000. Lastly, where possible, customers should negotiate caps on price increases to protect themselves from anticipated increases in labour costs.

14

Contracting for Year 2000 Services

Many organizations are contracting for the services of external service providers to assist with Year 2000 assessment, conversion and testing. An external provider of Year 2000 services can supplement internal resources and provide special expertise. Outsourcing components of a Year 2000 project may also enable organizations to keep their in-house staff focused on their core business.

Year 2000 services are being offered by system integrators (IBM, SHL, Andersen Consulting, EDS), the big accounting firms (KPMG, Price Waterhouse, Ernst & Young, Deloitte & Touche, Coopers & Lybrand, Arthur Andersen), consulting firms and tool vendors. These suppliers may provide valuable experience with the assessment phase, in managing conversions (including the use of specialized tools that can search existing software for segments that contain date-related functions) and with testing.

A Year 2000 project may be one of the largest projects undertaken by a particular organization. It will typically involve a substantial financial expenditure, high visibility and significant risks. It is therefore important to pay special attention to the agreements being signed to acquire such services.

An experienced Year 2000 service provider will have negotiated numerous agreements for such services. However, for many information system managers, the Year 2000 project may be their first experience in negotiating an agreement for a large scale "mission critical" project where a failure or delay may involve substantial potential risks and liabilities.[1] As well,

---

1 In some respects, an agreement for Year 2000 conversion services may be similar to a software development agreement, aside from the fact that the deadline is immovable.

certain aspects of an agreement for Year 2000 services may be unique and not immediately obvious even to persons who have otherwise been exposed to other large development projects and associated legal agreements. In many cases suppliers will also enjoy superior bargaining power.[2] Finally, a Year 2000 project may involve multiple agreements with multiple suppliers, each covering a different phase, and with each supplier trying to shift the risk of failures to others. Proper legal assistance is essential in such circumstances.

The following material discusses some of the general issues and provisions that should be considered in negotiating agreements for Year 2000 services. It is not intended to cover all provisions that should be included in such agreements or every possible issue that should be considered in drafting the particular provisions discussed. A discussion of standard terms commonly included in technology-related agreements is also omitted. Finally, this area is undergoing rapid change and terms that may be negotiable for customers that start their remediation projects early, may not be achievable as time grows shorter until the year 2000.

14.1 GENERAL ISSUES

There are a number of opportunists entering the Year 2000 conversion business.[3] Customers should confirm that their proposed supplier has adequate and relevant prior experience. Part of the due diligence in the selection of a supplier should include reviewing the supplier's track record on similar projects and its existing pool of available resources.[4] Customers should request and follow up on current and relevant references. Preference should be given to suppliers with significant experience in managing large projects. Specific Year 2000 experience is highly desirable. Suppliers may also desire to perform their own due diligence on potential customers (*i.e.*, whether the customer has a history of success using consultants, the level of executive commitment to the project, etc.)

---

2 The superior bargaining power typically results from the demand exceeding the supply in respect of Year 2000 services being requested from established suppliers.

3 It should be noted that some commentators have indicated that the Year 2000 problem has a number of ingredients that make it ripe for fraud opportunities. One area of potential fraud concerns the duping of investors to finance phony Year 2000 solution providers. Another concern are companies that may promise cheap solutions that don't necessarily correct a customer's Year 2000 problems. In the latter case, the fraud may not be discovered for some time (*i.e.*, until the year 2000).

4 However, the importance of this consideration will vary depending on whether or not the supplier can subcontract the performance of some or all of the services.

It should be noted that the Information Technology Association of America, an industry group, has a certification program in respect of Year 2000 solution providers. The Information Technology Association of Canada decided that it did not wish to risk incurring possible liability in certification of suppliers for Year 2000 services and has decided not to certify any company for such purposes in Canada.[5] In any case, these types of certifications typically only certify the process and method the supplier claims to use rather than certifying the delivered product.

The customer and supplier should ideally enter into the relationship with a shared set of assumptions. An important preventive measure to avoid litigation down the road is to ensure that the customer's expectations are in line with what the supplier intends to perform. In this respect, it would be desirable to have the proposed supplier perform some preliminary investigations of the customer's system and operations prior to execution of a definitive and legally binding agreement for the services. Of course, such investigations, and any preliminary exchange of information, should only be made pursuant to a non-disclosure agreement.

Risk allocation in Year 2000 remediation contracts can be particularly difficult to negotiate. Many Year 2000 providers may be reluctant to fully guarantee the results of their services due to the following factors:

♦ The application being converted may contain latent date-related problems or bugs other than strictly Year 2000 compatibility problems.
♦ In many situations, a Year 2000 conversion may be combined with other objectives, such as enhancing the functionality of the application.
♦ Test cases, required for the testing stage may be non-existent or out of date. Testing will require the use of a sufficient number and variety of target test cases in order to ensure an adequate comfort level.[6]
♦ Differences may exist between programs saved in libraries (*i.e.*, with source code) from the compiled versions being used in production systems. In some cases, source code or documentation may be missing.
♦ Services of Year 2000 service providers are in high demand, which tends to lessen their willingness to agree to assume risk.

Some Year 2000 service providers will only agree that they will provide services on a "best efforts basis" or on the basis that their liability for non-performance will be severely limited. Such suppliers approach Year 2000 remediation work as consulting assignments (*i.e.*, for the supply of a

---

5 W. Michael Fletcher, *Computer Crisis 2000* (Self-Counsel Press, 1998) at 195.
6 The customer will typically need to assume responsibility for testing.

defined amount of resources or effort) rather than as obligations to provide concrete deliverables or a guaranteed result. While this form of arrangement may be appropriate for some types of Year 2000 services, it may not be suitable, from the customer's perspective, for all. Companies undertaking Year 2000 conversion projects will want to contract for clearly defined results-oriented "deliverables" (*i.e.*, a system that is Year 2000 compliant and continues to conform to specifications). Customers will also want to tie deliverables to milestones on the project plan.

A Year 2000 project will typically have an immovable deadline. Therefore, the work must conform to a strict time line without the capacity for slippage that may be available for other types of information technology projects.[7] Some commentators have suggested that the traditional contracting approach, which incorporates a list of obligations coupled with liability to ensure performance, may not work well due to the high risk associated with failure and the strict time lines with which it must be compiled.[8] In such circumstances, it is suggested, customers need to instead focus on managing the process. This means incorporating:

♦ firm deadlines with incentives to meet or beat deadlines;
♦ frequent status checks to identify slippage as soon as possible; and
♦ an ability to terminate on short notice.

Other commentators have recommended a focus on remedial actions to be undertaken in the event of a breach rather than a focus on allocating liability for damages that may result. Such an approach merits consideration because, in many cases, customers will be more interested in fixing problems rather than obtaining monetary compensation.[9]

14.2 THE PARTIES

A number of consultants, developers and system integrators are setting up special-purpose subsidiaries to perform Year 2000 consulting and remedia-

---

7 Slippage can result from inadequate performance by a supplier. However, it may also occur as a result of a customer not performing its obligations on a timely basis. Suppliers will therefore want to condition their obligations on timely performance by the customer of its obligations.

8 For instance, see Gregory P. Cirillo, "Y2K Remediation Contracts: When Your Back is Against the Wall, You Do Not Need Leverage to Succeed" at <http://www.y2k.com/sequelgp.htm>.

9 Due to the scarcity of resources in this area, some suppliers may be more comfortable with liquidated damages rather than a commitment to remedy without limits.

tion work. Customers should keep in mind that a contract is only as strong as the legal entities who sign it. If the more financially viable parent will not be a party to the contract, customers may want to nevertheless seek to have the parent guarantee performance of the subsidiary that is to provide the Year 2000 remediation services or obtain other suitable security.[10]

14.3 SERVICES AND DELIVERABLES

It is essential that the agreement contain a clear and comprehensive definition of the deliverables to be provided by the supplier and/or the specific tasks and responsibilities to be performed by the supplier. This is important for both the customer and the supplier. In the event that the customer's precise requirements are not yet known, the development of such requirements may be the initial deliverable. However, in such cases, the customer should ensure that it can terminate the agreement if the charges or timetable proposed by the supplier for the subsequent phase is not acceptable to the customer.

The contract should clearly identify what is being acquired by the customer. As discussed previously, the parties will need to agree whether the customer is contracting for the contractor's expertise, to be provided on a "best efforts" basis, or for clear deliverables (*i.e.*, a Year 2000-compliant system). The parties need to address and clearly document whether the supplier will be responsible for finding and correcting all instances of non-compliant date codes. Suppliers that are retained to perform only specific Year 2000 activities will want to ensure that the agreement clearly limits the scope of their responsibility (*e.g.*, assisting in the organization in "scoping" the problem, finding date references, expanding date fields, or using specific automated tools and providing reports produced using such tools).

The following are other issues to consider:

♦ The agreement should provide for a clear allocation of responsibility. A "partnership approach" creates ambiguity as to which party is responsible if something does not work. While, some level of joint management may be necessary, the greater the desired level of customer

---

10 Of course, it will not be easy to obtain such guarantees from a corporate parent as that further insulation from liability was likely the reason for setting up the subsidiary in the first place. It should also be noted that any warranties from such purpose-specific entities may be devalued if the parent company decides to leave this line of business.

involvement in project decisions, the more the supplier will seek to share liability.

♦ Project management is an important component of the services being provided and is commonly listed as a deliverable. Customers will typically want frequent status updates. If the customer requires the supplier to use a particular project management tool then this should be documented.

♦ Suppliers will want to disclaim any responsibility for existing errors in the computer programs or data to be converted. Any additional time spent making necessary corrections in respect of such pre-existing problems may be chargeable to the customer.

♦ The scope of what is to be analysed, converted or tested should be set out. For instance, in most cases this will be a specific program or system (rather than the customer's entire enterprise).

♦ The agreement should set out any responsibility of the supplier to update the documentation applicable to any software that is being converted.

♦ The agreement should set out what obligations are being assumed by the supplier to identify date-related problems. Some suppliers limit their obligations to the conversion of date problems that are identified using specific Year 2000 tools. In such cases, responsibility for correcting other Year 2000 date problems that may be subsequently identified during testing or use needs to be allocated. One option is to share this responsibility, to some extent, by the supplier agreeing to provide a defined amount of additional resources, or agreeing to provide additional resources at favourable rates, in order to correct such problems.

♦ The work to be performed by the supplier should be characterized in a manner that is consistent with the accounting and tax treatment intended by the customer.

♦ The method to be used to convert date references should be set out.[11] Certain techniques utilized to achieve Year 2000 compliance may result in increased processing time. Customers will want to negotiate appropriate parameters on any decreases in performance.

♦ The agreement should include a definition of Year 2000 compliance. This definition should clearly include the correction of date problems

---

11 Several methods are available to convert date references. The most obvious solution is to convert all two-digit references to four-digit references (this technique is referred to as date expansion). If this solution is selected, both programs and data (current and historical) must be modified. This solution requires that all year references be expanded and will require an increase in storage capacity. Another popular technique is to retain all stored references to the year in two-digit form and to recalculate the date based on a 100-year time frame. While allowing the data to remain intact, this technique is not adequate for situations involving dates that extend beyond a 100-year window and may produce system degradation, particularly in systems that make extensive use of dates.

relating to the two-digit year problem, the use of dates as indicators, and the leap year problem. Definitions and compliance standards need to take into account other systems with which the system being converted will need to interface. Two systems can technically be "Year 2000 compliant" but unable to correctly transfer date data between them due to the way they were converted. Where a windowing technique is used to address Year 2000 deficiencies, all systems that exchange date data must utilize the same "pivot" year (*i.e.*, any year less than the pivot year is deemed to refer to a year in the 21st century). Those that use different pivot years will only operate correctly as long as information exchanged between them contains dates that are less than the smaller of the two pivot years or greater than the larger of the two pivot years. A clear definition of "testing" is also highly desirable.

♦ The agreement should include a definition for "line of code" if the supplier will be paying royalties based on line of code to its licensors of conversion tools and if such fees are to be passed on to the customer.

♦ With respect to "assessment phase" work to be performed by a supplier, the deliverables should include a determination of the extent of a customer's exposure to date-related problems and detailed analysis reports that identify how the problem can be solved. A customer may want a prioritization of recommended remediation work based on the importance of the systems to the customer's operation. Implementation plans for conversions may be required. Customers may also ask for backup documentation and data.

♦ Where a supplier is retained to perform assessment work only, the agreement should require the supplier to make itself available for consultation after completion of the assessment. The fee to be paid by the customer may include a specified number of hours for this purpose or such hours may be chargeable at the supplier's hourly rates.

♦ The agreement should set out which party will be responsible for developing testing plans, tools, scripts and test data. Most agreements require customers to assume responsibility for providing test data and writing testing scripts.

♦ The agreement should describe any special or proprietary methodology to be utilized. The use of a comprehensive and proven methodology can reduce some of the risks, and potentially some of the costs (through higher productivity), associated with a Year 2000 assessment and conversion effort. Where such a methodology is to be implemented, customers will want to see a clear contractual obligation that such methodology will be utilized by the supplier (and where applicable, this should flow down to any subcontractor).

♦ The agreement may also specify that the converted version of any customer application should continue to interface and integrate with all other existing systems in the same manner as prior to conversion. Any exceptions (such as changes in the format of dates) should be documented. Customers may also want suppliers to log all changes to customer applications.

♦ The agreement should reference any specifications that the converted application will need to meet or need to continue meeting. However, with some older systems, the customer may no longer have specifications (or they may not be up to date). In many such cases, the system itself may be the specification.

♦ An important consideration will be to allocate responsibility for the provision of a test environment and each party's responsibility for testing. In some cases, it may be more cost effective for the supplier to provide the test equipment, particularly if it is of a generic nature and can be re-used for other projects by the supplier.[12]

♦ Year 2000 remediation projects typically require strict delivery and performance schedules. The potential of delayed delivery should be dealt with in the agreement. A customer may want to consider the use of performance bonds, liquidated damages, or other payment structures that encourage completion of the work by the specified dates. However, as the time to the year 2000 grows shorter, and resources become more scarce, suppliers will likely become increasingly reluctant to assume liability for delayed implementations.

♦ It is likely that changes to the scope of services required from a supplier will be identified during the course of the project. It is therefore very important that the agreement incorporate a change management procedure so that changes can be made after execution of the agreement.

♦ The agreement should address whether or not the supplier will assume any responsibilities to investigate the Year 2000 compliance of the customer's suppliers (*i.e.*, sending out inquiry letters, testing third party products, etc.). If this type of work is to be performed by the supplier, customers may want to clarify that the supplier may not make legal decisions or waive any rights of the customer.

♦ Other responsibilities to be assumed by the supplier may include implementation of a quality assurance plan (which may include periodic quality reviews and/or additional testing), development of project budgets, and responsibility for cost control.

♦ The agreement will typically list certain obligations that are to be assumed by the customer. Timely performance by a customer of its

---

12 The customer will need to confirm that it has the right to operate any existing software licensed from third parties for non-production purposes on such a test system. Also, some licence agreements may differentiate between a system owned by the customer from a system owned by a third party such as a provider of Year 2000 services.

obligations may be important to the success of the project. A supplier may even want these listed on the project schedule. However, a customer will want the supplier to confirm that performance by the supplier does not require, and is not dependent upon, the customer providing any information or performing any services other than as set out in the agreement. The supplier will want to state that it is relying upon the accuracy and completeness of information to be provided by the customer.

♦ Suppliers will want to provide that their performance is conditional upon the performance by the customer of its obligations. Customers will want to restrict such a provision to a narrow list of specific customer obligations that may exonerate the supplier of a failure to meet its obligations. Customers will also want to require that any such failure on its part must be a direct and substantive factor in preventing the supplier from meeting its obligations as a condition of such exoneration.[13]

♦ Customers will want the supplier to agree that it will exercise reasonable care to prevent the loss or destruction of the customer's computer programs and data files. However, in such cases, suppliers will want to limit their responsibility due to such loss or destruction to the restoration of such programs or files from backups maintained by the customer.

(a) Staffing

A supplier's ability to retain its staff for the duration of the project should be considered. A customer may want the supplier to demonstrate that it has a history of retaining staff and has included strong non-compete provisions in agreements with its staff to control defections. It should be expected that some of the supplier's staff may nevertheless leave and customers should ensure that they select a supplier that has the size and professional depth to replace key personnel who leave or who cannot continue due to an illness or accident.

To the extent that a supplier is providing resources rather than results, customers will want to pay careful attention to documenting the supply of personnel by the supplier. In such cases, customers will want to:

♦ specify such personnel by name, if possible—if not, customers will want to document the number of full time personnel to be dedicated exclu-

---

13 The price to be paid will often be to provide reciprocal provisions in favour of the supplier.

sively to the customer along with their specific professional qualifications (skill sets and experience, prior Year 2000 experience, etc.);[14]

♦ restrict the ability of the supplier to change personnel without the customer's consent (not to be unreasonably withheld);

♦ require the supplier's personnel to work continuously each business day (and/or weekends) from the effective date of the agreement until completion of the project; and

♦ require the supplier to provide overtime or additional resources (at its own expense), if and when required, in order to address any slippage that may occur as a result of the supplier's non-performance.

Other considerations include:

♦ in appropriate circumstances, it may be desirable to specify where the supplier's personnel will be working (and if working at the customer's site, what resources must be provided by the customer);

♦ customers will need to be cautious about exercising too much control over the supplier's personnel as this may result in the customer potentially incurring certain employment-related obligations in respect of those personnel;

♦ both parties will likely have an interest in including a provision prohibiting the solicitation of each other's employees; and

♦ a customer may want to consider a right to interview and approve the personnel proposed by the supplier to work on the customer's remediation project.

14.4 CUSTOMER OBLIGATIONS

In most cases, the assistance of customers and their staff will be essential to a successful Year 2000 project. The agreement may contain specific responsibilities or obligations that are to be undertaken by the customer. However, customers will want to ensure that their obligations are not open-ended but rather are restricted to those specifically set out in the agreement.

Customer obligations may include:

---

14 This is very important as some suppliers may provide teams with an experienced leader but with other members who are recent graduates of a Year 2000 or COBOL "crash course."

- provision of the computer program or files to be converted by a specified date;
- performance of acceptance testing (however, the customer will want to specify any obligations of the supplier to assist);[15]
- timely reviews of any deliverables or work product submitted by the supplier;
- provision of internal resources to support the supplier's work; however, customers will want to put a reasonable limit on this—if possible, the extent should be documented in the agreement;
- provision of documentation and specifications for the applications to be converted;
- provision of facilities (*i.e.*, office space, LAN, etc.) and equipment (*i.e.*, test environment); however, the agreement should specify whether the supplier will be responsible for providing work stations to any supplier personnel working at the customer's premises;
- provision of up-to-date source code that corresponds to the system being used in production and that is free of material compiling errors;
- responsibility for maintaining adequate backups of the program and data files to be converted; and
- provision of a project plan for implementation of the remediated system.

While not intended to be an obligation under the agreement, it may be advisable for customers (or even suppliers) to establish a baseline of the system to be converted prior to any conversion activities. Such a baseline may be extremely important in the event a dispute arises down the road.

The supplier will want the customer to obtain all required consents needed to permit the supplier to access, use and/or modify third-party software programs.[16] Customers will need to review applicable agreements to ascertain their rights to modify third-party software and their ability to use third-party solution providers to make any required modifications.[17]

Consents from owners of any software licensed from third parties may be required in some circumstances. Even if the software being modified is owned by the customer, the supplier may require access to or use of

---

15 Suppliers will want customers to perform adequate and thorough testing of remediated systems.

16 Ideally, a supplier will want a customer to represent and warrant that the supplier's use of the customer's data, software systems and other technology will not infringe the rights of any other person.

17 Some suppliers may request the right to review such agreements themselves. However, in most cases, such agreements will be protected by non-disclosure obligations and therefore it may not be possible to provide access to these agreements.

third-party software licensed to the customer (for instance, development tools, database management systems, etc.).[18] Year 2000 solution providers will likely want an indemnity from the customer in respect of any claims for copyright infringement brought against them by owners of any such third-party software licensed to the customer. Suppliers may want a right to refuse to perform any obligation that will result in willful copyright infringement.

14.5 MANAGEMENT

Each party should appoint a person to represent that party and to manage and coordinate the day to day activities of its personnel and ensure that party's performance of its obligations under the agreement. This may be a "project sponsor" in the case of the customer and a "project manager" in the case of the supplier. Ideally, the project manager's position should be structured to provide sufficient independence to allow him or her to question any slippage or other issues.

The customer will want the supplier, through its representative, to keep the customer informed on a timely basis, regarding the progress of the project, the provision of services by the supplier, and any delays or other problems encountered or anticipated. These should also be documented on a monthly basis in a written status report. Each such report should review the progress achieved in the preceding month and should list any failure or deficiency of either party that occurred during such period. These reports should be due within a specified period (*i.e.*, five or ten business days) following the end of the applicable month.

Successful completion of a Year 2000 project involving an outside supplier will usually require a great deal of cooperation between the customer and the supplier. The need for open communications and coordination of services between the supplier and the customer suggests the need for a joint project management committee, particularly in the case of large projects. Such a committee should also be beneficial in helping to settle disputes that may arise between the parties.

Where the formation of a joint project management committee is contemplated, the agreement should specify the composition of such a committee and how often it will meet. However, notwithstanding the formation of such a committee, customers will want to ensure that the agreement contains

---

18 The same issue applies to the test environment and to the conversion environment.

clear obligations on the part of the supplier for the successful and timely completion of the project. Customers will also want to ensure that their participation in such a committee will not result in a sharing of responsibility for a failure of the supplier to complete its obligations on a timely basis.

14.6 PRICING AND PAYMENT TERMS

The fee structure should be clearly documented. Rates, limits, penalties and incentives should be set out.[19] While obtaining the lowest price may be important to customers, it is suggested that they also consider how the pricing mechanism will affect the behaviour of the service provider.

Customers frequently do not appreciate that a fixed price contract for a fixed amount of resources does not limit their risk. A fixed price arrangement is only achieved if the customer is to receive a specified result rather than a specified amount of effort from a supplier.[20]

Where a fixed price arrangement is desired by a customer, the project should be divided into phases and fixed prices negotiated for phases that follow the assessment phase (*i.e.*, after both parties have a better understanding of the work that will be involved). However, a fixed price arrangement will likely require a stricter definition of the services to be performed by the supplier and greater control by the supplier over the remediation solutions that are used.

The agreement should specify when fees will be payable. Customers will want to tie payments to successful completion of milestones applicable to the services.[21] Suppliers will prefer monthly invoicing for services rendered or an apportionment of the total amount due under the agreement.

In some cases, supplies may be required. If furnished by the supplier, these may be charged at "cost" plus an administrative charge (*e.g.*, 10-15%). However, customers will want to ensure that these will be provided at the supplier's actual cost plus the administrative charge (as opposed to the

---

19 Setting rates in advance may be very difficult for suppliers in this type of labour market.

20 However, guarantees of results will be much more difficult to secure in contracting for these services. A fixed price "deliverable" contract may be more achievable where the supplier has a pricing incentive.

21 In other words, suppliers will want to "front load" payments, for instance to individual deliverables, while customers will want to "backload" payments pending a final system acceptance test.

supplier's "standard cost" or other ambiguous definition plus the administrative charge).

The agreement may provide that the supplier will be entitled to late payment charges. However, the customer will not want to agree that the supplier has the right to suspend services based on a failure on the part of the customer to pay invoices on a timely basis, particularly if the amount of the invoices is in dispute. In such cases, suppliers will want customers to at least pay any amounts not in dispute when such amounts are due. Supplier may also want customers, upon request, to deposit any amounts in dispute into an escrow account.

Customers will want the agreement to set out the supplier's time and materials rate, and reasonable limits as to how often and by what percentage such rate may be increased. However, suppliers entering into longer term contracts will want to factor in the increasing cost of personnel and will want to incorporate escalation provisions that permit them to raise prices during the term of the contract.

The following pricing issues should also be considered:

♦ whether the customer will have a right to withhold a percentage of payments due pending timely and successful completion of specific deliverables and/or the entire project;
♦ whether the price being charged to the customer should reflect whether the customer is buying a particular result (*i.e.*, a Year 2000 compliant system), a process, or simply a supply of specified resources;
♦ whether withholding tax needs to be withheld if the services are to be provided by non-residents.

14.7 ACCEPTANCE TESTING

Where the services to be provided include conversion of customer software, the agreement should set out which party will be responsible for testing the deliverables[22] and permit sufficient time to effect such testing and the correction of any errors or deficiencies that are identified.

---

22 Acceptance testing will typically be performed by the customer with the assistance of the supplier. Suppliers will typically want the customer to be responsible for preparing the test data.

The supplier may seek to limit its obligation to correct errors to those that are reported to the supplier during a specified warranty period following delivery of corrected program code or completion of the acceptance test. From the customer's perspective, a long warranty period (*i.e.*, one which extends for a period past the year 2000) is preferable in order to address errors that are not identified until the program is used for production purposes during the year 2000.[23] A customer will also want to ensure that corrections will be made promptly and that such warranty obligations will survive the normal termination of the agreement.

Timely completion of acceptance testing by the customer will be an important factor in meeting tight schedules for Year 2000 projects. The supplier will want the acceptance test period to start within a specified period following delivery. Where this is the case, the customer should ensure that it will in fact have the required personnel and any inter-related systems available within that time frame. The customer may want the supplier to provide a certain period of advance notification prior to actual delivery in order to provide the customer with additional time to mobilize resources.

The agreement should also set out the length of the acceptance test period. An important consideration when setting out an acceptance test timetable or time frame is that revised programs may need to be integrated or tested with other customer components.

An acceptance testing procedure will likely require the customer to provide the supplier with notice, within a short period of the completion of the acceptance test, advising the supplier that either the deliverable complies with the acceptance test criteria (*i.e.*, conformance with specifications and no major errors or defects) and is therefore accepted by the customer, or that the deliverable does not comply and is rejected by the customer. Suppliers will want the agreement to provide that if such notice is not provided within the time stipulated, then the deliverable shall be deemed to have been accepted by the customer. Customers will want acceptance to be based on delivery by the customer of a certificate acknowledging successful completion of the acceptance test.

Any notice rejecting the deliverable may need to include reasonable details concerning the deficiencies claimed by the customer. Customers will want the supplier to correct such deficiencies as soon as possible and in any event, no later than a specified period after receipt of the notice. Retesting

---

23 Certain situations may not have been contemplated in the preparation of the test data for the acceptance test.

by the customer will be required following the making of corrections by the supplier.

The acceptance testing procedure should anticipate that the deliverable will contain a certain percentage of errors that will need to be corrected prior to acceptance. A customer may want to provide for a maximum number or percentage of such errors in order to ensure a certain level of quality by the supplier. A customer may also want to ensure that some limit is placed on how long the supplier has to correct any deficiencies notwithstanding multiple rounds of testing by the customer and correction by the supplier. As an alternative, the agreement may limit the number of permitted rede-liveries.

Suppliers will want to set the threshold for acceptance at a level less than "perfect tender." For instance, some may want the customer to accept the deliverable as long as there are no "material" errors present. The supplier would still be responsible for correcting any minor errors following accep-tance. In response to such an approach, customers may want to propose two payment milestones. The first at acceptance and the second following correction of any minor deficiencies that are identified during acceptance testing.

Another issue that may need to be addressed is whether the customer may terminate the entire agreement in the event that certain deliverables are not accepted by the customer. Some suppliers will want the remedy of termi-nation reserved for only a failure of those deliverables that are mission critical to the success of the conversion project.

14.8 RIGHTS, WARRANTIES AND OWNERSHIP

In the event the contract terminates, the customer will want ownership of all work product so that it can continue work without delay. Customers will want the agreement to specify that all work, including work in progress, belongs to and will be left with the customer (notwithstanding the reason for termination or if the agreement is terminated early). This may include:

♦ records and logs;
♦ work-in-progress;
♦ completed deliverables (including converted programs and data files and associated documentation); and

♦ copies of licences applicable to any tools or other software that are proprietary to the supplier or acquired from third parties for use in the customer's project (particularly if the latter were paid for by the customer). Supplier tools will be very important to the customer's ability to move forward with its Year 2000 project. The foregoing should include both code analysis tools and project control tools and data (for instance, database templates, data collected during the assessment phase, and other project management data).

Customers will want the supplier to acknowledge that it will not acquire any proprietary rights to, or any lien, encumbrance or other proprietary interest against the foregoing (other than the supplier's tools). Customers will also want the supplier to provide the customer with reasonable access to, including providing copies of, all such information and media in the possession of the supplier. However, suppliers may want assurances that all services delivered will be paid for in full before resolving these ownership issues.

The agreement should include appropriate intellectual property warranties and related indemnities for breach thereof:

♦ From the supplier, in respect of conversion work performed and all deliverables. As well, customers will want the supplier to warrant that it has the right to use any third-party conversion tools to be used to assist in diagnosis or conversion and to indemnify the customer against any damages or costs due to breach of such warranty. Where applicable, a waiver of moral rights should be obtained from the supplier's staff.
♦ From the customer, in respect of program code to be converted and access to be provided to the supplier.[24] However, customers will want to ensure that they do not over-indemnify. For instance, customers will want their indemnity to exclude activities that are beyond the scope of the suppliers' obligations under the agreement.

Customers will want the supplier to warrant that the deliverables (*i.e.*, the converted programs) will be Year 2000 compliant. However, customers should keep in mind that warranties regarding the quality of services to be provided and even explicit Year 2000 warranties will not be of much use if

---

24 Suppliers that are to be provided with data from a customer located in a jurisdiction with data protection or privacy legislation (such as the Province of Quebec in Canada or certain European Community countries) may also want to consider obtaining an indemnity in respect of any violation of such legislation that may occur by the supplier in carrying out the customer's instructions.

the supplier is well protected against liability in the contract. The ability to actually collect on the warranty should also be considered.

Explicit Year 2000 compliance warranties in respect of Year 2000 conversions were relatively easy to obtain in 1996 and in early 1997. They are now difficult to obtain from major suppliers. Suppliers may be particularly reluctant to provide warranties where encapsulation techniques are utilized to address Year 2000 problems in a particular application.[25]

In the case where a supplier is performing development work (*i.e.*, writing a new program) or replacing a customer's system with a new system being provided by the supplier, then it would be reasonable to expect an explicit Year 2000 warranty. However, suppliers may want to limit these warranties to specified periods (*e.g.*, 60 or 90 days). Extended warranties may be available for an additional fee.

Customers will also want to include some basic warranties in respect of the services to be provided by the supplier. For instance, customers may want the supplier to warrant that the services will be performed by competent personnel in a professional manner and in accordance with general industry standards. It should be noted, however, that the Year 2000 remediation industry is a new field that may lack clear established standards.

Customers may also seek to have the supplier warrant that its personnel, or at least its key personnel, have experience in prior Year 2000 engagements and are familiar and proficient in the use of Year 2000 assessment and conversion tools, including any specific tools whose use is contemplated in the agreement. Suppliers may also be asked to warrant the correctness of advice they provide, and where the supplier is responsible for performing an inventory of applications, a warranty that such inventory is complete.

14.9 LIABILITY/REMEDIES

The issue of remedies will likely be an area of significant negotiation because many Year 2000 service providers are not willing to accept the economic risk of failure. Suppliers will want to insert an exclusive remedy provision in the agreement. However, it may be difficult for customers to

---

25 Encapsulation methods involve "wrapping" a non-compliant program with a new program that performs any required translations on date data that is transferred to or received from the non- compliant program. The program code of the non-compliant program is not modified.

accept such a provision because unlike a traditional IT project where problems can be rectified and the project redelivered until it works, redelivery may not be a viable option in respect of a Year 2000 project if such redelivery cannot be made prior to the Year 2000 or other date after which the customer's system will experience a Year 2000 failure.

The supplier may seek to exclude its liability for any loss or damage caused by a delay in meeting any milestones specified in the agreement. While it may be difficult for a customer to obtain a supplier's agreement to assume liability for all economic losses resulting from a delay, customers will want to provide an incentive for the supplier to meet agreed upon milestone dates (or provide a disincentive for a failure to meet such dates).

Customers who are contracting for large scale Year 2000 projects are insisting on financial penalties (*i.e.*, liquidated damages) from the supplier in the event key milestones are not met. The following design considerations in the development of liquidated damage provisions may make them more acceptable for suppliers:

◆ liquidated damages should bear a relationship to the extra costs that a customer must assume to remedy the delay;
◆ liquidated damages may be structured based on a graduated scale where the amount is increased based on the length of the delay; and
◆ the applicability and the significance of liquidated damages may be differentiated depending on importance of the delayed component.

It will not likely be easy for customers to negotiate meaningful liquidated damage provisions given the current and anticipated future demand for Year 2000 conversion services, particularly from established suppliers. It may be easier to obtain the agreement of the supplier to provide liquidated damages if the supplier is given something in return. For instance, both parties could agree that the specified liquidated damages will be the sole and exclusive remedy during a specified late period (*i.e.*, the customer will be precluded from pursuing other remedies during this specified period).

Customers should also be aware that penalty provisions are not enforceable in some jurisdictions. A liquidated damages provision should therefore be drafted as a fair and reasonable estimate of damages rather than as a penalty. Careful attention to drafting of such provisions is required to ensure enforceability.

When confronted with a customer's demand for the inclusion of liquidated damages, many suppliers will ask for corresponding financial incentives for early delivery. In some cases, early delivery of a component from one supplier may not be of benefit to a customer, particularly if other necessary and inter-related components to be provided by the customer or other suppliers are not ready. However, where early delivery can provide a benefit to the customer then the provision of incentives may be in the interest of both parties.

A customer will want to ensure that it at least has as a remedy the ability to require the supplier to correct any deficiencies promptly (and preferably, at no additional cost) that are identified. Customers will also want to specify a specific time period for correction of any identified deficiencies.

Suppliers will want to include standard exclusions on indirect and consequential damages. They will also likely want to include limitations on their total liability to the amount paid by the customer under the agreement or a specified monetary amount.

Anticipated shortages, and the resulting hikes in fees, may encourage some suppliers to break agreements to secure higher paying work elsewhere. If penalties are limited to fees paid under the agreement, or that are paid in a certain period preceding breach, it may be commercially attractive for a supplier to break the agreement. Customers may therefore want to ensure that the penalty clauses and any limitations on damages are adequate to act as a sufficient deterrent to breach. A prudent customer will want to take as many steps as possible to ensure that their agreement will be the last one that the supplier will breach.

14.10 TERMINATION

Customers will want to ensure that they have the ability to terminate quickly in the event things are not working out. Customers may also want the supplier to provide post-termination assistance in such cases. For instance, the supplier's personnel may be required to remain on site or to be available for consultation by the customer.

Following termination of the agreement, customers may want the supplier to return, or if agreed to by the customer in writing, to destroy, all information or media remaining in its possession that contains proprietary customer information. In the event the supplier is permitted to retain any such material, customers will want it to be placed under an obligation of non-disclosure and restricted use.

14.11 DISPUTE RESOLUTION

The agreement should include a framework that can be used by the parties to settle any disputes in a quick and cost-effective manner, and while work continues. Customers will typically want the agreement to include a formal escalation procedure and require use of alternative dispute resolution in lieu of litigation.

Furthermore, the customer will want to ensure that the supplier will be required to continue its performance notwithstanding a disagreement and/or resort to the dispute resolution mechanism. Customers may therefore want to incorporate a provision such as the following:

> During resort to the foregoing dispute resolution procedures, the Supplier shall diligently proceed with the performance of the terms of this Agreement with the existing complement of staff provided. At no time during this Agreement shall the Supplier remove or replace any or all of its resources; doing so would cause an immediate and irreparable delay in the project and will result in a breach of this Agreement.[26]

The requirement to utilize the dispute resolution mechanism (including arbitration) should provide an exemption, and permit either party to commence a legal action, in order to prevent the disclosure of confidential information or to protect a proprietary right. The Agreement should specify which jurisdiction's laws and courts (or arbitration rules) will apply in the event of a dispute. The choice of jurisdiction may have important implications, including potentially limiting the availability of class action proceedings or the types of awards that may be available to a party.

14.12 OTHER ISSUES

(a) Insurance

In some situations it may be possible for customers to utilize insurance in order to obtain greater protection. Customers may prefer to contract only with Year 2000 service providers who are covered by errors and omissions ("E&O") insurance. However, it is likely that companies providing Year

---

26 A supplier will want the customer to continue to make payments as a condition to its agreement to such a provision.

2000 services will experience increasing difficulty in obtaining such insurance due to the high-risk nature of their business.

Errors and omissions insurance is generally "claims based," which means that coverage will only apply if the service provider is insured at the time that the claim is made rather than at the time when the error or omission occurs. Therefore, it will be important for customers to obtain assurances that the insurance will remain in effect until the last day on which any failure could occur. One approach could be to require prepayment of the policy. The customer may also want to consider obtaining the agreement of the insurance company that the policy will not be cancelled or altered in respect to the scope of coverage without notice and/or consent of the customer. It will also be important to carefully review the scope of any such policy, including applicable exclusions, to ensure that it will actually offer protection.

(b) Confidentiality

Customers will want to ensure that the supplier will treat all programs, data or other material furnished to the supplier, as well as other confidential or proprietary material that the supplier obtains access to in the course of performing the services, as confidential, and will not use or disclose such information other than as required to perform its obligations under the agreement. Likewise, suppliers will want to ensure that the customer will similarly treat as confidential, techniques and know-how utilized by them in performing the services.

Customers should keep in mind that certain information they possess may be subject to non-disclosure obligations that preclude disclosure to a supplier (or other party other than an employee of the customer) notwithstanding the agreement of the supplier to keep such information confidential.

(c) Use of Foreign Service Providers

Some organizations may decide to retain the services of an overseas Year 2000 service provider to assist with conversions. For instance, India, the Philippines and South Africa provide access to less expensive programmers. Some of the concerns that would need to be addressed before engaging the services of offshore service providers are:

◆ **Security.** Customers will want service providers to use encryption and passwords, and to implement proper security measures to protect valuable corporate programs and information. However, customers will need to review any software or technology being exported from Canada or the United States to ensure compliance with export controls. For instance, software containing cryptographic functions may require an export permit or confirmation of an applicable exemption.

◆ **Communications.** High speed network links are only one issue. Communication between people is also important. Ideally, customers will want the offshore service provider to provide the customer with the services of a full-time, on-site project manager.

◆ **Resources.** Customers will want to ensure that foreign service providers have the internal resources to manage a Year 2000 conversion from initial planning to final testing. Customers will want to avoid accepting assurances that the foreign service provider will be able to adequately subcontract testing or other obligations to another service provider.

◆ **Political.** Engaging the services of a foreign service provider must be handled delicately. Customers will not want to attract negative publicity by appearing to export high-paying jobs overseas.

◆ **Suitability of project.** Not all projects are suitable for outsourcing to offshore service providers. The prospects for success are best when requirements can be frozen. Offshore outsourcing may not work well for companies that may want to enhance or downsize mainframe applications to a client-server architecture at the same time as they address Year 2000 issues.

◆ **Governing law provisions.** Special attention should also be given to the governing law provisions contained in any contracts made with foreign Year 2000 service providers. Customers will want to have any dispute under the agreement interpreted by the courts in their own country and to have the foreign service provider submit to the jurisdiction of such courts. Customers should also review the following:

 – whether the foreign service provider has any assets in the local jurisdiction (particularly ones that are likely to remain);
 – whether a judgment of a court in the customer's jurisdiction is enforceable in the service provider's jurisdiction; and
 – whether the foreign jurisdiction where the service provider is located will respect the choice of law provision contained in the contract.

◆ **Privacy and Transborder Data Flow Restrictions.** Customers should ensure that any data that must be exchanged between the customer and the foreign service provider will not breach any privacy or transborder data flow restrictions. Customers in regulated industries, including banking, should also review any restrictions applicable to processing of certain types of information outside of the jurisdiction.

♦ **Withholding Tax.** Customers may be required to deduct, withhold and remit tax to the relevant taxing authority (*i.e.*, Revenue Canada or the IRS) in respect of payments made to non-residents to the extent such fees cover services performed within the jurisdiction (*i.e.*, Canada or the United States).

15

Mergers, Acquisitions and Financings

A company's ability to demonstrate its Year 2000-readiness will become an essential prerequisite for many business transactions. Just as environmental due diligence is now routinely required for most commercial real estate transactions, Year 2000 due diligence is likely to be seen as a basic requirement for financings, mergers, acquisitions, public offerings, asset and stock purchases, and other business deals that are the lifeblood of growing companies.[1]

15.1 THE ISSUES

The use of Year 2000 warranties, and the conduct of due diligence in respect of the Year 2000 problem, has become an important component of any significant corporate transaction such as acquisitions, mergers and major financings.

Vendors and companies looking for financing should commence their Year 2000 compliance programs well in advance of the transaction. A failure to resolve a Year 2000 issue can delay the transaction or result in a devaluation of the value attributed to the company by potential purchasers, lenders and investors.

Some companies may decide to deal with their Year 2000 problems by putting problem product lines or even entire divisions up for sale.[2] A party

---

1 Steven H. Goldberg, "How Lawyers Can Help Meet the Year 2000 Challenge" at <http://www.comlinks.com/legal/gold3.htm>.

2 According to Peter Brown, co-chair of the American Bar Association's Computer Litigation Committee, a number of companies are already disposing of existing divisions in anticipation of Year 2000 problems. See Joanna Glasner's "Millennium Bug Sparks Lawsuit" *Law Journal EXTRA!* (August 12, 1997).

contemplating an acquisition should deal with this issue as part of its due diligence and should incorporate appropriate Year 2000-related representations and warranties into the acquisition agreement. Additional investigation and testing may also be prudent.

A similar due diligence review, and use of appropriate representations and warranties, should also be considered as part of any major financing. To the extent that a company seeking financing may be exposed to substantial costs to deal with the Year 2000 problem, or the potential for significant legal liability or business interruption, and corresponding loss of value, due to a Year 2000 problem, an investor or financial institution will wish to obtain a proper assessment of that risk before investing in the company.

Canada's Task Force Year 2000 recommended that all lending institutions, whether federally or provincially regulated, should require the availability of a formal Year 2000 action plan from corporate borrowers as a prerequisite for loans (with a target implementation date of April 1, 1998).[3] The Task Force also recommended that all levels of government should make the existence of a formal Year 2000 action plan a condition for any company to secure grants, contributions, loans and loan guarantees from government programs.[4]

Numerous business failures are being projected, which can lead to a high proportion of loan losses unless such lenders take steps to investigate the Year 2000 readiness of their major commercial borrowers. The Year 2000 readiness of customers should also be of concern to suppliers who extend large unsecured trade credit.

The Canadian Bankers Association formed a Credit Risk Task Force to examine the banks' as lenders to customers who may experience Year 2000 problems.[5] The Task Force is considering appropriate processes for dealing with Year 2000 issues as part of their risk assessment and annual loan review. A number of Canadian financial institutions have implemented the use of Year 2000 reviews as part of their credit risk evaluation procedures.[6]

---

3 Task Force Year 2000, "A Call for Action" (February, 1998) Recommendation 3.

4 Task Force Year 2000 Recommendation 11.

5 It appears that this Task Force was set up following concerns expressed by the Office of the Superintendent of Financial Institutions regarding the exposure of Canadian financial institutions to customers who may default under loans due to Year 2000 problems.

6 The elements to be reviewed as part of a credit risk evaluation are likely to include: (i) awareness; (ii) inventory of affected equipment; (iii) external supplier risks; (iv) existence of a formal plan; (v) staff and budget needs; (vi) testing; and (vii) date targets. See Rick Davitt, "Risk Management of Client and Counterparty Year 2000 Risk in the

Financial institutions in the United States are expected to undertake similar reviews. The president of the Federal Reserve Bank of New York, in remarks before the Annual Membership Meeting of the Institute of International Finance (Hong Kong, September 21, 1997), urged that underwriting standards should require consideration of how customers are addressing the Year 2000 issue and that credit officers should monitor the progress of customers who rely on technology on a regular basis.

The Federal Financial Institution Examination Council ("FFIEC") advised federally supervised financial institutions in the United States that "[the] approach of the Year 2000 creates potentially adverse effects on the credit worthiness of borrowers. Corporate customers who have not considered Year 2000 issues may experience a disruption in business, resulting in potential financial difficulties affecting their creditworthiness. Financial institutions should develop processes to identify, assess, and control the potential Year 2000 credit risk in their lending and investment portfolio."[7]

Representations and warranties contained in commercial agreements for acquisitions and financings have focused on the Year 2000 compliance of the company's computers systems and equipment. However, such provisions need to be accompanied by adequate due diligence to address the Year 2000 compliance of all of the products sold to customers and the level of diligence the company has expended in ensuring that its major suppliers, customers and business partners are prepared for the next millennium. Additional representations and warranties should be considered following a review of the results of such investigations.

It may be desirable to engage the expertise of third parties with appropriate expertise to assist with such investigations. Such consultants should be requested to provide certification of their investigations. However, it is not likely that they will provide a certification that the company is compliant. Their report would likely be limited to a description of the investigations conducted and results obtained.

Where a company is unable to warrant that its systems are fully compliant, and where any Year 2000 warranties focus on activities the company is undertaking to address Year 2000 issues, lenders and investors will likely

---

Financial Services Industry" *The Year 2000 Computer Problem*, Insight Information Inc. (Toronto, February 19-20, 1998).

7 See Federal Financial Institutions Examination Council, "Safety and Soundness Guidelines Concerning the Year 2000 Business Risk" (December 17, 1997) at <http://www.ffiec.gov/federal.htm>.

want to incorporate an on-going right to confirm that a company's Year 2000 compliance efforts are proceeding in accordance with any agreed-upon plan. Lenders and investors may also want to explicitly provide for treatment of any failure to meet the milestones contained in the company's Year 2000 remediation plans as an event of default.

15.2 SAMPLE LANGUAGE FOR A YEAR 2000 WARRANTY

The following is a general representation and warranty that addresses the internal Year 2000 compliance of the products currently being used in the business of a target company, and that can be used by a purchaser, lender or investor as a starting point for an agreement to purchase a business, or to provide financing to a business. It is broad in nature and would need to be customized to the specific circumstances of the transaction or nature of the business. It does not, however, address issues related to products sold to customers or the efforts conducted by the target company to investigate the Year 2000 compliance of its suppliers, customers or business partners:

> [Vendor] represents and warrants that all computer software and all hardware and other products incorporating embedded software or microcode, used in the business of the [Vendor] (the "Systems"), including but not limited to the programs listed in Appendix A, are "year 2000 compliant" and, more specifically, (i) are designed to be used prior to, during and after the calendar year 2000 A.D. without error relating to date data, and shall operate transparently to the user during such time periods, (ii) are capable of operating without error relating to the product of date data which represents or references different centuries or more than one century, (iii) are designed such that all data fields, date-related user interfaces and other interfaces include the indication of century, and (iv) correctly recognize the year 2000 as a leap year. [Vendor] also represents and warrants that all data associated with the Systems to be used after the year 1999 and all historical data required for regulatory or business purposes after the year 1999 have been converted so as to be accessible by the Systems.[8]

A vendor, borrower or investee, would likely find it necessary to limit the scope of the representation and warranty based on the actual circumstances of the company and the extent to which it is fully aware of any Year 2000 or other date-related problems with its systems.

---

8 Part (iii) should be revised if a windowing technique is utilized to achieve Year 2000 compliance, as an explicit indication of century would not be used in such circumstances.

Additional representations and warranties should be considered, including that:

♦ the company has implemented a Year 2000 project, along with a detailed listing of the various components and the tasks to be performed (*e.g.*, review of products being resold, risk of disruptions to supply, EDI, key dependencies on third parties including customers, material contracts, potential liabilities, insurance, statements made to third parties, etc.);
♦ all costs associated with addressing the Year 2000 problem have been incorporated into budgets, forecasts, projections and financial statements; and
♦ the company has complied with disclosure obligations, including any disclosure obligations imposed by securities legislation, regulators and/or stock exchanges, if applicable.

Representations and warranties would need to be accompanied by an appropriate indemnity to deal with any costs, expenses or liability that may be incurred by the target company and any resulting depreciation in the value of the investment or loan. It may be appropriate to have the indemnity backed by a performance bond or guarantee by the parent. A purchaser should also consider a hold back of a portion of the purchase price until the company's Year 2000 remediation efforts are complete or until a period after the year 2000.

15.3 DUE DILIGENCE

Part of the due diligence relating to Year 2000 compliance in an acquisition, financing or other major transaction should include a review of the following (some of which may also need to be incorporated into representations and warranties):

♦ what computer systems are used in the company's business;
♦ whether the company has conducted an inventory of its systems (including any equipment or products that utilize embedded logic that may be susceptible to a Year 2000 date problem) and a full technical review of the Year 2000 compliance of such systems;
♦ whether the company has a Year 2000 compliance program and a plan to address the issue—the plan should be reviewed to confirm that it is realistic and that the company is meeting its targets;

♦ in the case of compliant systems, whether their operation or use may be adversely affected because they operate in conjunction with systems that are not compliant or that are no longer compatible due to remediation work performed on such systems or the company's systems.[9] This will require investigating the compliance of electronic trading partners and, where applicable, agreement on the interpretation of any two-digit year formats that will continue to be used;

♦ what recourses the company may have against third party suppliers under various agreements with respect to non-compliant systems;

♦ what costs the company might incur in order to become Year 2000 compliant and whether these have been factored into budgets and projections that are being relied upon;

♦ whether any write-downs for non-compliant assets have been reflected in the company's financial statements;

♦ whether major customers, suppliers and other trading "partners" of the company are Year 2000 compliant (or are taking adequate and reasonable steps to ensure compliance), and what problems the company may encounter if they are not compliant;

♦ what steps the company takes to ensure that all new acquisitions are Year 2000 compliant;

♦ what recourse third parties may have against the company as a result of the provision of products or services, currently and in the past, which may be susceptible to a Year 2000 problem;

♦ what statements have been made to customers, suppliers, auditors, regulators and other third parties, by or on behalf of the company, in respect of Year 2000 compliance;

♦ whether any reports addressing the Year 2000 compliance of the company, its products or otherwise addressing its potential exposure to the Year 2000 problem, have been prepared by the company, its parent or by other parties—if this is the case, then copies of the report, *including draft versions*, should be reviewed;

♦ what programs the company has implemented to retain key employees associated with its Year 2000 remediation efforts;

♦ what contingency plans have been developed;

♦ what insurance is in place and to what extent will it be applicable to possible Year 2000 problems; and

---

9 Two systems may be made Year 2000 compliant using different methods, and while each will be Year 2000 compliant, they may not be Year 2000 compliant or may not correctly transfer date information when used together. It would therefore be desirable to obtain a representation and warranty that all systems used by the company will accurately exchange date data with, and will accurately process date data exchanged with, the systems of all customers and suppliers with which the company currently exchanges or has any current plans to exchange information.

◆ whether any plans and proposals (including any draft versions) have been prepared by the company or third parties in respect of Year 2000 remediation to be performed by the company.

A purchaser, lender or investor may also wish to review copies of all requests made by or on behalf of the company, to its key suppliers, customers and trading partners for information relating to the recipient's Year 2000 compliance status and efforts, as well as comparable requests received by the company. In the case of an acquisition, if the company may have sold products in the past that were not compliant, the parties may wish to allocate responsibility in respect of any potential claims that may arise.

15.4 IDENTIFYING HIGH RISK COMPANIES

Certain characteristics may indicate greater vulnerability to Year 2000 problems:[10]

◆ companies that have grown through numerous recent acquisitions;[11]
◆ companies whose key systems utilize custom software or were internally designed;
◆ companies that are dependent on a large number of suppliers, and where a failure of a small number of suppliers may result in a major disruption (*e.g.*, automobile manufacturers);
◆ companies that have substantial contracts with or dependency on alliance partners;
◆ companies that utilize, manufacture, sell or maintain products where a potential failure or malfunction may result in personal injury or property damage (such as medical equipment);
◆ companies that provide maintenance of third party products (such as alarm systems and cash registers);
◆ companies that must carry high levels of accounts receivables or that provide financing to many other companies;

---

10 The following are generalizations. The specific circumstances of particular companies will need to be considered.
11 Such companies may have inherited a large assortment of different systems that will further complicate any Year 2000 remediation efforts. According to an article in the March 4, 1998 issue of the *Philadelphia Inquirer*, such problems were a major factor in convincing one bank, CoreState, to sell to another, First Union. According to CoreState's chairman, Terry Larsen, after a dozen years of making acquisitions, its computer systems had evolved into a patchwork of makes and models and CoreState faced a substantial risk and exposure in trying to address the Year 2000 problem in respect of those systems. First Union, on the other hand, was much further along in its remediation program.

- companies that are highly reliant on the use of technology and which may not be able to revert to manual systems and procedures even on a temporary basis;
- companies where an interruption in service provided to customers has the potential to result in significant losses to such customers (*e.g.* security monitoring services);
- companies that are dependent on key customers and/or suppliers located in foreign countries that are not addressing the Year 2000 problem as aggressively as in North America/United Kingdom/Australia.

Other characteristics that may be of concern include:[12]

- small and medium sized businesses that may have the same problems as large corporations but may lack the financial or human resources to address them in time;
- borrowers who borrow based on asset value and where the financial institution depends on accurate accounts receivable aging lists;
- retailers that are highly reliant on automated inventory systems and controls;
- companies with outsourced billings, payroll and collection processes; and
- companies with substantial owned or leased commercial real estate.

---

12 Rick Davitt, "Risk Management of Client and Counterparty Year 2000 Risk in the Financial Services Industry" *The Year 2000 Computer Problem*, Insight information Inc., February 19-20, 1998 (Toronto), at page 16. List courtesy of Robert Morris Associates.

16

Implementing a Year 2000 Compliance Project

It is important for organizations to establish a Year 2000 compliance program in order to reduce their exposure to the Year 2000 problem and establish a due diligence defence against claims by third parties that may arise in the future. It may also be necessary to establish such programs in order to comply with recommendations of regulators.[1]

16.1 YEAR 2000 STEERING COMMITTEE

A Year 2000 Steering Committee should be established with senior management representation from the various business units. The role of the Year 2000 Steering Committee would be to manage the process and:

♦ identify mission critical systems[2]
♦ audit legal and operational risks
♦ approve standards
♦ develop and implement the corporate Year 2000 communication plan
♦ develop and implement the company's Year 2000 compliance strategy
♦ allocate appropriate resources and implement measures to retain key personnel
♦ monitor Year 2000 activities

---

1 A number of regulators have provided guidance on steps to be followed by their regulated entities.
2 Some organizations are finding that there is insufficient time remaining to ensure that all systems can be made or confirmed to be compliant and are focusing their efforts on a smaller number of key or "mission critical" systems. Some systems may take precedent for "real time" operational or legal reasons. If not all systems can be converted in time then prioritization should be made by, or at least confirmed by, senior management.

A senior executive should also be appointed and given primary responsibility to ensure the company's Year 2000 compliance. The leadership of a high level executive is required to ensure that the project is given the required priority and cooperation throughout the company. Responsibility for the Year 2000 problem should not simply be left with the information technology department. Resolution of Year 2000 problems is likely to require substantial financial and human resources, and may necessitate deferral or cancellation of other business initiatives.[3]

16.2 YEAR 2000 PROJECT MANAGEMENT

> [t]here should also be a strong Y2K central team to coordinate and monitor all Y2K activities, provide tools, contract resources, develop standards, and establish processes.[4]

One component of a Year 2000 compliance program should be the establishment of a Year 2000 project management office. This office should establish effective project management with priorities, deadlines and appropriate follow-up action. It is important to recognize that unlike other types of projects, there is no flexibility in the deadlines for achieving compliance for a Year 2000 compliance project.

The Year 2000 project will need to include the following components:

◆ time tables
◆ bench marks
◆ reporting
◆ contingency plans[5]
◆ audit guidelines

In structuring an internal Year 2000 team, companies need to bring people together from many functional groups:

---

3 *Challenge 2000: Executive Guide to Year 2000 Computing Solutions*—Frequently Asked Questions <http://www.itac.ca/policy/survival>.
4 NASD Notice to Members (No. 97-16). NASD stated that one lesson it learned and wished to share with its members was that there should be a strong Year 2000 central team to coordinate and monitor all Year 2000 activities, provide tools, contract resources, develop standards and establish processes.
5 In a Notice to Members (No. 97-16), NASD advised:
   "It is likely that unforeseen events will occur that may affect a Y2K project's ability to meet its January 1, 2000 deadline. Consequently, a contingency plan addressing "worst case scenarios" must be developed, preferably during the planning and assessment phase of the project."

- line of business/user groups[6]
- information technology
- legal
- internal audit[7]
- risk management
- supply chain management
- sales
- business and system analysts
- external service providers[8]

Companies need to consider what material they can provide to demonstrate their Year 2000 compliance to other parties. Contractual warranties alone may not be sufficient for some customers of critical products or services. Many suppliers impose significant limits on their liability. Furthermore, there may not be much chance of recovery under contractual warranties if a non-compliant supplier goes out of business or is sued by a large number of customers.

Year 2000 activities should be fully documented. Some companies are implementing a mechanism to track employee time and other costs incurred in respect of Year 2000 compliance. Such tracking would be useful to demonstrate due diligence in the event of a future lawsuit against the company.

Periodic independent reviews of the project need to be carried out by designated functional units within the organization (*e.g.*, internal audit, compliance, supervisory specialists) to ensure that the project is on time and will be effective. Systems should be certified compliant by an independent control unit within the institution and the relevant business units as the development and acceptance testing phases are completed. A summary report to senior management and to the board from these business

---

6 It is important to include personnel from operations as well as IT units because the Year 2000 problem is not restricted to IT and ultimately each operations area will need to assume responsibility for mitigating the effects of the Year 2000 problem within its area of the business.

7 One component of Best Practices recommended by OSFI is periodic reviews by internal audit, compliance and supervisory specialists. CIBC's audit department reportedly uses a nine-step process to audit business units in respect of their Year 2000 compliance activities. In the case of mission critical systems, Year 2000 compliance must be demonstrated (*i.e.*, proved).

8 However, the involvement of third parties, particularly suppliers, must be carefully restricted to ensure they are not given access to information that could later be used against the company, particularly if a law suit is subsequently initiated by the company against that particular supplier.

units should confirm such compliance (including system interdependency and external linkages). For those systems or applications that fail certification, the institution should have a process in place to assess the impact, and implement a contingency plan.

16.3 TECHNICAL AND LEGAL AUDITS

Many companies are implementing projects to address their exposure to Year 2000 problems. Prudent organizations are conducting comprehensive audits to assess their vulnerability to liability claims and an assessment of possible recourse against existing suppliers. However, the first step is to conduct a technical audit to understand the scope of the Year 2000 problem as it affects the company.

The audit of existing systems should include an inventory of all computer software, hardware, and equipment, and of the company's equipment, and manufacturing and environmental systems that may contain embedded code. Following the completion of the inventory, the company should undertake a risk assessment to determine which systems are critical for the operation of the business. The risk assessment should take into account the company's dependencies on any key customers and suppliers.

An audit should also be conducted of products that have been or are being supplied to others to assess the potential date change problems with these products. Such an evaluation will also need to consider any components that are acquired from third parties and incorporated into the company's final product.

A legal audit should be performed following the technical audit to review the various agreements and to determine the company's legal position. The legal audit will require the collection of all agreements, past and current, relating to the acquisition of systems used within the company and where applicable, the ongoing maintenance of such systems. In some circumstances, the audit may include a review of the negotiations conducted by personnel involved in the procurement (including project managers).

Information from procurement staff should be requested by legal counsel as documents and reports created in the course or in anticipation of litigation may be protected as privileged communications (which will prevent the other party from obtaining access to such documents if litigation results).

Relevant contracts with suppliers of products that are incorporated into the company's products will also need to be reviewed. Once the supply-side audit is complete, the company will need to consider how to handle suppliers and what information should be disseminated to customers.

The information that results from a review of legal responsibilities concerning Year 2000 problems can provide the company with leverage in negotiating with its counter parties. Although a company may not intend to commence litigation against its suppliers, it is important for each party to understand its legal rights and obligations so that it can take appropriate action.

The legal audit should include the following components:

◆ Identification of all applicable contracts, amendments and related documentation such as:[9]
  – Product and service acquisition contracts such as purchase agreements, system agreements, software licences,[10] support and maintenance agreements, system integration agreements, software development agreements, consulting agreements, leases, and outsourcing/facilities management agreements. Agreements made with suppliers (whether for products acquired for use by the company or acquired for resale or to be incorporated into the company's products), as well as those entered into with customers of the company's products and services should be included;
  – Facilities-related contracts with suppliers including leases, contracts for the supply of utilities, facilities agreements, acquisition, and maintenance agreements for major equipment that may incorporate embedded logic;
  – Acquisition documents including purchase orders and standard form templates used in Requests for Information ("RFIs") and Requests for Proposals ("RFPs");
  – Customer agreements including standard form templates, major non- standard agreements, order confirmation and shipping docu-

---

9 It is very important to confirm that agreements being reviewed were not subsequently revised through an amending agreement, an agreement for another product or a letter agreement. Schedules to agreements should also be reviewed to determine if they contain provisions that are to prevail over any provisions in the main agreement.

10 Software acquired pursuant to shrink-wrap licence agreements or Web-wrap (*i.e.*, on-line agreements entered into over the Internet) must also be considered. The version that is reviewed should be that which was in effect at the time of the transaction rather than the current version. Unfortunately, these types of agreements are seldom retained.

ments, standard form templates for RFP Responses, product warranties;
- Merger and acquisition agreements;
- Advertising and promotional material;
- Manuals and other product documentation; and
- Agreements with trading partners.

♦ An analysis of contractual rights and obligations. The review should include an assessment of each party's responsibilities and the viability of potential claims by and against the company (whether for indemnification or direct damages). The review will involve identifying warranties and other obligations as well as provisions that limit each party's liability. A legal analysis of contracts should include a review of specifications for the operation of any system by legal counsel in consultation with technical staff.

♦ Analysis of statutory obligations and review of disclosure documents.

♦ Review of insurance policies.[11]

♦ Confirmation that adequate disclosure is being made to the board of directors.

♦ Review of record retention policies and practices to ensure retention of all required evidence of due diligence and actions taken by the company.

The legal audit is typically followed by letters to suppliers to ascertain the Year 2000 compliance of their products and services. If products and services are not already compliant, the customer must ascertain the supplier's plans to ensure that such products and services are made compliant.

16.4 CORPORATE POLICIES

A Year 2000 compliance program should also include a review of applicable corporate policies to implement or support a Year 2000 compliance program. Adoption or modification of corporate policies may be necessary to:

♦ require the use of standard Year 2000 warranties in agreements with suppliers;

---

11 Current insurance policies should be reviewed by a company's legal advisors to assess whether they will cover risks associated with the Year 2000 problem. As already discussed, common exclusions contained in many types of insurance policies may preclude claims relating to Year 2000 problems. Where appropriate, a Year 2000-specific policy should be considered.

- set out the authority of business units to make amendments to the Year 2000 warranty language to be included in agreements with suppliers; and
- set out the authority of business units to deal with inquiry letters from customers, suppliers and other parties.

It may also be helpful to develop guidelines for dealing with auditors and regulatory authorities.

16.5 INDUSTRY YEAR 2000 COMMITTEES

In some industries, a Year 2000 compliance program may include participation in a committee with representation from various companies. Industry committees can allow participants to explore the possibility of sharing testing facilities and efforts in order to minimize cost, time and effort. They may also provide customers with additional leverage in negotiations with suppliers.

The member agencies of the Federal Financial Institutions Examination Council encouraged federally regulated financial institutions in the United States to work collectively to address issues pertaining to the Year 2000 problem. According to the FFIEC:

> Effective industry cooperation can help reduce costs. By working together, financial institutions can share ideas, influence vendors, develop best management practices, and maintain their competitiveness with other industries . . . If the industry is to be successful in meeting the problems posed by the Year 2000, financial institutions will have to work cooperatively to share effective practices, common testing methodologies and other non-proprietary information.[12]

In early October 1996, the United States securities industry established a Year 2000 advisory group that included representatives of NASD, the NYSE, the American Stock Exchange, the National Securities Clearing Corporation, the Depository Trust Company and the Securities Industry Automation Corporation. The purpose of the group was to establish inter-organizational data interchange guidelines and a plan for "street-wide" testing to ensure that exchanges, stock markets, clearing corporations, depositories and securities firms perform data transfer and interface correctly when the millennium changes. The group was later expanded to

---

12 "Safety and Soundness Guidelines concerning the Year 2000 Business Risk" (December 17, 1997).

include representatives from member firms, regional exchanges and other similar organizations.[13] A similar industry Year 2000 committee has been established in Canada for participants in the securities industry by the Investment Dealers Association.

The Canadian Bankers Association ("CBA"), has formed a Year 2000 Interbank Working Group consisting of Year 2000 project managers from the domestic banks, Canada Trust, and the Bank of Canada. The Working Group is a user-oriented committee, and the members share information and solutions, identify common problems and service providers, and compare strategies for managing the internal conversion efforts of the various banks. The Working Group is also responsible for examining interfaces between the Canadian banks and key electronic networks such as Interac, Canadian Depository for Securities Ltd., SWIFT and the Canadian Payments Association. Sub-groups are responsible for examining the telecommunications infrastructure, vendor management issues and testing issues (*i.e.*, joint testing and the organization of street-wide testing).

It would be prudent for an industry committee to operate under a legal agreement whereby each participant agrees not to hold the other participants liable for any information provided, and agrees not to disclose or use for any unauthorized purpose any information provided by any other participant. As well, individual participants should be advised of the proprietary nature of certain information about the member they are representing and that such information should not be disclosed to other participants. Finally, the discussions that are held between such participants must be limited to Year 2000 issues and not extend to topics that may be viewed as anti-competitive or prohibited by anti-trust restrictions.

An important issue that must be considered by any industry group is that information obtained by one member in respect of a particular product or service, whether in respect of Year 2000 compliance issues or otherwise, may be subject to non-disclosure obligations imposed by the contacts under which such products or services were acquired. Disclosure of such information may be prohibited except to a company's own employees on a "need to know" basis. A disclosure of any information about a product or service, which may be deemed confidential information pursuant to such contracts, may constitute a breach of such contract and entitle the supplier to sue the customer for damages and/or terminate the applicable contract or relevant licences.

---

13 NASD Notice to Members, No. 97-16, March 1997.

Some member-owned organizations are being asked by their members to share information concerning the organization's Year 2000 compliance programs. Such organizations must carefully review the information that they disclose to their members because some members may be uniquely affected by a Year 2000 problem and may use the information obtained to make a claim against the organization. It may not be necessary for the organization to share detailed information concerning its Year 2000 compliance program, but instead, may provide information concerning data formats or standards used to exchange data with its members. In some cases, it may be sufficient to provide members with a summary of the organization's Year 2000 compliance efforts rather than providing a more detailed project plan.

Where an organization shares information concerning its Year 2000 compliance program (*i.e.*, project plan or status updates) with other parties, it should review the relevant documents to be disclosed. Ideally, recipients should be asked to execute an agreement that defines the use that the recipient may make of the documents, provides that the recipient will not utilize the information in any claim against the organization and restricts the further disclosure of the information to other parties. As well, it would be desirable for such organizations to include appropriate disclaimers on any documents being disclosed.

16.6 AWARENESS PROGRAM

An important component of a Year 2000 compliance program is the implementation of an awareness program to draw attention to the fact that Year 2000 compliance extends beyond the IT department and must include all equipment and devices that incorporate microprocessors or embedded logic. An awareness program should also highlight the importance of reviewing key supplier and customer dependencies. The assistance of all staff, particularly those in the "user" areas is required to identify all vulnerable products and relationships. A Year 2000 awareness program can also help raise the importance of the remediation project with directors, officers and senior management.

In many cases, companies are asking their legal advisors to conduct a seminar on Year 2000 compliance to assist the company in better understanding the problem and mitigating its legal risk associated with the problem. Such seminars can also be very helpful in assisting senior management to understand the scope of the problem and the importance of allocating sufficient resources to address the problem.

Even if no significant Year 2000 compliance problems are anticipated, a company's board should be briefed on Year 2000 issues and any potential risks. This will help show that the company took the issue seriously in the event that an unforeseen problem should subsequently arise.

Some of the activities that may be conducted, or resources developed, as part of an awareness program may include:

- internal seminars for all staff who deal with customers;
- Year 2000 awareness teleconferences for staff;
- Year 2000 Web site on the corporate intranet;
- brochures that describe the company's approach to the Year 2000 problem for distribution to concerned customers;
- responses (that have been reviewed by legal counsel) for distribution, on a request basis, to the media and to analysts; and
- notices that list products that are confirmed to be compliant and those with known Year 2000 problems.

It is important to identify all potential groups in the company who may need to be provided with special training regarding the Year 2000 problem due to the nature of the functions that they perform. These groups should include any personnel whose participation is necessary to ascertain Year 2000 issues being faced by the company, as well as those who have contact with customers, suppliers or regulators, and may include personnel from the following units:

- corporate acquisition/planning
- credit risk management
- contract administration
- public affairs
- corporate finance and investor relations
- risk management/insurance
- human resources
- sales and marketing

16.7 DOCUMENT RETENTION ISSUES

While a company's response to the Year 2000 problem must be reasonable, it is also important for a company to document the reasonableness of its actions and decisions. In this respect, companies will want to ensure that they implement a document management and retention system that provides for effective management of Year 2000 documentation.

The proper documentation of a company's Year 2000 efforts from the planning stage through to completion can be important in demonstrating that reasonable and adequate efforts were taken. Ideally, a company will want to have a written record to demonstrate a sufficient level of due diligence to enable the company to successfully defend any legal actions that may be brought. Such documentation should describe the company's Year 2000 compliance efforts including a summary of the Year 2000 problems that were identified, when and how each problem was resolved, and the person responsible for its resolution. Monthly status reports on Year 2000 activities, produced by project teams at larger companies, should be saved for this purpose. As well, board minutes should reflect, as appropriate, any material action taken by the board to address Year 2000 issues or concerns. In fact, most of the documentation produced in the course of addressing Year 2000 problems should likely be saved.

Companies should review the creation of internal documents for issues such as:

♦ who is creating documents related to the Year 2000 problem and for what purpose;
♦ whether the company's internal record is consistent with its public statements; and
♦ whether information being retained by the company would be understandable to a judge or jury in the event it must be disclosed as part of a claim against the company.

Any company that may have potential liability concerning the Year 2000 problem would be well advised to ensure that it does not create an internal record of containing expression of undue alarm. Internal documents should reflect proper concern regarding the Year 2000 problem and the due diligence activities being undertaken by the company, but should not include an admission of fault or liability. Care should be taken to avoid having persons without appropriate training or skill, or persons who do not have all the relevant facts, making statements of opinions or conclusions.

Expressions of concern should be stated in neutral language. Staff should understand that documents may be discoverable in future litigation and should utilize appropriate consideration concerning statements in order to avoid "smoking guns." Documents should also be drafted in a form that would be easily understood by a judge or jury.

Companies should also review what steps should be taken in order to reduce the potential for any incriminating documents being ordered released to another party in future litigation. The best approach is to involve the company's legal counsel at the beginning of the Year 2000 project. By being involved in the project on an ongoing basis, counsel may provide guidance as to the circumstance in which the company may wish to assert privilege with respect to certain documents and the steps required to be taken to obtain such protection.

The general rule is that communications between a lawyer and a client for the purpose of obtaining legal advice are protected from disclosure in legal proceedings (*i.e.*, a request for discovery). Privilege can also be used to protect reports prepared by employees and consultants provided they are prepared for the purpose of legal advice relating to actual or anticipated litigation.[14] Such reports must be requested by or prepared for the lawyer. Documents prepared for advice to be obtained from consultants, accountants or Year 2000 risk management advisors will not be accorded the same protection.

Any documentation relating to liability issues should be marked as confidential, and where appropriate, privileged. Access to such documentation should be restricted and never distributed to large circulation lists.

A company with an extensive Year 2000 compliance program may find itself accumulating a significant and possibly overwhelming quantity of documents. The time and cost of retaining and managing the voluminous number of documents related to Year 2000 compliance activities can be significant. While it may be appropriate in some circumstances to destroy some of these documents, such destruction should occur only in accordance with a formal document retention program that is designed with guidance from the company's legal advisor. Some of the issues that should be considered include statutory retention requirements, limitation issues, and evidentiary issues.

---

14 Consultants or other third parties engaged to prepare such reports should be subject to appropriate non-disclosure obligations.

17

Year 2000 Inquiry Letters

17.1 RELEVANCE

An important component of a Year 2000 compliance program for any organization involves sending inquiry letters to its suppliers to obtain information regarding any possible Year 2000 problems for products and services that have been or are being provided to the organization.

In many cases, organizations may require the assistance of suppliers to assess whether or not products, which may include software or any equipment that contains embedded logic, are susceptible to a Year 2000 problem. As well, organizations will want to ensure that services (including non-IT services) and suppliers being acquired are also not at risk of being disrupted due to a Year 2000 problem being experienced by the relevant supplier. Inquiry letters should therefore be sent to all key suppliers.

Many organizations are also reliant on third parties other than just suppliers. It is also important to write to customers and business partners in order to ascertain the vulnerability of such parties to Year 2000 problems and ask them to outline the action that they are taking to ensure compliance and reduce their exposure to Year 2000 problems. This is particularly important if these parties exchange data or otherwise communicate electronically with the organization or if their failure can have significant negative consequences to the organization.[1]

Inquiry letters serve several purposes: (i) they are a means of obtaining information regarding the other party's exposure to the Year 2000 prob-

---

1 Customers with substantial accounts payables should be assessed for Year 2000 compliance. Suppliers that are dependent on one or a few key customers for substantial portions of their sales should also consider the Year 2000 compliance of such customers, and if appropriate, seek ways of reducing the dependencies.

lem;[2] (ii) they allow a customer to compare its records of products and services acquired from a particular supplier with the records of the supplier (which can be especially important in the case of large organizations that may not have centralized records or an up-to-date asset management system); and (iii) they may enable the sender to obtain additional legal protection (*e.g.*, on the grounds that the response constitutes a collateral contract or gives rise to a claim of detrimental reliance based on the information provided concerning the respondent's readiness and plan of action.)[3] Some companies are also using inquiry letters as a subtle method of educating their suppliers to the less obvious areas that need to be addressed as part of a Year 2000 review. The sending of inquiry letters, and a process for follow up of responses that are received, may therefore constitute an important component of due diligence that should reasonably be exercised by organizations.

Another issue that should be considered by an organization is that while the products supplied to that organization may all be compliant, the supplier could still be sued because of other non-compliant products provided to customers. Therefore, it is important to consider the supplier's other products as part of a supplier viability assessment. It may also be prudent to ascertain a supplier's vulnerability to Year 2000 problems in all key products, even those not utilized by that particular organization.

One approach being considered by some organizations is to send an inquiry letter that simply requests information on what the supplier is doing regarding the Year 2000 problem and provides that the response will not be used for litigation purposes. The use of such a "without prejudice" request may result in a more comprehensive and useful response. Once the supplier's status is more clearly understood, the parties can then follow through with a binding agreement that actually does provide for legal obligations and remedies.

Organizations that send inquiry letters or use other mechanisms to monitor the Year 2000 compliance of their trading partners should ensure that their efforts will not prejudice their rights in the event the trading partner nevertheless experiences Year 2000 problems. Care must be taken to ensure that any involvement is not characterized as approval of the steps being

---

2 In the case of letters sent to suppliers, the objective is to obtain assurances that the products (or services) supplied to the customer will continue to operate (or be supplied) without anomalies or interruption due to Year 2000 problems.

3 An inquiry letter, in conjunction with a supplier's response can have legal consequences. It is therefore important to have inquiry letters reviewed by legal counsel.

taken, and potentially precluding remedies, if such steps fail to properly address the trading partner's Year 2000 problems.

17.2 SCOPE

The first issue to consider regarding supplier inquiry letters is scope. Inquiry letters should be sent to suppliers of telephone equipment, electronic office equipment, as well as other devices with "embedded" logic based on microprocessors (for instance, elevators and HVAC). Customers should also consider writing other key suppliers of products or services that are critical to the organization, even those that are not technical in nature. A problem with a key supplier can interfere with a company's ability to meet its own obligations to its customers.[4]

17.3 WHAT TO INCLUDE: STRUCTURE AND COMPONENTS OF AN INQUIRY LETTER

(a) Introduction

Many organizations begin an inquiry letter by including a description of what actions they are taking to address the Year 2000 problem. They may then request information concerning the supplier's Year 2000 compliance efforts in the context of facilitating their own compliance efforts. Such letters may begin with:

> [Customer] is in the process of assessing our Year 2000 compliance status. As part of this project, we are contacting you as one of [Customer's] third party suppliers to determine whether your products and/or services are Year 2000 compliant.

> or

> [Customer] has acquired products or services from your company for use in our business. [Customer] is in the process of confirming that the

---

4 For instance, CIBC expressed concern about power companies and telecommunications. If an armoured car service utilized by a financial institution has a problem then money cannot be delivered to automated teller machines or picked up from branches.

operation of such products and services will not be impaired by the advent of the year 2000.

However, a sender of an inquiry letter should consider that the recipient of the letter may rely upon such representations.

(b) Definition of Year 2000 compliance

Some customers include their own definition of Year 2000 compliance. For instance:

> [Software] is Year 2000 compliant if it functions without fault at all times prior to, during and after the calendar year 2000 without date error and without interruption relating to date data, including recognition of the year 2000 as a leap year.

> or

> [Software] processes dates after the year 2000 consistent with the manner in which it handles dates before the year 2000.

The definition of Year 2000 compliance can have important implications in respect of rights that can be asserted against a party's trading partners. A more comprehensive definition, such as the one included in Chapter 12, should also be utilized. Ideally, the definition should be customized for the particular product or service. However, this may not be economical in all cases.

(c) Expectations Regarding Compliance

Some customers set out their expectations that products acquired from the supplier are or will be made Year 2000 compliant by the supplier. For instance, they may provide:

> It is our expectation and understanding that all products will accurately recognize and accommodate the rollover to the year 2000, and will not experience date problems due to the year 1999 or the year 2000, if their functional specifications include recognizing and processing date information.

or,

> We expect all our suppliers to continue to deliver products and services without impact from Year 2000 problems.

See Chapter 12 for other suggestions.

Some customers are advising suppliers that they expect any non-compliant products to be made compliant by a specified date. For instance:

> If your product is not currently Year 2000 compliant, we require it to be compliant no later than [X].

It should be noted that some products and systems may begin experiencing problems sometime in the year 1999 (or earlier). Therefore, any date specified for compliance should take this risk into consideration.

Finally, while it may be questionable whether a response to an inquiry letter would be legally binding, it should be made clear that the sender will be relying on the response.

(d) Demonstration of Compliance/Assistance in Testing

In the case of products that are critical to a customer's business, the customer should not rely solely on a statement made by a supplier that its products are Year 2000 compliant. Instead, in appropriate cases, it should request the supplier to demonstrate such compliance. A customer may also request that the supplier provide test scripts or test data that can be used by the customer to confirm the Year 2000 compliance of the products.

Some organizations are also taking steps to confirm the Year 2000 compliance of the supplier's own suppliers. For instance, a customer that is highly reliant on telecommunication services may ask an equipment supplier such as Northern Telecom which versions of its products are Year 2000 compliant and then ask its telecommunications providers to advise which version of Northern Telecom's products that it is using.

(e) Identification of Products and/or Services

Inquiry letters may identify products and services that the customer's records indicate are being acquired from that particular supplier. For instance, the inquiry letter may state that "our inventory shows that the products and services you provide us include [X]." However, the customer will want to request that the supplier confirm or supplement any such listing provided by the customer.

Some standard-form inquiry letters do not attempt to identify particular products or services and refer to these in a generic manner. In such cases, the letter may simply refer to all products supplied to the customer or those delivered during a specified number of years prior to the date of the letter.

The inquiry letter may also explicitly extend the scope of the products referred to in the letter to include third party components embedded in the supplier's products, and all systems that interface electronically with the customer including any "feeder systems" (which therefore extends to any systems that directly or indirectly provide data to supplier's system). In many cases, extensive and time consuming due diligence would need to be performed by the recipient of such an inquiry letter in order to respond to the questions raised.

(f) Common Questions

Inquiry letters may include detailed questions and/or an attached question-naire that must be completed. The questions may seek information concerning the following:

♦ A listing of products or services that are utilized by that customer along with the status of their Year 2000 compliance including applicable version numbers. If customers do not attach their own definition of Year 2000 compliant then the definition used by the supplier should be requested;

♦ A request for detailed information on how the compliance was achieved, when it was achieved, test verification strategies that were utilized, and any supporting materials or technical literature. Customers may want to know whether the supplier's test procedures and results will be available for audit by the customer and whether the supplier has any testing tools or scripts that may assist the customer in validating the testing performed by the supplier. Some customers may want the supplier to agree that it will provide a demonstration of compliance (at no charge to the customer);

♦ Whether the supplier has produced a Year 2000 communications package;[5]

♦ If current releases of the products are Year 2000 compliant, whether other releases or versions are known to have processing problems when dealing with dates after the year 2000;

♦ If the products or services are not Year 2000 compliant, detailed information concerning the nature and scope of problems and a timetable for their correction;

♦ If a new Year 2000 compliant version of the product is contemplated, information concerning the "downward compatibility" of the new version with any existing versions, any applicable conversion procedures;

♦ A schedule for implementation of modifications or replacement products. Some customers may have firm deadlines for achieving Year 2000 compliance (which may have been set by regulators or industry associations) and may want an undertaking from suppliers to provide the Year 2000 compliant version of the product prior to any such deadline;

♦ Confirmation that any cost to be incurred to modify or enhance any product for Year 2000 compliance will be treated as part of normal maintenance and/or will be provided to customer at no additional cost;

♦ Whether any products are expected to fail before the year 2000;

♦ Any dependencies associated with or conditions applicable to the Year 2000 compliance of the products or services (*e.g.*, requirements for any products to be used with specific versions of operating systems, third party software or hardware);

♦ Specific compliance issues, such as:
  – whether dates are stored with an indication of century,
  – whether the product recognizes the year 2000 as a leap year;

♦ Information concerning the method of date manipulation used to convert an older software program (*i.e.*, windowing, field expansion to four-digit year, etc.);
  – If a windowing technique was used, information as to the pivot year that was utilized;[6]
  – Depending on the conversion method used, information about the conversion to be undertaken of existing applications that use the software program and/or historical data files. The same question

---

5 Many large suppliers, including IBM, HP and Digital, have developed a significant communication package, including a white paper, to help educate customers on the Year 2000 problem.

6 Note that the use of a windowing technique merely postpones the problem until a date with a year equal to the pivot year is encountered.

may be asked with respect to the backward compatibility of the Year 2000 compliant version of the software program. If conversion of existing databases or historical files will be required, customers will want to know whether facilities to assist with such conversion will be provided by the supplier;

♦ How the supplier deals with eight-character (*i.e.*, 01/01/99) date fields in screens and printouts (*i.e.*, will these be expanded or will the supplier be using special notations to denote dates in the year 2000 and beyond, (such as the use of superscripts to represent the next century "01/01^{2}03" for January 1, 2003);

♦ In the case of suppliers that are providing services, information concerning any changes that will be required in any data formats used to exchange data with such supplier;

♦ How the customer can acquire the Year 2000 compliant upgrade or new release of the software program and any operating environment, hardware (*i.e.*, RAM memory requirements), interface or other changes that are required for customer to implement the new upgrade;

♦ Name of supplier's executive responsible for Year 2000 compliance;

♦ Name and phone number of the supplier's project manager or lead technical representative who can be contacted to discuss Year 2000 compliance issues, and of the employee responsible for the Year 2000 compliance of the particular product or service.

In the case of a survey or questionnaire attached to the inquiry letter that the recipient is asked to complete, some customers ask the recipient to "declare," "warrant" or "confirm" that the information provided is correct and complete, and that the person responding has the authority to provide the information on behalf of the supplier to the customer. The recipient may also be asked to sign the survey, questionnaire or response letter.

(g) Other Issues

Certain software programs may contain internal expiration dates that can be avoided only if customers obtain licence keys on an annual or periodic basis from the supplier. Customers who intend to simulate future dates as part of their testing of such products for Year 2000 compliance should consult with the supplier and confirm that the product will continue to function during dates simulated in the future with any current licence keys in use by the customer.

If it is likely that the supplier will continue enhancing any products that have been made Year 2000 compliant, customers may want to seek assurances that the supplier will incorporate appropriate regression testing procedures to ensure such applications remain Year 2000 compliant.

Early versions of inquiry letters focused on ensuring that a supplier's products are or will be made Year 2000 compliant. However, in the case of key suppliers, customers may want to request more detailed information regarding the supplier's entire Year 2000 compliance program, including information concerning the Year 2000 compliance of its suppliers, products containing embedded logic, and other matters.

(h) Request for Response

A request for a written response to a particular customer contact person is usually included. A separate customer contact may be listed for dealing with any questions that the supplier may have.

A deadline for responses is usually included. Some inquiry letters state that a response must be received by a particular date. Other letters take a less stringent approach and may state that "in order for our Year 2000 project team to make the best use of your response, we would appreciate receiving your response by [X]." It is recommended that a specific deadline be included but that the time provided for the supplier to respond be reasonable in the circumstances. Small suppliers or suppliers of non-technology products may lack a process to respond to such letters and may require additional time to respond.

17.4 PROCESS FOR FOLLOW-UP

A procedure should be implemented to track and evaluate responses that are received to any inquiry letters. Simply filing the responses without further action is not enough. It is important to establish priorities, deadlines and follow-up procedures.

Customers with agreements containing contractual limitation periods should consider negotiating a "stand still" agreement with the supplier. Customers that may be subject to an upcoming statutory limitation period should consult with their legal advisors and take other appropriate action to ensure that they will not lose rights due to the passage of time.

Responses should be reviewed by someone with a good understanding of Year 2000 compliance issues and who can carefully evaluate the response, including any qualifications that may be present. Questionable responses should be referred to legal counsel.

Another letter or other action should be undertaken to deal with suppliers who fail to reply or that provide responses that are inadequate. One option is to deal with the matter from one CEO to the other. Other options that may be considered for placing increased pressure on suppliers to respond are to involve an industry association or form a user group with other customers.

If a product or service is not compliant, a customer will want to ensure that the supplier provides its plans and timetable to achieve compliance. It would be desirable to seek detailed information in order to confirm that proper steps have actually been considered and are being taken.

An important concern is that information regarding a particular product may change. A vendor may believe certain of its products to be year 2000 compliant, only to later discover that they are not. Also, time tables for future compliance may not be met.[7] It is therefore important to follow up with periodic requests for updates.

It should be noted that some suppliers are placing information concerning the Year 2000 compliance of their products on their Web sites. In some cases, replies to inquiry letters are directing the recipient to view these references on the Web rather than providing a response to the particular issues raised by the sender of the inquiry letter.

---

7 NASD advised in a Notice to Members (No. 97-16): "The Y2K arena resembles a minefield of hidden surprises. For example, contacting vendors for information about the Y2K compliance of their products and then verifying compliance will take longer than expected. Constant and careful communications with vendors is an absolute must because it is not unlikely that a vendor may reverse its position about whether it will or will not release a Y2K-compliant version of a particular product."

18

Responding to Inquiry Letters

Many companies who are sending out inquiry letters in their capacity as customers are also themselves suppliers to other companies and will find themselves on the receiving end of inquiry letters. The previous chapter considered the issue of inquiry letters from the perspective of customers whose interest is to obtain as much information and assurance as possible concerning the Year 2000 compliance of products and services acquired from third parties. This chapter considers the issue from the perspective of a supplier or other party being asked to respond to an inquiry letter and whose interest will be to minimize the assumption of any additional obligations or liability.

18.1 INTRODUCTION

The recipient of an inquiry letter will need to decide on the level of detail to be provided in the response. In some cases, especially where the recipient is still in the early investigative phase of its Year 2000 review, a standard generic response may be sufficient. In other cases, further investigation and a more detailed response may be required.[1]

In formulating a response to an inquiry letter, the recipient should:

---

1 A more detailed response may be required as time grows shorter and/or where necessitated by the business relationship between the parties.

- consider who in the company should be responsible for responding;[2]
- ensure that all responses provided by the company to the same sender are consistent between different divisions of that organization;
- ensure that the response is accurate and appropriate in the circumstances and takes into account the contractual and business relationship that exists between the parties; and
- consider whether the response will have different implications for different segments of the company (if necessary, this may require qualifying the response by area of business or specific types of products).

Recipients of an inquiry letter will want to strike a balance between not assuming new legal commitments while being responsive to the business relationship. Many companies are also increasingly reluctant to discuss the corrective work that they are performing for fear of providing information that may be used for purposes of future litigation in the event that their Year 2000 problems are not addressed in time. This highlights the need to have responses reviewed by legal counsel.

Suppliers must also consider to what extent they may be required to provide customers with information they may have regarding non-compliance of their products. In some cases, negligence or a failure to warn may constitute a basis for product liability claims.

18.2 GENERIC RESPONSES

The initial response may be very general in nature and may not address compliance issues associated with specific releases of the supplier's products. The initial response may advise that more detailed information is to be forthcoming in subsequent updates.

The following introduction could be incorporated into a generic response letter:

> [Supplier] recognizes the importance of addressing the Year 2000 computer problem. We have put in place a program to review our products and systems (including products supplied by third parties) to

---

2 A common practice is that the entity in the organization who "owns" something (which would typically be the operations or line of business unit) is the one responsible for ensuring Year 2000 readiness and for signing any responses to inquiry letters (subject to review by the legal department or external counsel).

assess the nature and scope of the problem and to take appropriate action.

or

We share your concern with respect to Year 2000 compliance and have given priority to this issue. In order to deal with this issue, we have established a corporate-wide Year 2000 program office and are channelling significant resources into this function. The objective of our Year 2000 program is to ensure that our internal systems and currently shipping products can be used in the next century with the least possible customer impact and cost.

or

A program has been established at [supplier] to address the Year 2000 issue and its possible effect on our internal systems and currently shipping products. We have prepared a special set of brochures for our customers to describe our Year 2000 compliance program

The supplier may state further:

[Supplier] will be working with our customers and suppliers in dealing with the problem so that we will continue to meet our commitments. As a result of the efforts now under way, we expect to avoid any disruption to our business, and minimize any impact on our customers to whom we may be supplying any products or services.

Suppliers may conclude by stating that they look forward to sharing the results of their Year 2000 program (as soon as they become available) in order to address the sender's concerns.

A supplier may wish to provide information concerning the organization and structure of its Year 2000 compliance program with a view to providing assurances to the customer that the supplier is making all reasonable efforts to address the issue. Such communication may inform the customer, as applicable, that the supplier's Year 2000 compliance program includes:

♦ establishment of a Year 2000 program office and cross-functional team from all supplier business units;
♦ management of the project by a full-time director or project manager;
♦ co-ordination through a central group of expert technical staff and a compliance steering committee;

♦ supervision by a committee that includes senior management and members of the board of directors;
♦ engagement in discussions with the supplier's suppliers regarding Year
2000 compliance;

A supplier may also highlight some of its accomplishments achieved to
date. These may include:

♦ completion of an inventory of supplier's date-affected programs;
♦ completion of the assessment phase;
♦ initial of conversion of certain critical programs.

Such generic responses are typically drafted in very general terms and do
not address any detailed questions that may be raised in a specific inquiry
letter. An important concern will be to ensure that the response does not
give rise to any new legal obligations on the part of the company responding. Some suppliers are also advising customers that, notwithstanding
actions being taken by the supplier, some level of product or service failure
may occur.

Some suppliers have developed a series of documents to communicate their
approach to the challenge posed by Year 2000 problems and to outline the
process by which the supplier intends to continue to provide Year 2000
related information on an on-going basis. Where available, such documents
may be sent along with a response to an inquiry letter.

One risk of using a generic response letter is that a failure to negate certain
statements that are made in the inquiry letter may imply agreement with
such statements. Ideally, any generic response letter should be customized,
as appropriate, to respond to statements or expectations contained in the
specific inquiry letter that may impose obligations or liability on the
recipient.

18.3 DRAFTING A DETAILED RESPONSE

A supplier may wish to exclude from its response any products for which
the supplier has completed its obligations.[3] The supplier's legal position
may be that it has no continuing obligations to the customer for these

---

3 This would include products that have been delivered by the supplier and accepted and
paid for by the customer and where supplier has no ongoing warranty or support
obligations.

products. However, this position may have to be modified due to the supplier's ongoing business relationship with the customer.

The contents of a detailed response will obviously depend on the specific products and services being supplied and the status of the supplier's compliance program. However, the following factors should be considered in drafting a detailed response:

◆ Consider a statement that the response letter does not represent the assumption of any liability or obligation beyond that set out in any existing contract between the parties. For instance:

> Nothing herein should be deemed to modify in any way any of the terms and conditions of any existing agreement to which we are a party in respect of our products or the assumption by us of any new obligations other than those contained in any existing agreements.

◆ If the supplier is asked to identify all products supplied to the customer, the supplier may want to indicate that it does not guarantee its records are accurate and complete and that customer should rely on its own records to confirm such information.

◆ Before the making of any statement as to whether the supplier's products already supplied to the customer are in fact Year 2000 compliant, the supplier would need to complete a detailed technical review. The supplier may wish to state that the information contained in the supplier's response is provided only to the best of the supplier's knowledge, is based on a preliminary technical review, and is subject to confirmation after a more detailed analysis. With respect to third party components, the supplier may wish to state that it is unable to make any statement, or alternatively that it is relying on information provided by third parties.

◆ A supplier may want to add appropriate qualifications concerning the interfaces between the supplier's products and any software or hardware to be used with these products. Examples of these qualifications are that in order for the supplier's products to operate without error past the year 1999, all information imported from other data sources must include complete four-digit year dates (or utilize the same pivot year in the case of two-digit years), and that such products must be used with hardware that supports dates past 1999. Where appropriate, suppliers will want to state that hardware, operating system and/or database system upgrades may be necessary. Others may want to state generically that they are not responsible for the integration or interface of other vendors' software systems or applications that are not Year 2000 compliant (or non-compliant data supplied to the supplier's product by such systems or applications).

♦ If a product incorporates a macro facility or programming language, it would be advisable to add a qualification that programming performed by customer personnel using such macro facility or programming language may have a Year 2000 problem even if the supplier's product itself is Year 2000 compliant.

♦ Even when a supplier is prepared to state that its product is Year 2000 compliant, it may wish to disclaim how the product may operate in a particular customer's environment.

♦ If a product has been customized by the supplier, or is designed to permit customization by the customer, the supplier may state that while the base version of their product is Year 2000 compliant, "many customer systems have altered the base capabilities of [Product] and may require Year 2000 compliance support." Customers in such situations could be advised to contact the supplier's consulting or professional services division.

♦ A supplier will wish to carefully consider its legal position before undertaking to perform any corrective action for products already supplied to customers that are not Year 2000 compliant. As noted above, the supplier may not wish to undertake the performance of any such work for any products for which it does not have any ongoing warranty or support obligations to the customer. The supplier will also wish to consider the cost of any corrective action and whether the customer should bear all or part of that cost. The supplier will want to have a specific agreement that addresses issues such as the scope of the work to be performed (*e.g.*, excluding any third party products from such work), the time frame for performing such work and appropriate disclaimers and exclusionary clauses.

♦ While suppliers may state that certain products are Year 2000 compliant, many are not providing a specific definition of this term. While there may be some benefit in omitting such a definition in some circumstances, a supplier that does not wish to be bound by any definition set out in the customer's letter should include its own definition.

♦ Some suppliers are providing a date by which they expect to achieve Year 2000 compliance. The supplier will want to state this date as a goal rather than as definitive date and include a qualification as to the scope of the expected compliance. For instance, a supplier may provide that their "goal is to have all of our mission-critical systems which directly affect customers to be Year 2000 compliant by [X]."

18.4 DESIGNATION OF PRODUCTS AS OBSOLETE

Some suppliers are advising that certain products "may not be fully compliant." If the supplier has previously announced that it would not be conducting further development of such products, the supplier may state that it will not be undertaking further investigation to determine the Year 2000 compliance of such products. In some cases, suppliers are explicitly stating that as their Year 2000 compliance program progresses, the supplier may declare additional products obsolete.

A supplier may be reluctant to declare products to be obsolete solely because they are not Year 2000 compliant. Suppliers may suggest other reasons, including:

♦ that the products have been or will soon be replaced with other announced products;
♦ that the products have not been enhanced or sold for some time;
♦ that the products have reached the end of their useful commercial life; or
♦ that there are capacity, performance or technology constraints that make the continued deployment of such products not viable.

Suppliers may advise customers that any products designated as obsolete should be considered to be obsolete the earlier of December 31, 1999 or the date specified on any notice of obsolescence. Customers may be told that the supplier will not offer any form of support or maintenance of such products after their "obsolete date." A caveat that should be considered by suppliers that have or are planning to designate products as obsolete is that a product that is designated as obsolete as of December 31, 1999, may experience a Year 2000-related problem prior to such date. A supplier that does not intend to correct a problem with a product that does not correctly recognize or process a date (of January 1, 2000 or beyond) that is encountered on or before December 31, 1999 should make its position clear.

18.5 THIRD-PARTY PRODUCTS

For some suppliers, addressing the Year 2000 problem may require coordinated action with several thousand suppliers of hardware, software, data and other services. As a consequence, in most cases, suppliers will want to assume little responsibility for the Year 2000 compliance of any components supplied by third parties. Their efforts may be restricted to contacting such suppliers and exercising reasonable efforts to determine the nature and extent of those suppliers' efforts. An obligation to test third-party products is seldom assumed.

Some suppliers may be very dependent on third-party suppliers, particularly for hardware, operating system software, and the network. Where such third-party products are supplied to a particular customer by the supplier, the supplier may undertake to conduct limited investigation, testing and/or modifications to address Year 2000 compliance issues with such products, particularly as they may impact the supplier's own products. Where such products have been acquired and are maintained by the customer then the customer will generally be responsible for any necessary Year 2000 revisions.

A supplier's efforts with respect to the Year 2000 compliance of any third party products may be focused only on those functionalities and capabilities that their own products require (and therefore, specifically on any interfaces). In such cases, suppliers may not be addressing the Year 2000 compliance of other functionality of such products supplied by third parties. If such products are used by customers with other products, or for other purposes, such customers should be advised to conduct their own additional investigation.

18.6 APPROACHES

♦ Rather than simply sitting back and waiting for inquiries from customers, some suppliers have been proactive in alerting their customers of the need to take action to address the Year 2000 problem and assisting their customers in obtaining information about potential problems. For instance, IBM wrote its customers and suggested that they request a complimentary "Year 2000 SoftCheck." This is a customized report that itemizes the IBM software currently installed on the customer's S/390 system and indicates whether or not the software is Year 2000 ready. For any software that is not Year 2000 ready, the report will also identify which version or release is required.

♦ A number of suppliers are advising customers that the next release of their product will address Year 2000 issues and that the customer should have received or will receive the Year 2000 compliant release if they are covered by a current maintenance contract. Some of these suppliers are advising those customers that are not covered by a current maintenance contract that they will first need to sign up for maintenance prior to receiving the updated release.

♦ A number of suppliers have been unwilling to provide explicit Year 2000 warranties. For instance, Microsoft's position, as set out in its Year 2000 FAQ, is that "contractual warranties specific to Year 2000 readiness are not appropriate given the true nature of Year 2000 issues and the simple fact that a single technology provider, even one as well prepared for the year 2000 as Microsoft, cannot solve all issues related to the transition to the Year 2000."

♦ A prudent practice adopted by some suppliers is to log every Year 2000 query received from customers and a listing of documentation or other disclosure that was provided to each customer. Such logs may be very useful in the event of subsequent litigation to show what the supplier may have promised, and also what information a particular customer was given and therefore, upon which may have reasonably been required to act.

18.7 POSTING OF YEAR 2000 MATERIALS ON WEB SITES

A number of organizations are posting information concerning the Year 2000 problem and/or the steps they are taking to address the Year 2000 problem on their Web sites. While Internet Web sites may be efficient mechanisms for dissemination of information, caution should be exercised in respect of the type of information that is made available from such Web sites.

Any such information could be used in a future claim against the organization. Specifically, such information could be relied on by third parties as evidence of certain actions taken by the disclosing organization. Many organizations that are providing information on public Web sites concerning their Year 2000 efforts are including disclaimer notices with such information.

18.8 DISCLAIMERS

Prudent suppliers have been including disclaimers on their Year 2000-related publications. The following extracts are examples:

Subject to Change
This document reflects [COMPANY]'s current understanding of and

intentions with respect to the matters discussed in this document. However, the information provided is subject to change since it relates to matters that are in a state of evolution. The information contained in this document is based on the current status of the [COMPANY]'s Year 2000 compliance program and on the information the [COMPANY] has been provided on the Year 2000 status of third party components on which the [COMPANY] or its products rely.

No Legal Effect/No Warranty
This document is intended to support the internal business purpose of [COMPANY] and should not be relied upon by any other entity or for any other purpose. [COMPANY] makes no warranty that the information contained herein is complete or accurate.

or

The information contained in this document does not constitute any form of warranty, representation or undertaking. This document does not have any legal effect and is provided for information purposes only. Nothing in this document should in any way be deemed to alter the legal rights and obligations contained in agreements between [COMPANY] and customer.

Microsoft's Web site contains a disclaimer that the information it is disseminating about Year 2000 readiness does not constitute an extension of any warranty for Microsoft products. IBM's Web site states:

> IBM's assessment of Year 2000 readiness is an ongoing effort, and the information regarding Year 2000 is changing rapidly. The information provided in the database reports may not be exhaustive. It is intended for informational purposes only, and does not constitute a certification or warranty, expressed or implied, of any kind.

Such disclaimers may also be appropriate for pre-printed materials and other communications intended to be widely disseminated.

18.9 OTHER CAVEATS

Companies will want to avoid stating that they will ensure or guarantee that all systems or operations will be Year 2000 compliant or will not be adversely affected by the Year 2000 problem. It is preferable to state that the company is taking reasonable steps to reduce or eliminate the risk of the Year 2000 problem on its systems and operations. However, more specific commitments may be necessary in some circumstances.

Even in cases where a supplier may be prepared to provide a warranty or other assurances that a particular product is or will be made Year 2000 compliant, it may still be necessary to caution the customer that the product in question does not operate in isolation (*i.e.*, because it is reliant on third-party software, systems, communication systems, etc.) and may still be susceptible to a disruption. The supplier may also want to indicate that it plans to take appropriate action to review such other systems on which its product is reliant and follow up with key suppliers who could affect the operation of the product in question.

Suppliers that market their products internationally may employ the services of local distributors who may customize the products to meet local requirements. Such suppliers will want to restrict any statements that they make concerning the Year 2000 compliance of their products to the base products and note that such statements may not apply to any products that have been so modified to meet local requirements. Customers may be advised that information concerning any locally modified versions of a supplier's product may be available from its local subsidiary or local distributor.

A final caveat concerns the need to educate employees that only designated persons in the organization may make statements concerning its Year 2000 compliance. Many suppliers have developed templates to respond to Year 2000 inquiries from customers. These are often carefully considered and reviewed by legal counsel. However, in some instances, sales representatives may add notes that are not as carefully considered, and which may be relied upon by a customer who subsequently experiences a Year 2000 problem.

Reviewing Responses to Inquiry Letters

The following is intended to indicate the types of responses being received from suppliers that have been sent inquiry letters. The examples that follow, which were derived from actual responses, should help illustrate the type of responses that may require further action.

19.1 IDEAL RESPONSES

Customers will want the responses to their inquiry letters to contain clear and unambiguous statements, as indicated in the following examples:[1]

- [Supplier] warrants that all of its products, including but not limited to [Product], used prior to, during and after the calendar year 2000, are designed so that the user shall not experience software abnormally ending, invalid and/or incorrect results from the software relative to calendar year and leap year calculations.[2]
- Current versions of [System] are already Year 2000 compliant.
- This letter is to certify that all our products are Year 2000 compliant and operate correctly before, during and after the year 2000.
- Our [Product] has been Year 2000 compliant since its creation. No modifications or any changes need to be made on your part.
- Our [Product] has been tested exhaustively and confirmed to be Year 2000 compliant.

---

1 Customers will also ideally want to see any supplier that states its product is Year 2000 compliant, to provide a detailed definition that sets out exactly what such Year 2000 compliance means.

2 Ideally, the letter would be signed by an officer of the supplier.

- All previous, current and future versions of [Products] are fully Year 2000 compliant and will operate after December 31, 1999 exactly as they do now. The [Products] were designed and programmed from inception using year date fields that handle the year 2000 dates, and that meet all year 2000 requirements, including . . . Our products do not have to be upgraded or converted in any way to be Year 2000 compliant.

It should be noted that in some cases, a supplier may use a particular version number when referring to a Year 2000 compliant release of a product. This may or may not mean that earlier releases are not Year 2000 compliant. However, unless confirmation of compliance of earlier releases is obtained, it is suggested that customers should assume that such earlier releases are not Year 2000 compliant.

19.2 PROBLEMATIC RESPONSES

Some responses, while positive, may warrant further clarification. For instance, consider the following:

- We confirm that [System] has been tested to run without any problems after December 31, 1999.[3]
- The following [Systems] currently support Year 2000 processing.[4]
- The following products were designed to accommodate the year 2000.[5]
- The [System] is capable of handling dates up to 2099.

Some suppliers, while stating that certain of their products are Year 2000 compliant, nevertheless may advise customers that:

- Any functional errors will be treated as 'bugs' and resolved according to our standard maintenance and support policies.

---

3 Such a statement, without more, does not appear to cover the use of dates as indicators and any date-related problems that may occur prior to the year 2000. It also does not provide a warranty of compliance.

4 This statement does not indicate that the systems will continue to support processing of Year 2000 dates after the year 1999.

5 This statement does not actually say that the products are compliant or that the supplier has conducted any testing to verify compliance. Such a statement also does not appear to cover the use of dates as indicators and any date-related problems that may occur prior to the year 2000. It also does not constitute a warranty of compliance.

- Though we've exerted considerable effort to be Year 2000 compliant and have conducted significant testing, bugs are still possible, in date-handling code as in any other code. That is why we, like others in the industry, do not make any legally binding warranties that our software will be free from bugs, even those related to processing of dates in the year 2000 or beyond.
- The software may not always correctly resolve all Year 2000 issues without an impact on functionality or without an additional cost to the customer.
- Customer applications that are not programmed using specified functions or according to procedures documented by the supplier may experience problems.

In many cases, suppliers utilize third-party software in their own products. Such suppliers may be very reluctant to warrant compliance of their suppliers and may state that:

- Our third-party vendors have already addressed the Year 2000 issue and either have the problem solved or are working on upgrades. We will continue to keep track of all relevant third party software vendors and their programming efforts, to ensure that their software can accommodate dates in the year 2000 and beyond.
- Interfaces to other vendors may need to be modified. Should there need to be a change to those interfaces, [Supplier] will perform such changes under your support contract.[6]

Some suppliers may respond by not making any commitments themselves regarding the Year 2000 compliance of their system. For instance, consider the following response:

- [System] was developed using [XYZ development tools]. We are enclosing an article which describes how dates are handled in the [XYZ environment].

Suppliers may also attempt to shift at least some of the onus of confirming Year 2000 compliance onto their customers. For instance, consider the following responses:

- As a precaution, we recommend that a test account be set up for the purpose of testing the [System] with transactions containing dates

---

6 This means that there may be problems with existing interfaces and a further inquiry by the customer would be in order.

in the year 2000. This will confirm that the [System] will properly handle dates in the year 2000.

- We recommend that our customers check limitations, if any, of databases, middle- ware or other software components they use in conjunction with [System].

In cases where a supplier's product may not be Year 2000 compliant, the supplier may respond that:

- A future enhancement of [Product] will be Year 2000 compliant. This enhancement is scheduled for release in [X] quarter, 1998.
- We are taking the necessary steps to ensure that [Product] accepts and recognizes dates in the year 2000 and beyond, and that all applications will be made Year 2000 compliant.
- [Product] will require some minor changes and we are in the process of determining what these will be. Our goal is to complete any required changes by [X].

Rather than undertaking to make products Year 2000 compliant by a certain date, some suppliers are simply stating that they "currently plan to include that particular product in their Year 2000 compliance program" or that "if any modifications are necessary, these will be provided as part of the regular release cycle." This approach provides less of a commitment and allows the supplier the flexibility of changing its plans or even designating any problem product as "obsolete" sometime prior to the year 2000.

Some suppliers are responding that due to the volume of requests that they receive from customers concerning Year 2000 compliance, they cannot respond to individual customer requests and have enclosed a copy of their white paper. Others direct customers to check the supplier's Web site in order to ascertain which of the supplier's products are Year 2000 compliant.

Customers will want to ensure that any supplier statement regarding Year 2000 compliance actually speaks to the compliance of current products rather than new products that are under development. For instance, one supplier has stated that its research and development group has a mandate to implement and verify Year 2000 compliance on all products under development. It also stated that it has tested and corrected a number of problems with its existing products. These statements do not provide very much assurance that Year 2000 issues with all existing products are being adequately addressed.

Some suppliers are providing information to their customers in respect of the types of tests that they have conducted or will be conducting. In such cases, customers may want to review whether such tests are adequate to identify all possible Year 2000 problems.[7] As well, in cases where suppliers may provide customers with access to pre-release Year 2000 compliant versions of their applications, customers should note that in some circumstances they may be placed under an obligation to conduct testing of such applications, and to report any deficiencies to the suppliers.

19.3 CONDITIONS AND RESTRICTIONS

All responses must be carefully reviewed to ascertain how much reliance can be placed on them. Even an explicit Year 2000 warranty mentioned by a supplier in its response to an inquiry letter, or posted on its Web site, may be restricted in a number of ways. Examples of such restrictions include those that provide that the Year 2000 warranty is:

♦ subject to all exclusionary clauses contained in the agreement pursuant to which the product was acquired or subject to supplier's "standard terms";
♦ only applicable to products that are designated by the supplier as "Year 2000 compliant" or "Year 2000 ready";
♦ only applicable to new products where the warranty is explicitly included in the agreement, and not retroactive to prior acquisitions;
♦ conditional upon all customer and third party products, applications and networks properly exchanging accurate date data with the [System].

In the case of Year 2000 warranties that are subject to exclusionary clauses contained in the agreement with the supplier or subject to the supplier's "standard terms," the remedies available to customer may, depending on the terms found in the foregoing:

♦ be limited to the supplier correcting problems following notice provided by the customer of specific problems (which means that the customer could suffer an interruption and then need to wait weeks or months until the problem is corrected);
♦ preclude recovery of indirect or consequential damages incurred due to a Year 2000 related failure of the product;

---

7 Some suppliers are advising customers that they will provide copies of their compliance specifications and test results for those customers who require such documentation. It is recommended that such documentation be requested and reviewed where available.

♦ be limited damages to a maximum cap, which might be the total fees paid to the supplier under the contract, or the fees paid in respect of a specific module or component of the total product that experiences the problem or failure—in the case of maintenance, outsourcing or master agreements, damages may be further limited to fees paid in a specified period (*e.g.*, the one year period preceding the occurrence of the problem); and

♦ be subject to short limitation periods.

19.4 CONCLUSIONS

In some cases, responses to Year 2000 inquiries or to other statements made by a supplier (in brochures, "white papers" or posted on its Web site) may contain disclaimers that may preclude a customer from relying on such statements. Even where such disclaimers are not present, following the preliminary exchange of letters, a customer should consider requesting the supplier to execute a compliance agreement in order to clarify the supplier's obligations and avoid disputes relating to the enforceability of any promises made by the supplier.[8] The use of a compliance agreement is particularly important in the case of products and services that are critical to the business of a customer. Of course, in most cases, a supplier will be under no legal obligation to execute such an agreement and such an agreement may only be agreed to where a supplier is obtaining sufficient value from the on-going relationship to justify becoming subject to additional binding obligations.

---

[8] Generally speaking, an enforceable agreement requires an exchange of promises or consideration. However, some exceptions may exist. Other issues may also need to be considered. For example, the agreement may require any amendment to be in writing and signed by each party.

20

Year 2000 Litigation

I think the litigation is inevitable. The only question is to what degree it will occur.[1]

I will be surprised if there are less than 100 lawsuits filed where people are suing vendors, vendors are suing other vendors, and everybody is suing everybody else. There will be equipment failures, and companies will be looking to blame somebody for it.[2]

Lawyers will become rich. It's not a prediction, its just a simple forecast of what's going to happen based on the fact that lawyers sue people for things that go wrong, and the year 2000 is something that's going to cause things to go wrong.[3]

20.1 INTRODUCTION

There is no quick or easy fix for the Year 2000 problem. Date-related elements are spread throughout software programs including firmware found in many types of equipment.

As discussed earlier, the costs of dealing with the Year 2000 problem can be substantial and are likely to be revised upwards as companies proceed with their compliance efforts. Many organizations will likely be actively looking to claim at least some of their Year 2000 related costs against other companies by means of legal recourse.

---

1 Philip Lian, manager of Millennium Risk Management Service of On Risk Services, quoted by Suzanne King, "Year 2000 could bring new era of lawsuits" *Kansas City Business Journal* (September 1, 1997).

2 Lou Marcoccio, Year 2000 research director for Gartner Group, quoted by Sougata Mukherjee, "Look for Year 2000 issue to fill courts" *Triangle Business Journal* (November 10, 1997).

3 Peter de Jager, a recognized Year 2000 authority, quoted by Laura Pratt in "Year 2000" *The National* (November 1997) [published by The Canadian Bar Association].

Numerous articles have been published that predict that substantial litigation will occur as a result of the Year 2000 problem. Some American lawyers have predicted that the Year 2000 problem will lead to some of the biggest class action[4] lawsuits by customers suing suppliers as a result of non-compliant products and investors suing directors over stock market declines resulting from business disruptions. Some commentators have predicted that total legal and liability costs may exceed US$1 trillion, far exceeding prior environmental, asbestos and savings and loans related litigation.[5]

An article in *Computer Weekly*, which was subsequently referenced in the *London Times*[6] indicated that a American law firm, active in the Year 2000 area, was contemplating filing a $5 billion class action law suit against the PC industry over the Year 2000 problem. Although the law firm in question quickly denied the allegation, other class action lawsuits have been started.

The lack of court decisions dealing with the Year 2000 problem makes it difficult to ascertain the legal arguments that will be made and a particular court's response. However, the results of Year 2000-related litigation are expected to be very fact specific. Much will depend on the exact nature of the relationship between the parties and what took place between them.

When cases end up in litigation, an important factor will likely be a comparison of what the defendant did to achieve Year 2000 compliance in comparison to what other companies did. A plaintiff would want to show that the defendant was negligent in that its efforts were inadequate, it started late, it did not allocate sufficient resources, or it did not perform proper testing. Legal questions will centre on what kind of implied or express warranty was in effect and any applicable duty of care.

One issue that may be relevant to the imputation of liability is when suppliers should have become generally aware of the problem. Although

---

4 A class action is a lawsuit brought on behalf of a large number of similarly situated claimants. Each claimant's individual damages may be relatively small, however, the damages of the multiple claimants together may be significant and may justify a lawsuit that would otherwise not have been economically feasible if each claimant had to conduct their own lawsuit. However, it should be noted that certain requirements may need to be met before a class can be "certified."

5 See Rex Nutting, "Y2K Could Cost $1 Trillion in Legal Costs" in *TechWire* (March 20, 1997). See also Jon Swartz, "Year 2000 Computer Bug Expected to Cost $1 Trillion-Grim report from Lloyd's of London" in the *San Francisco Chronicle* (Friday, June 20, 1997) at A9.

6 December 4, 1997.

there was a surge in awareness concerning the Year 2000 problem in the mid-90s, the problem was recognized and written about prior to that time frame.[7] An early alarm bell was sounded by Peter de Jager in an article called "Doomsday," which was published in the September 6, 1993 issue of *Computerworld*.[8] Numerous articles in computer-related publications followed in 1994 and 1995. However, serious attention in the non-computer press did not appear until approximately 1996 and 1997.[9]

As discussed earlier, potential plaintiffs must take reasonable steps to mitigate their damages. These steps should attempt to reduce the likelihood of damages occurring as well as attempt to keep damages to a minimum in the event they do occur. Aggrieved parties should be able to demonstrate that they had taken reasonable steps to address the Year 2000 problem including implementation of a reasonable compliance program and taking steps to convince suppliers of non-compliant products or services to make the necessary changes. Where this was not possible, such parties should have attempted to take any steps they could take themselves to address the problem, including, if necessary, replacement of the product or sourcing of the service from another vendor.

An interesting project was initiated in December 1997 by Peter de Jager.[10] Called Project Damocles, it involves the gathering of information about suppliers who have knowledge that their systems or products will fail and are reluctant to make that information public. Persons with first hand knowledge of a system that will fail, whether an embedded system, software application, or computer platform, and where the supplier refuses to fix the problem or announce publicly that a problem exists, are asked to e-mail the information to de Jager.[11] The information submitted will then be sent by registered mail by de Jager to the legal department of the company in question. Once the sender of the report is verified, all record of who has submitted the report will be removed from the copy kept on file by Project Damocles. Should the information reported turn out to be true, and failures

---

7 For instance, see DataPro Research Corp., "Computer Processing of Dates Outside the 20th Century" (April 1987).

8 An earlier article, "Time's a Wasting and the Clocks Keep on Tickin'" was published in the May 1993 issued of *Info Canada*, Volume 18, No. 5.

9 An extensive Year 2000 bibliography has been compiled by Larry E. Towner and is accessible at <http://www.io.com/~deweerd/year2000/biblio.html>.

10 See <http://www.year2000.com>.

11 It should be noted, however, that doing so may result in a breach of confidentiality obligations, owed by the employee to the employer, that arise from contract, statute and/or common law.

do occur accompanied by lawsuits, these files are to be made available to the lawyers as part of the discovery process.

Peter de Jager offers some examples of tips he has received:

- ♦ a list of 30 medical devices, including model numbers, and a description of how they will fail;
- ♦ a large manufacturer of computer chips that has identified embedded systems that will fail but is leaving the decision on whether or not to inform its customers to the marketing department; and
- ♦ a chemical plant that has an embedded chip problem that, if not corrected, will cause explosions involving chlorine gas.

20.2 ACTUAL LITIGATION

There have been several instances of date-related disputes in the past. However, Year 2000-specific lawsuits did not appear to commence until about 1996.

An article in *Forbes* referred to a Year 2000 lawsuit that involved an international magazine publisher who claimed that an external computer service provider failed to supply it with an adequately updated software system. The lawsuit was settled under seal, with the supplier reportedly paying out more than $4 million.[12]

The first widely-reported Year 2000-related lawsuit was filed by the Produce Palace, a Warren, Michigan-based produce supplier.[13] Produce Palace alleges that the computerized cash register system it acquired is unable to process credit cards containing expiration dates after 1999. The lawsuit names as defendants both the manufacturer, All American Cash Register Inc., as well as the vendor, TEC-America Cash Register Inc. Shortly after the lawsuit was filed, the cash register vendor filed suit against the manufacturer for indemnification.

Produce Palace is seeking "an amount in excess of $10,000." Its two owners, Mark Yarsike and Sam Katz, paid about $100,000 in April 1995 for the system and allege that the system problems have cost them more

---

12 Susan Adams, "The bug bar" *Forbes* (July 28, 1997).
13 *Produce Palace International v. TEC-America Cash Register Inc., and All American Cash Register Inc.*, case No. 97-3330-CK (Michigan, June 12, 1997).

than $50,000 in additional wages and hundreds of thousands of dollars in lost business.[14]

According to the claim, of the first five hundred days the system was in place, it was down over one hundred times, and a good majority of the problems involved the failure of the computer to process credit cards during business hours. Specifically, the use of credit cards with expiration dates beyond 1999 would result in an "improper transaction" error being reported, and almost immediately, the entire cash register network consisting of ten registers would crash for hours.[15]

The lawsuit alleges nine separate counts, which may be illustrative of the types of claims that may appear in future Year 2000 related actions. They are:[16]

- Breach of warranty. These claims include an allegation that the defendant breached implied warranties of merchantability, as well as certain express warranties and representations made to the plaintiff, both orally, and in writing designed to encourage the plaintiff to purchase the system. The express warranties were alleged to have been breached by the defendants' failure to deliver the system free from defects and by their failure to repair the defects within a reasonable time.
- Violation of the *Magnusson-Moss Warranty Act*.[17] The plaintiff alleges that it is a "consumer," the defendants are "suppliers" and the registers are a "consumer product" as defined in the Act. The defendants, having had a reasonable opportunity to remedy the defects in the system, but having failed to do so are required to refund the purchase price to the plaintiff.
- Breach of warranty of fitness. The plaintiff alleges that at the time the parties executed their contract, the defendants had reason to know the particular purpose for which the plaintiff desired to use the system, and that the plaintiff relied upon the defendant's expertise in selecting the system to confirm to the plaintiff's needs and requirements. As a

---

14 "Year 2000 suit launched" *The Ottawa Sun* (Friday, August 8, 1997).

15 David M. Nadler and Kendrick C. Fong, "Year 2000 Lawsuits Begin" in *Infotech and the Law* (October 9, 1997).

16 However, it should be noted that some of the following claims may be specific to the United States or to Michigan and may not be applicable in a Canadian jurisdiction. It should also be noted that the attorney representing the plaintiffs appears to practice primarily in the area of automobile litigation and the claims appear to be adaptions of those typically made in cases of those type.

17 15 U.S.C. § 2301(3).

consequence, the defendants impliedly warranted that the system would be fit for the purpose the plaintiff intended.

- Failure to accept revocation. The plaintiff alleges that due to the system's repair history and continuing defects, it had previously sought to revoke acceptance and the return of the purchase price of the system and that the defendants have refused to comply.
- Breach of duty of good faith. The plaintiff alleges that the defendants breached their duty of good faith in the transaction by (a) breaching express and implied warranties, (b) selling the plaintiff a system with defects of which they know or should have known, and (c) failing to repair the defects the first time during the warranty periods.
- Negligent repair. The plaintiff alleges that it has made the system available to the defendants for repairs of the defective conditions, that the defendants attempted repair and that the defendants owed a duty of care to the plaintiff to perform the repairs in a good and professional manner within a reasonable time. The plaintiff alleges that the defendants breached this duty in that, the attempted repairs of the plaintiff's system were done negligently, carelessly, and recklessly as to substantially impair the system's use and value in its operation. After each repair attempt, the defendants represented to the plaintiff that the repairs were complete, but, the plaintiff alleges that these representations were false.
- Misrepresentation. The plaintiff alleges that (a) the defendants had a duty to perform repairs or cause repairs to be performed properly, professionally and in a reasonable time, (b) the defendants had a further duty to disclose to the plaintiff if any defects or non-conformities were not repaired or could not be repaired within a reasonable time, and (c) that contrary to these duties, the defendants represented and continued to represent that the defects and/or non-conformities could be repaired when they knew, or should have known, that this was not the case or not true.
- Breach of contract.
- Violation of the Michigan *Consumer Protection Act*.[18] The plaintiffs alleges numerous breaches of this Act, which include:
  - representation that the system would be of good, merchantable quality, free of defects, when in fact it was not;
  - representation that the system had been properly repaired when in fact the defendants knew or should have known that it had not;
  - representation that the repairs would be performed properly and within a reasonable time, when the defendants knew, or in the

---

18 M.C.L.A., chapter 445.

> exercise of reasonable care, should have known that this was not the case;
> - failing to make proper repairs on a warranted item;
> - failing to offer a refund or replacement of the system on revocation;
> - failing to reveal material facts, including the cause of the defects and non-conformities;
> - entering into a consumer transaction in which the consumer waives or purports to waive a right, benefit, or immunity provided by law, unless the waiver is clearly stated and the consumer has specifically consented to it.

The case is interesting both for the various Year 2000 claims it raises in respect of Year 2000 problems, but also, in that it may help shed some light onto the possible allocation of liability between a manufacturer and its retailer (particularly if it proceeds to trial).

Class action lawsuits regarding the Year 2000 problem have also been commenced. On December 2, 1997 Atlaz International filed the first Year 2000 class action law suit against Software Business Technologies and its subsidiary, SBT Accounting Systems, alleging breach of warranty, fraud, and fraudulent and unfair business practices.[19] In support of its breach of warranty claim, Atlaz alleges that the Year 2000 deficiencies breach a five year express warranty that the software will operate in compliance with its written specifications. Atlaz alleges SBT is improperly requiring customers to pay substantial fees to purchase upgrades in order to fix software that is not Year 2000 compliant while other software companies are correcting such problems without charge. SBT indicated that it plans to offer a free patch in 1998 to address Year 2000 problems in its software. SBT also claims that the suit is in retaliation for a suit filed by SBT against Atlaz for breach of a reseller licence agreement.

A number of class action law suits have been filed against various defendants (including Symantec and Macola Inc.) by the law firm of Milberg Weiss Bershad Hynes & Lerach. The complaints allege breach of implied warranties and related claims in circumstances where the defendant software vendors have required their customers to purchase upgrades in order to remedy Year 2000 defects.

Class action lawsuits are more likely to arise in American jurisdictions than in Canadian jurisdictions for a number of reasons:

---

19 *Supra*, at Chapter 2, note 23.

♦ Class action lawsuits are an established practice in the United States;
♦ In the United States, if an action fails, both parties are responsible for their own costs. In Canada, generally, the loser must pay the winner's costs, a rule that tends to discourage lawsuits, especially by smaller defendants;[20]
♦ American law firms can provide legal services on a contingency basis. The law firm can take up to a third of the award if it succeeds with the rest held in trust for affected parties.[21] In Canada, a plaintiff would generally need to fund the action on their own.

Many legal authorities and industry analysts predict that these lawsuits are just the tip of the iceberg. According to Lou Marcoccio, Gartner Group Inc.'s research director for application development and management, lawyers have been brought in on more than two hundred Year 2000 disputes (93% of such disputes involve complaints against software vendors by their customers). Two of these disputes were settled (one for US$8.5 million and the other for US$2.5 million).[22]

20.3 YEAR 2000 PRACTICE GROUPS

Providing advice concerning Year 2000 issues can involve numerous legal fields. Many large full-service firms have put together special practice groups or teams that include a multidisciplinary team of "Year 2000-aware" practitioners specializing in:

♦ Commercial law, particularly computer-related contacts (breach of contract)
♦ Litigation
♦ Tort (product liability, professional negligence)
♦ Corporate law (liability of directors and officers)
♦ Insurance law
♦ Intellectual property law
♦ Securities law (disclosure obligations)

---

20 It generally costs at least $50,000 to prosecute even a small matter. Therefore, in many cases, particularly where a class action is not an option, damages resulting from Year 2000-related problems will need to be significant before litigation can become a serious option.

21 This is the trend for actions brought in federal court. In some state courts, including California, contingency fees are based on hourly billings with a multiplier applied to compensate for the risk assumed by the law firm. However, the total fees are usually significantly less under this approach.

22 "Millennium Mess" *Information Week* (April 13, 1998).

- Bankruptcy law (priorities between competing claims)
- Employment law
- Criminal law

The Year 2000 practice group or team is typically headed up by a co-ordinator with a commercial law background. This individual should possess an advanced understanding of the Year 2000 problem and be capable of marshalling together and managing the necessary legal specialists, as required, to solve a particular problem.

A Year 2000 practice group can provide a law firm's client with best-of-class advice regarding legal issues specifically related to the Year 2000 problem. As well, they can help ensure that Year 2000-related provisions in mergers, acquisition, financing and other transactional agreements are properly drafted to provide the best possible protection and advantage for the firm's clients.

20.4 CONCLUSIONS

The full repercussion of the Year 2000 problem is not expected to occur until the early part of the year 2000. Most companies are currently focused on reducing their vulnerability. However, once the year 2000 arrives, they will likely become more concerned with the allocation of costs rather than risk management. Although negotiated settlements may settle many disputes, it is nevertheless likely that the Year 2000 problem will result in significant litigation.

Not all Year 2000 potential problems can be solved or even anticipated. Companies that expect to be targets of litigation, especially large commercial enterprises, are taking steps now to prepare to defend the anticipated law suits.

Appendix

1. SAMPLE YEAR 2000 WARRANTY

(a) Long Version

Year 2000 Warranty. [Licensor] represents and warrants that the [Program] is designed to be used prior to, during and after the calendar year 2000 A.D., and that the [Program] will operate during each such time period without error relating to date data, specifically including any error relating to, or the product of date data, which represents or references different centuries or more than one century ("Year 2000 Compatible"). Year 2000 Compatible shall also mean:

(i) that the [Program] will not abnormally end or provide invalid or incorrect results as a result of date data, specifically including date data which represents or references different centuries or more than one century;

(ii) that the [Program] has been designed to ensure year 2000 compatibility, including, but not limited to, date data recognition, calculations which accommodate same century and multi-century formulas and date values, and date data interface values that reflect the century;

(iii) that the [Program] includes "year 2000 capabilities", which means the [Program]:

    (1) will manage and manipulate data involving dates, including single century formulas and multi-century formulas, and will not cause an abnormally ending scenario within the application or generate incorrect values or invalid results involving such dates;

    (2) provides that all date-related user interface functionalities and data fields include the indication of century; and

    (3) provides that all date-related data interface functionalities include the indication of century;

(iv) that all date processing by the [Program] shall be performed using an indication of century;

(v) that the [Program] recognizes the Year 2000 as a leap year;

(v) that any facilities or interfaces in the [Program] which permit the use of two-digits to represent the year shall be documented and any translation between two-digit and four-digit representations for the year shall be performed by the [Program] in conformance with such documentation;

(vi) that the [Program] does not use date fields as indicators or for purposes other than to store valid dates; and

(vii) that the [Program] will continue to be Year 2000 Compatible.

An indication of century for the purposes of the foregoing may be accomplished either through use of a four digit year format (*i.e.*, the first two digits to designate the century and the second two digits to designate the year within the century) or may be accomplished through the use of unambiguous algorithms or inferencing rules. In the latter case, the [Program] must respond to two-digit year dates in a way that resolves the ambiguity as to the century in a disclosed, defined and pre-determined manner.

(b) Short Version

Year 2000 Warranty. [Supplier] represents and warrants that the [Product] is designed to be used prior to, during and after the calendar year 2000 A.D., and that (i) the [Product] will operate during each such time period without error relating to date data, specifically including any error relating to, or the product of date data, which represents or references different centuries or more than one century; (ii) that the [Product] will operate without a difference in functionality or perform-ance during each such time period; (iii) that the [Product] recognizes the Year 2000 as a leap year; (iv) that the [Product] does not use date fields as indicators or for purposes other than to store valid dates; and (v) in all interfaces and data storage, the century in any date is specified either explicitly or by unambiguous algorithms or inferencing rules (and in the latter case, the [Product] must respond to two-digit year dates in a way that resolves the ambiguity as to the century in a disclosed, defined and pre-determined manner).

2. YEAR 2000 DEFINITIONS

(a) Standards Organizations

A number of different standards applicable to representations of dates currently exist. Many of these are not compatible and a system may be said to be "Year 2000 compliant" and may conform to one of these standards and yet not be capable of exchanging date-related data with another Year 2000 compliant system that conforms to a different standard. Some of the competing standards include those adopted by:

♦ the American National Standards Institute ("ANSI") which permits a date field formal of MM-DD-CCYY
♦ the International Organization for Standardization ("ISO")
♦ the National Institute of Standards and Technology ("NIST")

The United States has a Federal Information Processing Standard and there also exists a European Standard.

With respect to definitions and standards specific to the Year 2000 issue, the British Standards Institute has issued *"DISC PD-2000-1* A Definition of Year 2000 Conformity Requirements," which provides a definition of the expression and the requirements that must be satisfied in equipment and products that use dates and times.[1] The purpose of the document is to allow checks to be made, and discussions to be held, between organizations on the basis of a common understanding. It provides:

Year 2000 conformity shall mean that neither the performance nor functionality is affected by dates prior to, during and after the year 2000. In particular:

Rule 1: No value for current date will cause any interruption in operation.

Rule 2: Date-based functionality must behave consistently for dates prior to, during and after year 2000.

Rule 3: In all interfaces and data storage, the century in any date must be specified either explicitly or by unambiguous algorithms or inferencing rules.

---

[1] Document: DISC PD2000-1. See <http://www.2k-times.com/y2k-p110.htm>.

Rule 4: Year 2000 must be recognized as a leap year.

The above mentioned document contains further explanations and commentaries regarding the above rules. It should be noted that Rule 3 may be satisfied either by explicit representation of the year in dates (*e.g.*, by using four digits or by including a century indicator) or by the use of inferencing rules (*e.g.*, two-digit years with a value greater than 50 implying 19xx, those with a value equal to or less than 50 implying 20xx).

Where a generally applicable definition—such as that set out by the British Standards Institution—is available, then it may be incorporated by reference into applicable agreements and representations. Many institutions are developing their own standard definition of compliance. For instance, the University of Florida has defined a standard level of cross-century date compliance for computerized information systems that are to apply to any and all individual components of an information system, including in-house and vendor-supplied application software, utilities, operating systems and physical device processors.[2]

(b) Vendor Definitions

A number of suppliers have adopted their own definitions. For instance, IBM uses the term "Year 2000 ready" and provides the following information on its Web site:[3]

> IBM considers a product Year 2000 ready if the product, when used in accordance with its associated documentation, is capable of correctly processing, providing, and/or receiving date data within and between the 20th and 21st centuries, provided that all products (for example, hardware, software and firmware) used with the product properly exchange accurate date data with it. We have updated the specifications of our ready products that do not include a readiness statement in the appropriate product specifications.

Intel Corporation uses the term "Year 2000 Capable," which is defined as:[4]

> An Intel product, when used in accordance with its associated documentation, is "Year 2000 Capable" when, upon installation, it accurately stores, displays, processes, provides, and/or receives date data from, into, and between the

---

2 University of Florida, "Year 2000 Definition of Compliance" at <http://www.is.ufl.edu/bawb050h.htm>. The definition explicitly states that *no existing system should be considered compliant based upon the fact that all year elements contain four digits.*

3 <http://wwwyr2k.raleigh.ibm.com/>

4 <http://support.intel.com/support/year2000/microprocessor.htm>

twentieth and twenty-first centuries, including leap year calculations, provided that all other technology used in combination with the said product properly exchanges date data with it.

NCR utilizes the term "Year 2000 Qualified."[5] Oracle utilizes a superset of the Year 2000 conformance requirements set out by the British Standards Institute in order to meet its definition of "Year 2000 Compliance." Five main factors must be satisfied with respect to date datatype processing pursuant to Oracle's requirements:

1. Correctly handle date information before, during, and after 1st January 2000 accepting date input, providing date output and performing calculation on dates or portions of dates.
2. Function according to the documentation before, during and after 1st January 2000 without changes in operation resulting from the advent of the new century assuming correct configuration.
3. Where appropriate, respond to two-digit date input in a way that resolves the ambiguity as to century in a disclosed, defined and pre-determined manner.
4. Store and provide output of date information in ways that are unambiguous as to century.
5. Manage the leap year occurring in the year 2000, following the quad-centennial rule.

For a particular Oracle product, the stated compliance may be one of four defined levels:

1. Fully Compliant. ("The current production version of the product is intended to fully comply with all five of the factors . . .").
2. Partially Compliant (1). ("The current production version of the product does not fully comply with all five of the factors. , . . However, Oracle intends to provide full compliance in a future release of the product.")
3. Partially Compliant (2). ("The current production version of this mature product does not comply with all five of the factors . . . and Oracle has not plan to provide further compliance in the future.")
4. Not Compliant ("The current production version of the product does not comply with the factors [. . .] and Oracle does not intend to provide any further compliance in the future.")

---

5 The requirements that must be met for an NCR product to be designated as Year 2000 Qualified are set out in NCR's "Year 2000 Qualification Requirements Definition" at <http://www.ncr.com/year2000/y2k-qual.htm>.

3. YEAR 2000 SOURCES OF INFORMATION ON THE INTERNET

- **Year 2000 Computer Crisis Legal Guide—Online Site <http://www.gahtan.com/year2000/>**

- AICPA Year 2000
  <http://www.aicpa.org/members/y2000/intro.htm>

- Cassandra Project
  <http://millennia-bcs.com/CASFRAME.HTM>

- CIO Magazine
  <http://www.cio.com/forums/year2k.html>

- CIO Subcommittee on Y2K/GSA Home Page
  <http://www.itpolicy.gsa.gov/mks/yr2000/y201toc1.htm>

- CIPS position paper and executive checklist prepared by the Information Technology Association of Canada (ITAC) and the Canadian Information Processing Society (CIPS)
  <http://www. cips.ca/ y2k.htm>

- CMP Techweb Year 2000 site
  <http://www.techweb.com/wire/technews/year2000.html>

- Comlinks Year 2000
  <http://www.comlinks.com/>

- Computer Information Center Year 2000
  <http://www.compinfo.co.uk/y2k/manufpos.htm>

- Computerweekly
  <http://www.computerweekly.co.uk>

- Computer World
  <http://www.computerworld.com/year2000/>

- Datamation
  <http://www.datamation.com/>

- CSSA Year 2000
  <http://fm6.facility.pipex.com/cssa/new/millen.htm>

- Datamation IS Managers' Workbench—Year 2000
  <http://datamation.com/PlugIn/workbench/yr2000/year.htm>

- Digital Equipment Corporation—Year 2000
  <http://ww1.digital.com/year2000/>

- Federal Financial Institutions Examination Council
  <http://www.ffiec.gov/y2k>

- Federal Reserve Board Year 2000 Initiatives
  <http://www.bog.frb.fed.us/y2k/>

- Federal Year 2000 Commercial Off-the-Shelf (COTS) Product Database
  <http://y2k.policyworks.gov/>

- IBM
  <http://www.software.ibm.com/year2000/>

- IBM Canada
  <http://www.can.ibm.com/year2000/>

- Industry Canada
  <http://strategis.ic.gc.ca/year2000>

- Info2000 (Treasury Board of Canada)
  <http://www.info2000.gc.ca/>

- Information Society Project Office (ISPO)—Y2KEURO
  <http://www.ispo.cec.be/y2keuro/>

- Information Technology Association of America—Year 2000 Home Page
  <http://www.itaa.org/year2000.htm>

- IOSCO Year 2000
  <http://www.iosco.org/year_2000.html>

- General Services Administration
  <http://www.itpolicy.gsa.gov/>

- Information Technology Association of America
  <http://www.itaa.org/>

- Management Support Technology
  <http://www.mstnet.com/year2000/>

- Microsoft Year 2000 site
  <http://www.microsoft.com/year2000/>

- Mitre Company
  <http://www.mitre.org/research/y2k>

- National Bulletin Board for the Year 2000
  <http://www.it2000.com/>

- ◆ Platinum Technology Y2K Library
  <http://www.platinum.com/products/year2k/library.htm>

- ◆ Peter de Jager's Year 2000 site
  <http://www.year2000.com/>

- ◆ RX2000
  <http://www.rx2000.org/>

- ◆ United Kingdom's Taskforce 2000
  <http://www.taskforce2000.co.uk/>

- ◆ Westergaard Year 2000
  <http://www.y2ktimebomb.com/>

- ◆ Year 2000 MCRB
  <http://www.year2k.com>

- ◆ Year 2000 Resource
  <http://www.deweerd.org/year2000/>

- ◆ Year 2000 Support Centre
  <http://www.support2000.com/>

- ◆ The Y2K Site
  <http://www.y2k.com/>

- ◆ Y2K Times
  <http://www.2k-times.com/y2k.htm>

INDEX

The Year 2000 Computer Crisis Legal Guide

Alan M. Gahtan, M.B.A., LL.B.

❏ YES! Please send me ____ copy(ies) of **The Year 2000 Computer Crisis Legal Guide** for a 30-day risk-free examination. I understand that if I am not completely satisfied with my order, I may return it within 30 days for a full refund.

Order # 9260111-XXX   **$50**

Softcover   1998   approx. 250 pages   0-421-26011-1

❏ Please advise me of further publications in this field.

Name _____

Title _____

Company _____

Address _____

City _____ State _____ Zip Code _____

Telephone # (   ) _____ Fax # (   ) _____

e-mail _____ www _____

BILLING OPTIONS

❏ Bill me   ❏ Bill my firm/company   ❏ Payment enclosed _____

❏ Charge my Carswell Account # _____

P.O.# _____

❏ Charge my   ❏ VISA   ❏ Mastercard   ❏ American Express

Card # _____ Expiry Date _____

Signature _____

(ORDERS MUST INCLUDE SIGNATURE AND TELEPHONE NUMBER TO BE PROCESSED.)

Please use an envelope when sending credit card information.

Shipping and handling are extra. Price subject to change without notice and subject to applicable taxes.

3 EASY WAYS TO ORDER

Please quote **Order # 9260111-XXX**

1. TELEPHONE—TOLL FREE:

1-800-387-5164

2. FAX

(416) 298-5082

3. ELECTRONIC:

orders@carswell.com

For more information on these or any other products from Carswell, please contact your local Account Representative.

YOUR SATISFACTION GUARANTEE

Your satisfaction with any Carswell product is guaranteed. If you are not completely satisfied with any Carswell product, simply return it within 30 days of receipt, along with the invoice marked "cancelled".

CARSWELL
Thomson Professional Publishing

One Corporate Plaza, 2075 Kennedy Road,
Scarborough, Ontario, Canada M1T 3V4
www.carswell.com